AN ALPHABETICAL INDEX OF

Revolutionary Pensioners

Living in Maine

By Charles Alcott Flagg

CLEARFIELD COMPANY

Originally Published
Dover, 1920

Reprinted
Genealogical Publishing Co., Inc.
Baltimore, 1967

Reprinted for Clearfield Company, Inc.
by Genealogical Publishing Co., Inc.
Baltimore, 1992

Library of Congress Catalogue Card Number 67-28604
International Standard Book Number 0-8063-0111-2

Made in the United States of America

An Alphabetical Index of Revolutionary Pensioners Living in Maine

Compiled by Charles A. Flagg, Librarian, Bangor (Maine) Public Library

INTRODUCTION

For a quarter century past the popularity, growth and activities of our patriotic-hereditary societies have been features of American life. It is now considered the proper thing to cherish and prize the names and mementoes of the men of '76; perhaps even to idealize them and their services. And many who have never applied for admission to any of the various societies of Revolutionary descendants, take a just pride in knowing that they are eligible, and of the blood of the heroes who established our independence.

Maine, of course, was a part of Massachusetts at the time of the Revolution.

Very little has been done even yet in the publication of regimental histories and personal narratives of Revolutionary service— lines that have been so enormously expanded in the case of the Civil war. The histories of two or three Maine regiments which the late Nathan Goold prepared, and Dr. Frank A. Gardner's notable series of Massachusetts regimental histories, now running in the "Massachusetts Magazine" of Salem, being practically all there is available in that field.

But when it comes to individual service, Massachusetts people are particularly fortunate because that state has, at enormous expense, printed all her Revolutionary muster, pay and other rolls, as "Massachusetts soldiers and sailors of the Revolutionary war" in 17 large quarto volumes. No other state has done nearly as much in this direction.

But even these records, full as they are, leave much to be desired. Families were usually large and in the old home towns it was more the rule than the exception to find several contemporaries of the same name (middle names being very rare). In using the above work it is not uncommon to find two or more soldiers bearing the name of the ancestor one is in search of, from the town we known he lived in; and still others of the same name whose residence is indeterminate.

Unless it can be conclusively established that no other of the name could have served from that town at the time, or our family tradition is more definite than is usually the case, we really have found no evidence at all. Here is where the value of the pension lists come in. While we may not know in whose company or regiment, or in what capacity the Revolutionary ancestor served, we can usually find out where he lived in later life, and if he survived to old age and drew a pension, the necessary link to the chain of evidence is often secured so one can identify the actual military service of the ancestor in "Massachusetts soldiers and sailors."

The U. S. Pension Office at Washington is a veritable mine of information, and once an ancestor is located on the pension roll, it is worth while to secure direct from the Office and at some expense, a copy of all papers relating to the claim.

It may be added that the Pension Office authorities give no very cordial endorsement of the printed pension rolls, having found them to contain numerous errors. It must also be added, however, that some of the lists preserve records whose originals have been lost in the destruction of the Capitol by the British in 1814 or in other ways. The important things to realize are that the printed lists are so useful and so largely used that a consolidated list like the following will be valuable; and that once the name desired is found it will almost certainly be worth while to write to the Pension Office for full details of service.

The difficulty in using the various printed pension lists springs from the fact that not one is strictly alphabetical, and they are so rare now that only the large libraries have them all.

Before we take up the various pension lists in print, it may be well to devote a little time to consideration of Revolutionary pensions in general, and fortunately Columbia University studies in history, economics and public law, Volume XII, No. 3 (History of military pension legislature in the United States by W. H. Glasson) gives us an exhaustive sketch.

Classes of Pensioners

Revolutionary pensioners really fall into four classes.

I. *Invalid pensioners.*

The first national U. S. pension law passed Aug. 26, 1776, promised half pay for life or during disability to every officer, soldier or sailor, losing a limb or being so disabled in the service of the U. S. as to be incapable of earning a livelihood. Proportionate relief was promised to such as were partially disabled. April 23, 1782, it was enacted that Continental soldiers who were sick or wounded and unfit for duty were to be discharged and be pensioned at the rate of five dollars per month. An act passed June 7, 1785, further provided that when so disabled as to be unable to earn a livelihood, commissioned officers should be allowed a half pay pension and non-commissoned officers and privates five dollars a month, proportionate rates being allowed for partial disability.

This act was afterwards amended to include later disability resulting from wounds, to include state troops and militia as well as Continentals, and the rates were somewhat increased.

Invalid pensioners surviving at the dates of the service pension acts of 1818 and 1832 usually found it advantageous to secure entry under them.

II. *Half pay or commutation pensioners.*

As a result of Washington's appeal at a time when the depreciation of the continental currency and the gloomy outlook in the field were preventing the re-enlistment of many officers and men at the termination of their periods of service, Congress on May 15, 1778, voted to all American commissioned officers who should continue in service to the close of the war half pay for seven years after its conclusion; to all common soldiers who served to the end of the war a gratuity of eighty dollars. As these measures failed to secure the full results expected, Washington again appealed to Congress, which on October 21, 1780, voted that all officers who should continue in service to the end of the war, should receive half pay for life. These measures are believed to have been of the utmost importance in keeping the army together till the end of the struggle, but they were immensely unpopular, especially in New England, while opposition to Congress was very strong.

To the irritation aroused in the officers' minds at the suspicion that Congress intended to repudiate these obligations were attributable their "Memorial to Congress" of December 1782 and the more celebrated "Newburgh addresses" of March, 1783.

Washington once more prepared an urgent appeal for recognition of the army's claims, and on March 22, 1783, Congress adopted a compromise known as the "Commutation act," substituting for the half pay for life, five years full pay in money or interest bearing securities.

As the Confederation had no funds, the officers received not money but "commutation certificates," but with no provision for paying principal or interest, these depreciated like the continental currency and soon came into the hands of speculators who profited when the first Congress under the Constitution provided for the refunding of these certificates.

The survivors of this group and their friends felt that justice had not been done and petitions were introduced into Congress from time to time until on May 15, 1828, just 50 years after the original act, a measure was passed giving full pay for life, beginning March 3, 1826, to the surviving officers of the Continental line who had been entitled to half pay under the act of 1780, and the same allowance was made to the non-commissioned officers and privates entitled to receive the gratuity of eighty dollars promised in 1780. This act was executed by the Secretary of the Treasury rather than by the Secretary of War, who administered the other pension laws until in 1835 it was transferred from the former to the latter office.

III. *Service pensioners.*

March 18, 1818, was passed the first service pension act, which provided that every resident of the U. S. who had served in the Revolutionary war until its close or for the term of 9 months or longer, at any period of the war, on the Continental establishment or navy, and who was by reason of his reduced circumstances in need of assistance, should receive a pension; if an officer, twenty dollars a month, if a private eight dollars. Claimants were required to give up invalid and all other pensions. So many frauds were perpetrated under this act that in 1820 Congress required of all pensioners under the act, sworn schedules of their property and income, and under this ruling thousands of names were stricken from the rolls.

In June, 1832, a still more sweeping service pension measure became law. It granted to all who had completed a total service of two years in Continental line, state troops or militia, or the navy, and who were not entitled to pensions under the Commutation law of 1824, full pay according to rank, to commence May 15, 1828, and not to exceed a captain's pay. All who had completed a service of not less than six months were to receive the same proportion of their full pay that their service bore to two years. Here again enormous frauds were unearthed.

IV. *Widows and Orphans.*

Augusta 24, 1780, Congress extended the half pay for seven years to the widows or orphan children of officers who had died or should die in the service. This act was renewed under the Constitution in 1792 but nothing further was done till 1836 when provision was made that if any soldier who would be entitled to a pension under the service act of 1832 (see preceding paragraph) died leaving a widow whose marriage took place before the expiration of his service, she might receive his pension as long as she might remain unmarried. Varied later acts were passed supplementing and extending the above.

The report of the Commissioner of pensions for 1874 gives some interesting figures.

Soldiers in the Revolutionary army (estimate)		289,715
Revolutionary pensioners		57,623
Under act of 1818	20,485	
" " " 1828	1,200	
" " " 1835	33,425	
		55,110

Leaving a balance 2,513, pensioned under early invalid acts or by specific measures. The Commissioner also stated that there were 39,295 widows who received Revolutionary pensions.

Penion Lists

Including the principal lists published by the U. S. government, as far as we have noted them. There seems to be no index available to special pensions granted after 1840. It is well known that Revolutionary pensioners were on the rolls over a quarter century later. The venerable William Hutchings of Penobscot was present as an honored guest at the Bangor 4th of July celebration in 1865.

1792. Invalid pension claims. Communicated to the House of Representatives, Dec. 14, 1792. (American state papers. Class IX. Claims. p. 56-68.)

Tabular. Arranged by states (including District of Maine). Alphabetic by initial letter only. 7 columns: Names; Rank; Regiment; Disability; Date from which annual pension commenced; Monthly allowance; Arrears due.

1794. Invalid pension claims. Communicated to the House of Representatives April 25, 1794-[1795]. (American state papers. Claims. Washington, 1834. p. 83-122, 125-128, 135-145, 150-172).

Tabular. Arranged by states (including the District of Maine). Not alphabetic. Usually in 7 columns:—Names; Rank; Regiment or company or ship; Disability; When and where disabled; Residence [town]; To what pension entitled [or Monthly allowance and Arrearages]; Remarks.

'*20.* Letter from the Secretary of war, transmitting a report of the names, rank and line of every person placed on the pension list, in pursuance of the act of 18th of March, 1818, &c. . . . . . . Washington, Printed by Gales & Seaton, 1820. 672 pages.

(16th Congress, 1st session. House. Doc. No. 55)

Tabular. Arranged by states of residence in 1820. Alphabetic by initial letter only: 3 columns:—Names; Rank; Line.

Practically all the names in this list are reprinted in the 1835 list, but occasionally there is a variation in spelling name or added detail of service.

'*28.* Officers on the pension list. Letter from the Secretary of war, transmitting a list of officers on the pension roll of the U. S. designating the states to which the officers severally belong. January 30, 1828. . . . . . . Washington: printed by Gales & Seaton, 1828. 29 pages.

(20th Congress, 1st session. House. Doc. No. 124.)

Tabular. Arranged by states; two classes under each: Invalid pension list, and Revolutionary pension list. Alphabetic by initial letter only. Gives name and rank only; no particulars of service or present residence. These "Revolutionary pensioners" are those officers pensioned under the "service" act of 1818 who were living in 1828.

'*29.* Officers, &c. pensioned under act of 1828. Letter from the Secretary of the treasury, transmitting a list of the names of pensioners under the law of May 15, 1828. January 13, 1829. [From Treasury Dept.] 16 pages.

(20th Congress, 2d session. House. Doc. No. 68.)

Tabular. Alphabetic by initial letter only. 5 columns:—Names; Line; Rank; Sum annually; State or Territory of residence at time of application.

'*31*. Rejected applications for pensions, &c. Letter from the Secretary of war, transmitting a report respecting rejected applications for pensions. January 6, 1831. 84 Pages.
(21st Congress, 2d session. House. Doc. No. 31)

In two parts, each subdivided by state: *a*. Persons whose claims to pension on account of Revolutionary service have been rejected (3 columns: Name, Rank and Reasons for rejection); *b*. Revolutionary pensioners placed on the rolls under the act of March 18, 1818, and who have been stricken from the pension list under act of May 1, 1820, not being considered in indigent circumstances (2 columns: Name and Rank).

The veterans in the second part would regularly be found in the '20 and '35 lists also.

'*35*. Report from the Secretary of war, in obedience to resolutions of the Senate of the 5th and 30th of June, 1834, and the 3d of March, 1835, in relation to the pension establishment of the United States. Washington: Printed by Duff Green, 1835. 3 volumes.
(23d Congress, 1st session. Senate. Doc. No. 514.)

Tabular. Arranged (1st) by state, (2d) by class of pensioners: *a*. Invalid pensioners; *b*. Heirs of non-commissioned officers, privates, &c. who died in the U. S. service who obtained five years' half pay in lieu of bounty land, under the second section of the act of April 16, 1816; *c*. Pensioners under the act of March 18, 1818; *d*. Pensioners under the act of June 7, 1832, (3d) by county. Alphabetic by initial letter only. Section [*a*] contains very few Revolutionary pensioners and [*b*] gives heirs of soldiers killed in the War of 1812. Sections [*c*] and [*d*] are confined to Revolutionary pensioners; names are alphabetic under county by initial letter of family name only. 9 columns:—Names; Rank; Annual allowance; Sums received; Description of service; When placed on the pension rolls; Commencement of pension; Age; Remarks. Sections [*c*] and [*d*] include all veterans who had been pensioned under these two acts; many had died before 1835 but full entry is made, with date of death.

'*40*. A census of pensioners for Revolutionary or military services; with their names, ages, and places of residence, as returned by the marshals of the several judicial districts, under the act for taking the sixth census. Washington: printed by Blair and Rives, 1841. 195 pages.

Tabular. Arranged by states, sub-arrangement by counties and then by towns. Names not alphabetic. 3 columns: Names of pensioners; Ages; Names of heads of families with whom pensioners resided 1840.

There is no mark of distinction between the Revolutionary and the other military pensioners. The latter are evidently very few.

This list includes a considerable number of widows.

CLAIMS

While the foregoing lists include the veterans who were pensioned under the general laws and many others, they do not by any means give *all* Revolutionary pensioners; many of course died before the date of our earliest lists; and many must have been pensioned by special act between the date of the last list (1840) and the death of the last Revolutionary veteran in the late "sixties."

Fortunately each House of Congress publishes from time to time indexes of private claims brought before them and these claims include special pension bills. Furthermore these indexes are strictly alphabetical and therefore easy to consult (as the pension lists are not).

Such House lists are:

1st-31st Congress, 1789-1851 (32d Cong. 1st session. House misc. doc. [unnumbered] serial No. 653-655).

32d-41st " 1851-1871 (42d Cong. 3d session. House misc. doc. No. 109. Serial No. 1574).

14th-46th Congress, 1817-1881 (46th Cong. 3d session. Senate misc. doc. No. 14. Serial No. 1945-1946).

NOTES

In connection with the use of following list and the various pension lists to which it serves as an index, there are several things to bear in mind. In the first place this index is intended to cover all the most important facts recorded, and at the same time, definitely locate the original entry in case completer history is desired.

As to "service," first there were the Continental regiments raised by Congress, such as Harrison's artillery, the Commander-in-Chief's guard, etc., and the various continental regiments raised by the individual states and turned over to Congress, such as the 16th Mass., etc.; (indicated by "Mass. line," etc.) There was also the Continental navy. Then came the state line and state navy, raised and supported by the states for home defence when the Continental army and navy was engaged elsewhere (indicated by "Mass. state," "R. I. navy," etc.) Finally came the militia of the states—citizens called out for temporary or special service (N. H. mil, etc.)

The "residence" ("County" having a column for itself, and town being given in "Remarks" column if reported) in each case is the place of domicile at date of list; most of the lists giving no intimation at all where soldier resided or enlisted 1775-81. The 1835 list which does contain particulars of service has no more than the *state* pensioner served from, Maine men of course being accredited to Massachusetts. Indeed there is no list in print as far as known giving Revolutionary soldiers who enlisted from Maine, save as one might dig some information out of "Records of Mass. soldiers and sailors," already alluded to.

The "age" is of course age reported at time list was made; date of birth being approximated by subtracting age given from date of list;

c. g. Obadiah Abbee, the first pensioner on our list was born *about* 1765 (1835—70=1765).

As to Maine counties, at the time of the first list giving county of residence (that of 1835) the state was divided into the following: York, Cumberland, Lincoln, Hancock, Washington, Kennebec, Oxford, Somerset, Penobscot and Waldo. Before the 1840 list appeared there were three new counties. Franklin and Piscataquis (1838) and Aroostook (1839) and since that date Androscoggin, Knox and Sagadahoc have been formed. So it follows that a man might live in the same place, and still be recorded in one county in 1835, in another in 1840 and still another at time of death.

No special effort has been made to identify different holders of the same name. If they lived in same county by the record and ages would approximately correspond the ——— has been used for entries after the first. In cases where there could be the least doubt, separate entries have been made.

Names from the 1820 and '31b lists ar not given separate entry save in cases where name is not found in 1835 list; ('20) or ('31b) in remarks column for names in '35 list signifying that name occurs in former list, any variations in form of name or additional information being noted.

The county abbreviations will be obvious. Other abbreviations are: d. for died, res. for residence, and Pri., Corp., Lieut., Capt., Surg., for private, corporal, etc.

Widow's names are italicized.

Aside from the works already referred to one should consult Saffell's "Records of the Revolutionary war," 1858, pages 401-467, which contains a full treatment of the Half-pay or commutation pensioners, and an extensive list of officers killed in the war or possessed of right to half pay at the end.

Maine also, since statehood, has made liberal provision for her Revolutionary veterans, as attested by "Names of soldiers of the American revolution who applied for state bounty under resolves of March 17, 1838, March 24, 1836 and March 20, 1836 as appear by record in the Land Office........ Compiled by Charles J. House." Augusta, Burleigh & Flynt, 1893. The introduction gives text of the resolves, and as the names are alphabetical, they are not entered in this index.

List.	Name.	Service.	Rank.	Age.	County.	Remarks.
'35d	Abbee, Obadiah....	Mass. mil....	Private....	70	Kennebec...	
'35d	Abbree, William....	Cont. navy..	Lieutenant.	87	Washington..	Washington
'40	*Abbott Betsey*.........	....	....	73	Waldo......	Res. with Joel Abbot, Montville.........
'40	Abbot, Henry......	....	....	85	Lincoln....	Same as Abbot, Henry Residence Boothbay.
'35d	Abbott, Isaac......	Mass. line...	Private....	72	Oxford......	
'40	———	....	....	78	Oxford......	Res. Fryeburg.
'35c	Abbot, John, 2d....	R. I. line....	Private....	74	Lincoln.....	('20 as Abbott) died April 18, 1824.
'35c	Abbot, Jonathan...	Mass. line...	Private....	75	Cumberland.	
'35d	Abbot, Joseph......	Mass. state..	Private and Corporal	80	Oxford......	Died Nov. 30, 1832.
'35	Abbot, Nathaniel...	Mass. line...	Private....	86	Cumberland.	('20) d. April 8, 1830.
'35d	Abbot, Philip......	H. N. mil....	Private....	77	Oxford......	
'40	———	....	....	83	Oxford......	Res. Rumford.
'35c	Abbot, Abner......	N. H. line...	Private....	73	Oxford......	('20) d. Sept., 1823.
'35d	Abbott, Daniel.....	Mass. line...	Private....	86	York.......	('20 and '31b, as Abbot.)
'35c	Abbot, Henry......	R. I. line....	Private....	77	Lincoln.....	('20) same as Abbot, Henry.
'35	Abbott, John......	Mass. line...	Private....	76	York.......	('20 and '31b as Abbott).
'35	Abbot, Silas.......	Mass. line...	Sergeant...	83	York.......	Died June 30, 1826.
'35c	Acorn, Geo. Michael	Mass. line...	Private....	77	Lincoln.....	('20) d. Feb. 27, 1823.
'35d	Adams, Amos......	Mass. line...	Private....	87	Kennebec...	
'40	Adams, Amos......	....	....	94	Somerset...	Res. Madison.
'35d	Adams, James......	Mass. state..	Private....	90	Somerset...	
'35c	Adams, Jedediah...	Mass. line...	Private....	83	Lincoln.....	('20) d. July 17, 1832.
'40	*Adams, Jemima*...	....	....	83	Lincoln.....	Res. Union.
'35c	Adams, Joel.......	Mass. line...	Private....	....	Lincoln.....	('20).
'35c	Adams, Joseph 1st..	Mass. line...	Private....	71	Lincoln.....	('20) d. June 25, 1818.
'35c	Adams, Joseph 2d.	Mass. line...	Private....	68	Oxford......	('20).
'40	Adams, Joseph.....	....	....	74	Franklin....	Res. Jay.
'35c	Adams, Samuel....	Mass. line...	Sergeant...	89	Lincoln.....	('20 as surgeon) d. March 6, 1819.
'35d	Adams, Samuel.....	Mass. line...	Private....	76	Lincoln.....	('20, 31b).
'40	———	....	....	83	Lincoln.....	Res. Bowdoin.
'40	*Adams, Susan*......	....	....	99	Penobscot...	Res. Corinna.
'35d	Adams, Solomon...	Mass. line...	Private....	75	Kennebec...	Died Nov. 4, 1833.
'40	*Adams, Susannah*..	....	....	72	Kennebec...	Res. Greene.
'40	Addison, John.....	....	....	89	Cumberland.	Res. Freeport.
'35d	Additon, Thomas...	Mass. mil....	Private....	71	Kennebec...	
'35c	Adley, Peter.......	N. Y. line...	Private....	78	Somerset...	
'40f	Adley, Peter.......	....	....	79	Franklin....	Res. Berlin.
1794	Airs, George.......	Crane's a r t. regt.	Matross....	....	....	Res. Arundel. Wounded at Brandywine.
'35c	Akley, Samuel.....	Mass. line...	Private....	76	Oxford......	Tr'sf'rred from Windham Co., Vt., 1827.
'40	Akley, Samuel.....	....	....	76	Oxford......	Res. Rumford.
'35c	Albee, Jonathan...	Mass. line...	Private....	90	Somerset...	('20).
'31a	Albee, William....	....	....	....	....	Rejected as not serving in Cont. regiments.
'35d	Alden, Silas.......	N. H. line...	Private....	69	Oxford......	
'40	*Aldrich Mary*.....	....	....	79	Cumberland.	Res. Freeport.
'35c	Aldrick, Henry....	Mass. line...	Private....	72	Oxford......	Died 1822.
'35d	Aldricks, Nathaniel.	Mass. line...	Private....	82	Cumberland.	Died March 5, 1834.
'40	Allbee, Jonathan...	....	....	97	Somerset...	Res. Lexington.
'35d	Allen, Amos.......	Mass. line...	Private....	74	Lincoln.....	('20, '31b).
'35d	Allen, Barsham....	N. H. state..	Private....	72	York.......	
'40	———	....	....	76	York.......	Res. South Berwick.

List	Name	Service	Rank	Age	County	Remarks
'40	Allen, Cynthia			81	Kennebec	Res. Greene.
'35d	Allen, Daniel	Mass. line	Private and Corporal	87 or 81	Kennebec	('20 and '31b, Daniel 1st.)
'40				86	Kennebec	Res. Winthrop.
'40	Allen, Daniel, 2d	Mass. line	Private	71	Lincoln	Res. Bowdoin.
'35c	Allen, Ebenezer	N. H. line	Private	71	Waldo	('20.)
'40	Allen, Ebenezer			80	Waldo	Res. Montville.
'35c	Allen, Ephraim	See Alley, Ephraim				
'35c	Allen, Hezekiah P.	Mass. line	Private	65	Lincoln	('20) d. Feb. 3, 1826.
'35d	Allen, Isaac	Mass. line	Private	82 or 77	Cumberland	('20.)
'40	Allen, Isaac			83	Cumberland	Res. Minot.
'35d	Allen, Jacob, 2d	N. H. line	Private	75	York	('20, '31b.)
'40				82	York	Res. No. Berwick.
'35d	Allen, Jacob	Mass. line	Private	71	Cumberland	('20, '31b.)
'40				76	Cumberland	Res. Scarborough.
'35c	Allen, James	Cont. navy	Seaman	79	York	('20, frig. "Raleigh.")
'35d	Allen, Job	Mass. line	Private	71	Cumberland	('20.)
'40				77	Cumberland	Res. Pownal.
'31a	Allen, John		Private			Rejected as not serving in Cont. reg.
'35c	Allen, John	Mass. line	Private	86	York	('20) d. Feb. 27, 1832.
'35d	Allen, John	N. H. state	Private and Corporal	76	York	
'35d	Allen, John	Mass. mil	Private and Sergeant	75	Kennebec	
'40			Private	81	Kennebec	Res. Vienna.
'35d	Allen, John	Mass. line	Private	73	Kennebec	
'35c	Allen, Joseph, 2d	N. H. line	Private	79	York	
'35c	Allen, Joseph	Mass. line	Private	75	Cumberland	('20.)
'40				81	Cumberland	Res. Gray.
'35d	Allen, Nehemiah	Mass. mil	Private	81	Cumberland	
'40				87	Cumberland	Res. Pownal.
'35c	Allen, Peter	Mass. line	Private	76	Lincoln	
'40	Allen, Susannah			69	Lincoln	Res. Bowdoinham
'35d	Allen, William	Mass. mil	Private	82	Cumberland	
'35d	Allen, William	Mass. line	Corp. and Sergeant	81 or 87	Penobscot	('20.)
'40	Allen, William			83	Cumberland	Res. Poland.
'35c	Allen, Wright	Mass. line	Private	80	Oxford	('20) d. Jan. 2, 1832.
'35c	Alley, Ephraim	Mass. line	Private	74	Lincoln	('20) ('35c as Allen.)
'40				80	Lincoln	Res. Boothbay.
'40	Alven, Silas			74	Franklin	Res. Jay.
'40	Alvin, Eliphalet			80	Oxford	Res. Waterford.
'40	Ames, Deborah			79	Waldo	Res. Camden.
'35c	Ames, Eleazer	Mass. line	Private	76	Kennebec	('20) d. Jan. 20, 1825.
'35d	Ames, Jacob	Mass. mil	Private	76	Kennebec	
'40	Ames, Jacob			83	Hancock	Res. Brooksville.
'35d	Ames, John	Mass. line	Private	77	Oxford	Died Sept. 30, 1833.
'35d	Ames, Samuel	Mass. state	Drummer	75	Oxford	
'40				81	Oxford	Res. Norway.
'35d	Anderson, Robert	Mass. mil	Sergeant	78	Kennebec	
'40	Anderson, Robert			84	Lincoln	Res. Lewiston.
'35d	Anderson, Robert	Mass. mil	Private	73	Cumberland	
'40				79	Cumberland	Res. Otisfield.

List.	Name.	Service.	Rank.	Age.	County.	Remarks.
'40	Andrews, Ephraim.			83	Piscataquis..	Res. Guilford.
'35c	Andrews, Jeremiah.	Mass. line...	Private....	77	Oxford......	('20) d. Feb. 25, 1827.
'35c	Andrews, John.....	Mass. line...	Corporal...	78	Oxford......	('20) d. Feb. 7, 1828.
'35d	Andrews, Robert...	Mass. line...	Private....	82	Cumberland.	
'40	Andrews, Robert...			81	Cumberland.	Res. Bridgton.
'35d	Andrews, Sam., 2d	Mass. line...	Private....	80 or 77	Penobscot...	('20 and 31b as Samuel.)
'40	Andrews, Samuel...			85	Kennebec....	Res. China.
'35c	Andrews, Samuel E.	N. H. line...	Private....	69	Oxford......	('20) d. Jan. 1, 1822.
'35c	Andrews, Stephen..	Mass. line...	Private....	78	York........	('20.)
'35d	Andrews, William..	R. I line...	Private and Sergeant.	79	York........	('20 as private.)
'35d	Applebee, Simeon..	Cont. navy..	Private and Marine.	74	York........	('20, ship "Ranger," '31b.)
'40	Applebee, Simeon..			88	York........	Res. North Berwick.
'35c	Arbour, Michael...	Mass. line...	Private....	80	Somerset....	
'35c	Arno, John........	Mass. line...	Private....	87	Kennebec....	('20) d. June, 1831.
35d	Arnold, Nathaniel..	Mass. line...	Private and Corporal.	75	Kennebec....	Died Oct. 13, 1833.
'35c	Arnold, Robert....	Mass. line...	Private....	87	Somerset....	('20.)
'35c	Arskine, Alexander.	Mass. line...	Private....	84	Lincoln......	('20) d. 1826.
'35c	Artherton, Joel....	Mass. line...	Private....	73	Oxford......	('20) same as Atherton.
'40	Aspenwall, Nancy..			77	Waldo......	Res. Unity.
'40	Atherton, Joel.....			77	Oxford......	Same as Artherton. Res. Waterford.
'35d	Atherton, John....	Mass. line...	Corporal...	72	Oxford......	('20.)
'35c	Atkinson, William..	Mass. line...	Private....	73	Lincoln......	('20.)
'40	Atkinson, William..	Mass. line...	Private....	75	Lincoln......	Res. Lewiston.
'40	Atus, Lunun.......				Washington.	Res. Machias. Same as Atys.
35c	Atwood, Nathan...	Mass. line...	Private....	77	Hancock....	('20.)
'40				82	Hancock....	Res. Bucksport.
'35d	Atys, London,.....	Mass. state artillery.	Private....		Washington..	
'35d	Aunes, Stephen....	N. H. state..	Private and Sergeant.	79	York........	
'35c	Austin, Benjamin..	Mass. line...	Private....	72	York........	('20.)
'35c	Austin, John......	Mass. line...	Private....	100	Kennebec...	('20) d. Jan. 16, 1820.
'35c	Austin, Jonah.....	Mass. line...	Private....	81	Cumberland.	('20, '31b.)
'35d	Austin, Stephen...	Mass. mil...	Private....	71	Kennebec....	
'35c	Averell, Ezekiel...	Mass. line...	Private....	78	Lincoln......	('20.)
'40	Averill, Ezekiel....			85	Lincoln......	Res. Wiscasset.
'35c	Averill, Moses.....	Mass. line...	Private....	74	Kennebec....	('20.)
'40	Averill, Moses.....			85	Franklin....	Res. Wilton.
'20	Avery, John.......	N. H. line...	Private....			Not in '35 under Me.
'35c	Avery, Samuel.....	N. H. line...	Private....	78	Lincoln......	('20.)
'35d	Ayer, Benjamin...	Mass. line...	Private and Musician.	70	Waldo......	(20.)
'40	Ayer, Benjamin....			76	Kennebec....	Res. Monmouth.
'35c	Ayer, Moses.......	Cont. navy..	Marine....	85	Somerset....	('20, ship "Hancock,' '31b.)
'35c	Babb, Peter.......	Mass. line...	Private....	72	York........	('20.)
'35c	Babbage, Courtney.	Mass. line...	Private....	73	Hancock....	('20, Babbidge.)
'35d	Babcock, Benjamin	Mass. mil...	Private....	•75	Lincoln......	
'40				82	Lincoln......	Res. Boothbay.
'35c	Babcock, Jeremiah.	Mass. line...	Private....	78	Kennebec....	('20, '31b.)
'35c	Bachelder, David..	N. H. line...	Sergeant...	67	Cumberland.	Died Jan. 8, 1829.
'35d	Bachelder, Phineas.	N. H. mil...	Private....	73	Penobscot...	Same as Batcheld
'40	Bachelder, Stephen			85	Penobscot...	Res. Exeter. Same. Bacheldor, S.?
'35d	Bacheldor, Stephen	N. H. line...	Private....	79	Somerset....	Same as Bachelder, S.?
'35d	Bacon, Josiah.....	Mass. line...	Private....	72	Kennebec..	
'35c	Bacon, Timothy...	Mass. line...	Private....	70	Cumberland.	('20.)
'40				70 to 80	Cumberland.	Res. Gorham.
'20	Bailey, Eliphalet..	Penn........	Private....			
'35c	Bailey, Eliphalet..	Mass. line...	Private....	77	Kennebec....	('31b.)
'35d	Bailey, Eliphalet }	Mass. line... N. H. state..	Private.... Artificer...	77 77	} Kennebec..	
'35c	Bailey, Israel.....	Mass. line...	Private....	70	Cumberland.	('20) d. May 22, 1830.
'35c	Bailey, John, 2d...	Mass. line...	Private..\..	78	Cumberland.	('20) d. Aug. 31, 1822.
'35c	Bailey, John.......	Mass. line...	Private.\...	71	Oxford......	('20) d. July 19, 1833.
'20	Bailey, Joshua.....	Mass........	Private....			('31b) see also Bailey, Josiah.
'35c	Bailey, Josiah.....	Mass. line...	Private....	80	Lincoln......	'20.)
'35c	Bailey, Josiah.....	Mass. line...	Private....	71	Lincoln......	Error for Bailey, Joshua?

List.	Name.	Service.	Rank.	Age.	County.	Remarks.
40	Bailey, Lucy			73	Cumberland	Res. Minot.
'35c	Bailey, Prince	Mass. line	Private	78	Kennebec	('20.)
'40	Bailey, Rebecca			91	Cumberland	Res. Portland.
'35c	Bailey, Samuel	R. I. line	Musician	78	Penobscot	('20) d. May 11, 1829.
'35d	Bailey, Thaddeus	Mass. mil	Private	74	Kennebec	
'40	Bailey, Thaddeus			80	Waldo	Res. Palermo.
'40	Baker, Asa G			50	Lincoln	Res. Boothbay.
'35c	Baker, John	Mass. line	Private	66	York	('20) d. Dec. 17, 1820.
'35c	Baker, Joseph	Mass. line	Private	91	Oxford	Died Dec. 19, 1833.
'40	Baker, Mary			8!	York	Res. York.
'40	Baker, Mary			71	Cumberland	Res. No. Yarmouth.
'35d	Baker, Samuel	Mass. mil	Private and Sergeant.	8!	Kennebec	
'40	———			85	Kennebec	Res. Albion.
'35c	Baker, Samuel	Mass. line	Private	73	Cumberland	('20.)
'35c	Baker, Silas	Mass. line	Private	75	Somerset	('20.)
'40	Baker, Silas			82	Franklin	Res. Strong.
'40	Baldwin, Nahum			78	Somerset	Res. Mercer.
'35c	Ball, John	Mass. line	Private	76	Somerset	('20) d. Sept. 3, 1823.
'40	Ballard, Betty			83	Franklin	Res. Temple.
'35c	Ballard, Frederick	Mass. line	Private	76	Oxford	Transf. from Strafford Co., N. H., 1829. Died March 4,1832.
'40	Ballard, Frederick			77	Oxford	Res. Greenwood.
'35c	Ballard, Jonathan	Mass. line	Private	72	Kennebec	('20) d. Nov. 28, 1830.
'35c	Ballard, Uriah	N. H. line	Private	74	Oxford	('20.)
'40	———			80	Oxford	Res. Fryeburg.
'35c	Baloon, Samuel	Mass. line	Private	74	Lincoln	Also given Maloon. Died Jan. 16, 1828.
'35c	Banks, John	Mass. line	Private	76	York	('20.)
'35c	Banks, Moses	Mass. line	Lieutenant	88	Cumberland	('20) d. Oct. 10, 1823.
'40	Banks, Sarah			88	York	Res. York.
'35d	Barbarick, John	21st reg't	Corporal		Lincoln	Pensioned, 1785. Died June 25, 1827.
35c	Barber, Solomon	Mass. line	Private	77	Hancock	('20, '31b) d. June 12, 1827.
35	Barker, Benjamin	Mass. state		79	Oxford	
'40	Barker, Benjamin			77	Oxford	Res. Newry.
'35	Barker, Daniel	Mass. line	Private	89	Oxford	('20.)
'35	Barker, Daniel, 2d	Mass. line	Private	78	Kennebec	('20) d. Aug. 22, 1820.
'35	Barker, James	Mass. line	Private	75	Cumberland	Pensioned, 1825.
'35	Barker, James	Mass. line	Private	74	Cumberland	Pensioned, 1818.
'40	Barker, James			80	Oxford	Res. Greenwood.
'31r	Barker, James					Deserted.
35d	Barker, Jesse	Mass. line	Private	92	Oxford	
'40	Barker, Jesse			75	Oxford	Res. Newry.
35c	Barker, Jonathan	Mass. line	Private	70	Cumberland	('20) d. Feb. 11, 1824.
35c	Barker, Samuel	Mass. line	Private	73	Oxford	('20, '31b.)
20	Barnard, Daniel	N. H.	Private			
'35c	Barnard, Daniel	Mass. line	Private	72	Cumberland	
'35c	Barnard, Nathan	Mass. line	Private	67	Lincoln	('20, '31b.)
'40	Barnard, Sarah			80	Lincoln	Res. Union.
'35c	Barnes, Abraham	Mass. line	Private	65	York	('20.)
'35c	Barnes, Joseph	Mass. line	Private	70	Washington	
'35c	Barrett, James	Mass. line	Private	66	Cumberland	('20) d. June 30, 1819.
35c	Barrett, John	Mass. line	Private	75	Somerset	('20.)
'35c	Barrett, Nathaniel	N. H. line	Private	69	Somerset	Retransf. from Rutland Co., Vt., 1830.
'40	———			74	Somerset	Res. Fairfield.
'35d	Barrows, Asa	Mass. mil	Private	83	Oxford	
'35c	Barrows, Ephraim	Mass. line	Private	72	Oxford	('20.)
'20	Barrows, Peter	R. 1	Private			
'35c	Barrows, Peter	Mass. line	Private	79	Waldo	Originally on invalid pension roll, 1789.
'40	———			85	Waldo	Res. Camden.
'35d	Barrows, William	Mass. line	Private	78	Oxford	('20.)
'35d	Barry, Jonathan	Mass. mil	Private	78	Washington	
35c	Barstow, Benjamin	Mass. line	Private	62	Lincoln	('20, '31b.)
'35d	Barstow, Timothy	Mass. mil	Private	72	Cumberland	
'35c	Barter, John	N. H. line	Private	74	Lincoln	('20)
'40	Barter, Joseph			57	Lincoln	Res. St. George.
'40	Barter, Mark			54	Lincoln	
'35c	Barter, Pelatiah	N. H. line	Private	93	Lincoln	('20, Peletiah)d. Mar. 1, 1825.
'35a	Bartlett, Benjamin	Rev.?			York	Pensioned, 1807. Died, 1825.
'35c	Bartlett, Caleb	Mass. line	Private	65	Cumberland	('20)d. Aug. 23, 1820.

List.	Name.	Service.	Rank.	Age.	County.	Remarks.
'35c	Bartlett, John	Mass. line	Private	82	Oxford	('20.)
'40				89	Oxford	Res. Sumner.
'35c	Bartlett, Joseph	Mass. line	Private	80	Lincoln	Died June 2, 1828.
'35c	Bartlett, Joseph	Mass. line	Private	75	Lincoln	From Mass. Died June 2, 1828.
'35c	Bartlett, Malachi	Mass. line	Private	76	Kennebec	('20) d. Feb. 29, 1832.
'35d	Bartlett, Thaddeus	Mass. mil.	Private	75	Oxford	
'40				81	Oxford	Res. Bethel.
'35d	Barton, Benjamin	R. I. line	Captain	75 & 94	Waldo	
'35c	Barton, John	Mass. line	Private	82	Lincoln	('20.)
'35c	Bassett, David	Cont. navy	Mariner	85	Lincoln	('20, ship "Warren".)
'35d	Bassett, Samuel	Mass. state	Private and Sergeant.	86	Kennebec	Res. Vassalborough.
'40				94	Kennebec	
'35c	Basteen, Joseph	R. I. line	Private	84	Washington	('20.)
'35c	Baston, Jonathan	Mass. line	Private	80	York	('20) same as Boston?
'20	Baston, Thomas	Mass.	Private			Same as Boston, T.
'40	Batchelder, Phineas			80	Penobscot	Res. Garland. Same as Bachelder, P.
'35c	Batchelder, William	N. H. line	Private	71	Kennebec	('20.)
'40	Batchelder, William	N. H.		79	Kennebec	('20, William, 2d). Res. Pittston.
'35c	Batcheldor, Gideon	Mass. line	Private	87	York	('20, Bacheldor.)
'35d	Bates, Doughty	Mass. mil.	Private	73	Kennebec	
'35d	Bates, Jabez	Mass. line	Private and Seaman.	73	Kennebec	
'40	Bates, Jabez R.			79	Kennebec	Res. Leeds.
'35d	Bates, Jacob	Mass. line	Private	74	Cumberland	
'40				80	Cumberland	Res. Minot.
'40	*Bates, Mary*			77	Kennebec	Res. Leeds.
'40	*Bates, Susannah*			82	Somerset	Res. Fairfield.
'35d	Bates, Thomas	Mass. mil.	Sergeant and Fifer.	77	Kennebec	
'40				83	Kennebec	Res. Waterville,
'35d	Battles, Asa	Mass. mil.	Private	69	Oxford	
'35c	Baxter, Benjamin	N. H. line	Private	74	Somerset	Died Oct. 17, 1831.
'35c	Baxter, John	Mass. line	Private	79	Somerset	('20, '31b.)
'40	*Baxter, Reliance*			84	Kennebec	Res. Vassalborough.

Burnham Tavern, Machias, Me., of Revolutionary Fame.

List.	Name.	Service	Rank.	Age.	County.	Remarks.
'35c	Beal, Daniel	Mass. line	Private	72	Cumberland	('20) Died Sept. 4, 1825.
'40	Beal, Elizabeth T.			78	Cumberland	Res. Freeport.
'35d	Beal, Job	Mass. mil	Private and Sergeant.	74	Cumberland	
'35c	Beal, Joseph	Mass. line	Private	77	Waldo	('20) Died Oct 29 1830.
'35d	Beales, Isaac	Mass. mil	Fifer, matross and drummer	74	Kennebec	
'35c	Beall, Benjamin	N. H. line	Private	76	Lincoln	('20) d. July 26, 1823
'40	Beals, Lydia				Kennebec	Res. Greene.
'35d	Bean, Daniel	Mass. line	Private	75	Oxford	
'20	Bean, Ebenezer	R. I.	Private			
'35c	Bean, Ebenezer	Mass. line	Private	96	York	Died 1824.
'40	Bean, James R.			67	York	('35a) Res. Hollis
1792	Bean, John	3d N. H. regt.	Corporal			Wounded 1779. Pensioned 1789.
1794		3d N. H. regt.	Corporal			Res. Washington.
'20	Bean, John	N. H.	Private			('31b)same as Beans, J.
'35c	Bean, Jonathan	Mass. line	Private	79	Oxford	('20) d. Nov. 19, 1826.
'35d	Bean, Josiah	N. H. line	Private	75	Kennebec	('20, '31b).
'40	Bean, Margaret			82	Oxford	Res. Bethel.
'40	Bean, Oliver			42	Kennebec	Res. Readfield.
'35c	Bean, Samuel	R. I. line	Private	70	Lincoln	('20) d. Aug. 14, 1818.
'35a	Beans, John	N. H. line	Private		Kennebec	Transf. from Mass., 1819.Same as Bean, J. d.Nov.12,1832.
'35c	Bearce, Elemezer	Mass. line	Lieut	79	Lincoln	('28 as Ebenezer). d. May 3, 1827.
'35d	Bearce, Gideon	Mass. state	Marine	76	Oxford	
'40				82	Oxford	AsBearseRes.Hebron
'35c	Bearce, Levi	Mass line	Private	77	Oxford	('20) d. Dec. 17, 1826.
'35c	Beckey, Magnus	N. H. line	Private	72	Somerset	('20 as Beckley). d. May 19, 1824.
'35d	Beckford, William	Mass. mil	Private	72	York	
'35c	Beckler, Daniel	Mass. line	Private	86	Oxford	('20) d. Sept. 4, 1833.
'35d	Beedle, Henry	Mass. state	Private	75	York	
'40				80	York	Res. S. Berwick.
'20	Beeman, John	Mass	Private			Same as Buman ?
'35d	Belcher, Supply	Mass. line	Priv'te and Sergeant	82	Kennebec	
'35c	Bemis, Jacob	Mass. line	Private	76	Cumberland	('20).
'40				83	Cumberland	Res. Pownal.
'35c	Bemis, Thaddeus	Mass. line	Private	75	Oxford	('20).
'40				81	Oxford	Res. Fryeburg.
'35c	Benjamin, Samuel	Mass. line	Lieut	82	Oxford	('20, '31b).
'35c	Benner, Christopher	Mass. line	Private	78	Washington	('20).
'40				84	Washington	Res. Dennysville.

List	Name	Service	Rank	Age	County	Remarks
'35c	Benner, Peter	Mass. line	Corporal	72	Kennebec	('20). d. Sept. 9, 1833.
'40	Bennet, John			58	Cumberland	Res. Brunswick.
'35c	Bennett, Andrew	Mass. line	Private	81	Waldo	('20).
'35c	Bennett, Moses	Mass. line	Private	78	Cumberland	('20) d. Feb. 12, 1832
'35c	Bennett, Samuel	Mass. line	Private	86	Somerset	('20).
'35d	Benson, Ichabod	Mass. line	Private	77	Oxford	Died Aug. 1, 1833.
'40	Benson, Jeptha			81	Hancock	Res. Brooksville.
'35d	Benson, Robert	Mass. mil	Drummer	79	York	Died July 1, 1833.
'40	Berdens, Timothy			76	York	Same as Burdeen. Res. S. Berwick.
'40	*Berry, Abigail*			73	York	Res. York.
'35d	Berry, George	Mass. line	Private	78	Kennebec	('20, '31b).
'35d	Berry, Jonathan	Mass. line	Private	78	York	
'35c	Berry, Joseph	Mass. line	Private	78	York	('20).
'35d	Berry, Josiah	Mass. state	Private	73	Cumberland	('20).
'35c	Berry, Josiah	Mass. line	Private	75	Lincoln	
'40	Berry, Josiah			78	York	Res. Limerick.
'35c	Berry, Nathaniel	Mass. line	Private	78	Kennebec	('20).
'40				84	Kennebec	Res. Pittston.
'35c	Berry, Pelatiah	Mass. line	Private	74	Cumberland	('20).
'35c	Berry, Thomas	Mass. line	Lieut	92	Lincoln	('28). d. Jan. 27, 1828.
'35d	Berry, Thomas	R. I. state	Private	72	Oxford	
'40				78	Oxford	Res. Buckfield.
'35c	Berry, Timothy	Mass. line	Private	82	Oxford	('20)
'40	Berry, Timothy			87	York	Res. Cornish.
35d	Berry, Zebulon	Mass. mil	Private	74	Cumberland	
'40				80	Cumberland	Res. Scarborough.
35d	Besse, Jabez	Mass. mil	Private	72	Kennebec	
'40				75	Kennebec	Res. Wayne.
'35c	Besse, Joseph	Mass. line	Private	74	Oxford	('20).
'40					Oxford	Res. Paris.
'35d	Bessee, Ebenezer	Mass. line	Private	81	Somerset	
'35d	Bett, Amzi	Mass. mil	Private	72	Oxford	
'35d	Bettis, Jeremiah	Mass. line	Priv'te and Sergeant	71	York	('20 as Bettes).
'35d	Beveridge, Matthew	Mass. mil		68	Waldo	
'35d	Bibber, James	Mass. mil	Private	78	Cumberland	
'40				84	Cumberland	Res. N. Yarmouth.
'35d	Bickford, Ben amin	Mass. mil	Private	91	Kennebec	
'35c	Bickford, John	N. H. line	Private	75	York	('20).
'40	Bickford, William			84	Lincoln	Res. Lewiston.
'35c	Bickmore, John	Mass. line	Private	76	Waldo	('20) d. Sept. 4, 1832.
'35d	Bicknell, Abner	Mass. mil	Private	70	Waldo	
'40				76	Waldo	Res. Frankfort.
'40	*Bicknell, Olive*			89	Oxford	Res. Hartford.
'35d	Bigge, David	Mass. mil	Private	85	Oxford	
'35d	Billings, Abel	Mass. mil	Private	78	Hancock	
'35c	Billington, Issac	Mass. line	Private	70	Kennebec	Died Dec. 16, 1829.
'35c	Bisbee, Elisha	Mass. line	Lieut	78	Oxford	('20). d. Dec. 4, 1826
'35d	Bishop, Enos	Mass. mil	Private	87	Cumberland	
1794	Bishop, Squire	M'Cobb's mil regt.	Private			Wounded 1779. Res. Washington.
1792	Bishop, Squire, Jr.	S. Webb'srgt.	Private			Wounded 1779. Pensioned 1792.
'35a		Blunt's Co.			Kennebec	
'40	Bishop, Squire			85	Kennebec	Res. Vassalborough.
'35d	Bishop, Zadock	Mass. line	Private	85	Kennebec	
'40	Bishop, Zadoc,			91	Kennebec	Res. Leeds.
'35c	Biter, Peter	Mass. line	Private	79	Kennebec	('20) d. Mar. 4, 1827.
'35c	Black, Henry	Mass. line	Private	76	York	('20).
'35c	Black, Joab	Mass. line	Private	81	Cumberland	('20, '31b).
'31a	Black, Joseph		Private			Rejected on account of amount of his property.
'35d	Black, Josiah	Mass. state	Private	84	York	('31a).
'40				89	York	Res. Limington.
'35c	Black, Moses	Mass. line	Private	83	Hancock	('20) d. Dec. 22, 1829.
'35c	Blackington, James	Mass. line	Private	70	Lincoln	('20).
'35d	Blackston, William	Mass. mil	Sergeant	79	Kennebec	
'35c	Blackstone, John	N. J. line	Private	75	Lincoln	('20) d. Dec. 20, 1818.
'40	*Blackstone, Rebecca*			79	Lincoln	Res. Richmond.
'35c	Blackwood, James	Mass. line	Private	90	Washington	('20) d. Mar. 1827.
'35c	Blair, James	Mass. line	Private	81	Lincoln	('20).
'35c	Blake, Benjamin	Mass. line	Private	69	Oxford	('20).

List.	Name.	Service.	Rank.	Age.	County.	Remarks.
'40	Blake, Deborah			70to 80	Cumberland	Res. Gorham.
'35d	Blake, James	Mass. state	Private	71	Cumberland	
'35d	Blake, John	N. H. line	Ensign and Lieut.	77 & 79	Penobscot	('20, '31b).
'40	——			86	Penobscot	Res. Brewer.
'35d	Blake, John	Mass. line	Private	72	Kennebec	('20).
'40	Blake, John			80	Kennebec	Res. Gardiner.
'35c	Blake, John	Mass. line	Private	66	Cumberland	
'35c	Blake, Joseph	Mass. line	Corporal	76	Cumberland	('20).
'40	Blake, Josiah			80	Franklin	Res. Phillips.
'35d	Blake, Robert	Mass. mil	Private	82	Kennebec	
'40	——			87	Kennebec	Res. Fayette.
'35d	Blake, Willing	Mass. line	Priv'te and Sergeant.	72	Lincoln	('20).
'40	——			78	Lincoln	Res. Warren.
'40	Blanchard, Sarah			86	Lincoln	Res. Richmond.
'35d	Blanchard, Seth	Mass. mil	Private	74	Cumberland	
'40	——			81	Cumberland	Res. N. Yarmouth.
'35d	Blanchard, Solomon	R. I. mil	Priv'te and Art.	72	Lincoln	
'40	——			77	Lincoln	Res. Dresden.
'31b	Blanchard, Theoph.		Private			Same as Blancher.
'35d	Blanchard, Timothy	R. I. line	Priv'te and Sergeant.	79	Lincoln	('20, '31b).
35c	Blancher, Theophilus	Mass. line	Private	70	Lincoln	('20) same as Blanchard.
'35c	Blasdell, Daniel	Mass. line	Private	86	Lincoln	('20) d. Feb. 4, 1829.
'35c	Blethen, Increase	Mass. line	Private	76	Somerset	('20).
'31a	Blodget, Jonathan		Private			Reg't. not on Continental establishment.
'35d	Blodget, Jonathan	N. H. line	Private	78	Oxford	
'40	——			83	Oxford	Res. Gilead.
'40	Blue, Hannah			78	Kennebec	Res. Monmouth.
'35c	Boas, James	Mass. line	Private	73	Cumberland	('20 as Boaz).
'40	Booker, Aaron			88	York	Same as Booker, A. Res. York.
'20	Boden, Theodore	Mass	Private			Same as Booden, T.
'35a	Bodwell, Ebenezer		Corporal		Oxford	From Mass. in 1817.
'40	——			55	Oxford	Res. Andover.
'35c	Bogues, Samuel	Mass. line	Private	76	Lincoln	Misspelled Rogues. ('20).
'35c	Boice, James	Va. line	Mariner	77	York	('20 ship "Ranger").
'35c	Bointon, Joseph	N. H. line	Private	80	Oxford	Same as Boynton, J.
'35c	Bointon, Pelatiah	Mass. line	Private	77	Kennebec	('20 as Boynton, P.) Same as Boyington, P. ?
'35c	Bois, John	N. H. line	Private	74	Somerset	('20) d. Mar. 16, 1833.
'35c	Bolden, John	Va. line	Private	88	Lincoln	('20).
'35c	Bolton, David	Mass. line	Private	64	Kennebec	Same as Botton ? d. Feb. 4, 1828.
'35c	Bolton, Solomon	Mass. line	Private	78	Penobscot	
'40	——			82	Penobscot	Res. Orrington.
'35c	Bompus, Morris	Mass. line	Private	78	Oxford	Same as Bumfries ?
'35c	Bond, Jonas	Mass. line	Private	74	Washington	
'40	——			80	Washington	Res. Robbinston.
'40	Bonney, Isaac			85	Oxford	Res. Sumner. Same as following ?
'35d	Bonneys, Isaac	Mass. line	Private	79	Oxford	Same as preceding ?
'35c	Booden, Ebenezer	R. I. line	Private	67	Hancock	
'35c	Booden, Theodore	Mass. line	Private	70	Penobscot	Same as Boden, T. and as Bowden,T?
'35c	Booffee, Thomas	N. H. line	Ensign	84	Lincoln	('20) d. Jan. 10, 1820
'35d	Booker, Aaron	Mass. line	Private	80	York	Same as Booker, A.
'40	Booker, Anna			75	Lincoln	Res. Richmond.
'35c	Booker, Isaiah	Mass. line	Private	72	Somerset	d. Feb. 27, 1833.
'35c	Booker, Josiah	Mass. line	Private	78	Kennebec	('20) d. Feb. 27, 1823
'40	Boothby, Elizabeth			80	York	Res. Limerick.
'35c	Boothby, William	Mass. line	Private	76	York	('20, '31b).
'35d	Bornhumen, Jacob	Mass. mil	Priv'te and marine.	69	Lincoln	Same as Burnheimer.
'40	Boster, Jonathan			86	York	Same as Baston, J. ? Res. Kennebunk.
'35d	Boston, Elijah	Mass. line	Private	81	York	('20, '31b).
'35d	Boston, Shebruel	Mass. mil	Private	78	York	
'35d	Boston, Thomas	Mass. line	Private	74	York	Same as Baston, T.

List.	Name.	Service	Rank.	Age.	County.	Remarks.
'40	————			77	York	Res. Kennebunkport ('20).
'35c	Bosworth, Daniel...	Mass. line...	Private...	74	Washington..	
'40	————			79	Washington..	Res. Dennysville.
'35c	Bosworth, Jonathan	Mass. line...	Private...	76	Somerset....	('20).
'20	Botton, David.....	Mass......	Private....			Same as Bolton, D.?
'20	Bouden, Amos.....	Mass......	Private....			Same as Bowden, A.
'20	Boulter, Nathaniel..	Mass......	Private.....			Same as Butler, N. ?
'35d	Bourne, John......	Mass. mil...	Private....	74	York......	
'35c	Bowden, Amos.....	Mass line....	Private....	62	Hancock.....	Same as Bouden, A. d. Dec. 23, 1823.
'40	Bowden, Theodore..			76	Hancock....	Same as Booden, T? Res. Penobscot.
'40	Bowen, Samuel....			76	Waldo......	Res. Brooks.
40	*Bowen, Sarah*......			77	Waldo......	Res. Vinalhaven.
'35c	Bowers, Benjamin..	Mass. line...	Private....	75	Penobscot...	Transf. from Caledonia Co. Vt. 1825
'20	Bowing, Jabish.....	N. H......	Private....			
'35c	Bowing, Jabish.....	Mass. line...	Private....	77	Somerset....	
'40	Bowing, Jabes......			82	Somerset....	Res. Starks.
'35c	Bowker, Levi......	Mass. line...	Private....	71	Washington..	('20).
'40	————			77	Washington..	Res. Machias.
'35d	Boyd, Samuel......	Mass. line...	Priv'te and Drummer	81	Kennebec...	
'40	Boyington, Peltiah..			82	Somerset....	Same as Bointon.P.? Res. Mercer.
'28	Boynton, Joseph...		Lieut.....			
'29	Boynton, Joseph...	N. H. line...	Lieut. Inf....			('20). Same as Bointon, J.
'35e	Boynton, Joseph....	3d N. H. line.	Lieut......	—	York......	
'35c	Bracey, James.....	Mass. line...	Private....	91	York......	('20).
'35d	Bracket, Joshua....	Mass. state..	Private....	76	York......	Same as Brackett, J.
'35d	Bracket, Joshua....	Mass. mil...	Private....	72	York......	Same as Brackett, J.
'35c	Bracket, Josiah.....	Mass. line...	Private....	64	Cumberland	Same as Brackett, J. d. Aug. 8, 1820.
'35d	Bracket, Peter.....	Mass. line...	Pvt. of Art.	78	Cumberland	
'35d	Bracket, William...	Mass. state..	Priv'te and Sergeant	82	Oxford.....	Same as Brakett, W.
'35d	Brackett, James....	Mass. mil...	Private....	70	Oxford.....	('20).
'40	Brackett, James....			76	Franklin....	Res. Berlin.
'35d	Brackett, John.....	Mass. line...	Private....	83	Cumberland	('20, '31b).
'40	Brackett, John.....			79	Cumberland	Res. Harrison.
'40	Brackett, Joshua...			82	York......	Same as Bracket, J. Res. Acton.
'40	Brackett, Joshua...			78	York......	Same as Brackett J. Res. Limington.
'20	Brackett, Josiah....					Same as Bracket, J.
'35d	Brackett, Nathan...	Mass. state..	Private....	80	Oxford.....	
'40	Brackett, Nathan...			55	Kennebec....	Res. Clinton.
'35d	Bradan, Robert....	Mass. state..	Private....	89	York......	Died Jan. 4, 1833.
'35d	Bradbury, Paul....	Mass. line...	Priv'te and Corporal	77	Kennebec...	
'35c	Bradford, Elijah....	Mass. line...	Private....	73	Lincoln.....	Died Nov. 23, 1829.
'35d	Bradford, Peabody.	Mass. line...	Corporal...	76	Cumberland	('20).
'40	————			82	Cumberland	Res. Minot.
'35d	Bradford, Peter....	Mass. mil....	Sergeant...	89	Kennebec...	Died Jan. 11, 1834.
'35d	Bradley, Samuel....	Mass. line...	Private....	72	Kennebec...	
'40	Bradley, Samuel....			74	Franklin....	Res. New Sharon.
1792	Bradstreet, Dudley.	Invalid's regt	Private....			Wounded 1777. Pensioned 1792.
1794	————	Col. Francis' regt...	Private....			Res. Portland.
'35c	Brag, Nicholas....	Mass. line...	Private....	82	Cumberland	Same as Bray, N. ?
'40	Bragden, John.....			86	York......	Res. Kennebunk. Same as Bragdon, J. ?
'35c	Bragdon, Aaron....	Mass. line...	Private....	74	Penobscot...	('20) d. Oct. 22, 1832
'40	————			83	Penobscot...	Res. Corinth.
'35d	Bragdon, Arthur...	Mass. line...	Priv'te and Corporal	78	Oxford.....	('20, '31b).
'35c	Bragdon, Daniel....	Mass. line...	Private....	99	York......	('20) d. 1821.
'35c	Bragdon, Ezekiel...	Mass. line...	Private....	86	York......	('20) d. June 19, 1827.
'35c	Bragdon, John.....	Mass. line...	Private....	77	York......	('20) Same as Bragden, J. ?
'35c	Bragdon, John, 2d..	Mass. line...	Private....	74	Cumberland	('20).
'40	Bragdon, John.....			80	Cumberland	Res. Poland.
'35d	Bragdon, John.....	Mass. line...	Private....	71	York......	
'35c	Bragg, Joab........	Mass. line...	Private....	76	Kennebec...	('20).

List	Name	Service	Rank	Age	County	Remarks
'40	Bragg, Lydia........			71	Kennebec....	Res. Vassalborough.
'35d	Brainard, Church....	N. H. state..	Priv'te and marine	77	Kennebec....	
'40	Brakett, William...			88	Oxford......	Same as Bracket, W. Res. Dixfield or Peru.₂
'35d	Brand, Jeremiah....	Mass. mil....	Private....	76	Lincoln......	
'40	Branscomb, Rebecca.			95	Hancock....	Res. Mt. Desert.
'35c	Branscum, Charles..	Mass. line...	Private....	85	Hancock....	('20 as Branscom). d. Sept. 18, 1825.
1794	Brawn, Daniel.....	Col. E.Phinney's mil. rgt	Private....			Wounded 1777. Res. York.
'35c	Bray, Joseph.......	Mass. line...	Private....	68	Somerset....	('20).
'40				76	Somerset....	Res. Anson.
'40	Bray, Nicholas.....			89	Cumberland	Res. Harrison. ('20). Same as Brag, N.?
'40	Breck, Patience.....			75	Kennebec....	Res. China.
'35d	Breman, Aaron.....	Mass. line...	Private....	71	Cumberland.	
'40	Breth, Amsi.......			79	Oxford......	Res. Paris.
'35d	Brewster, Darius...	Cont. navy..	Seaman...	70	Lincoln......	
'40				76	Lincoln......	Res. Thomaston.
'40	Brewster, Lucy.....			89	Waldo......	Res. Camden.
'35d	Bridgeham, John...	Mass. line...	Sergt. and Ensign & 74	80	Cumberland	Same as Bridgham, J.
'35c	Bridges, Daniel.....	N. H. line...	Private....	72	York........	('20).
'40				79	York........	Res. York,
'35c	Bridges, Edmund...	Mass. line...	Private....	71	Hancock....	('20).
'40				77	Hancock....	Res. Castine.
'40	Bridgham, John....			86	Cumberland	('20) Same as Bridge ham. Res. Minot.
'40	Bridgham, Lucy....			74	Cumberland	Res. Minot.
'35c	Bridgham, Samuel..	Mass. line...	Private....	71	Oxford......	('20 as Bridgman.)
'35d	Bridgham, William..	Mass. mil....	Private....	78	Cumberland	
'35d	Briggs, Abner......	R. I. line....	Private....	71	Cumberland	(20).
'35c	Briggs, Aden.......	Mass. line...	Private....	67	Somerset....	('20) d. Feb. 14, 1828
'35c	Briggs, Jesse......	Mass. line...	Private....	75	Oxford......	('20) d. Feb. 8, 1833.
'40	Briggs, Naomi.....			78	Oxford......	Res. Paris.
'35d	Briggs, Samuel.....	Mass. line...	Private....	70	Somerset....	
'35c	Briggs, William....	Mass. line...	Captain...	83	Kennebec....	('20) d. Aug. 11, 1819.
35c	Brimigion, Thomas.	Mass. line...	Private....	79	Lincoln......	('20) same as Briniyion.
'40	Briniyion, Thomas..			85	Lincoln......	Same as Brimigion. Res. Bowdoin.
'35c	Britt, John........	Md. line....	Private....	80	Kennebec....	('20) d. 1833.
'35e	Britton, John.......	4th Va. line..	Private....		Lincoln......	
35d	Brocklebank, Joseph	Mass. mil...	Private....	71	Cumberland	
'35c	Brooks, Samuel....	Mass. line...	Sergeant...	77	York........	('20) d. June, 1826.
'35c	Brooks, Samuel, 2d.	Mass. line...	Private....	62	Oxford......	('20) d. Apr. 1825.
'40	Brooks, Widow of Sa	muel........		75	Oxford......	Res. Porter.
'35d	Brooks, Solomon...	Mass. line...	Private....	80	York........	
'35d	Brooks, William....	Mass. mil....	Private....	79	York........	
'35c	Brown, Amos......	Mass. line...	Private....	81	Oxford......	('20) d. Dec. 1827.
'35c	Brown, Amos, 2d...	Mass. line...	Private....	74	Oxford......	('20) d. Jan. 11, 1826
'35c	Brown, Andrew....	Mass. line...	Private....	74	Lincoln......	
'40	Brown, Andrew....			79	Kennebec....	Res. Litchfield.
'35d	Brown, Andrew....	Mass. state..	Private....	71	Cumberland	('20).
'40	Brown, Asenath....			76	Waldo......	Res. Palermo.
'35d	Brown, Cyril......	Mass. mil....	Priv'te and Sergeant	78	Hancock....	('31a as Cyrel).
'40	Brown, Cyril......			84	Waldo......	Res. Searsmont.
'35c	Brown, David.....	Mass. line...	Private....	80	Lincoln......	('20).
'35c	Brown, Enoch.....	Mass. line...	Private....	82	Penobscot...	('20).
'40	Brown, Enoch.....			89	Piscataquis..	Res. Sebec.
'35c	Brown, Ezekiel....	Mass. line...	Surgeon....	90	Kennebec....	('20, '31b as private)
'35c	Brown, Ezekiel....	Mass. line...	Surgeon....	78	Hancock....	Perhaps identical with preceding.
'35c	Brown, Jacob......	Mass. line...	Private....	76	Lincoln......	('20) d. Dec. 2, 1831?
'35c	Brown, Jacob......	Mass. line...	Private....	73	Oxford......	Died Dec. 2, 1831 ?
'40	Brown, James......			83	York........	Res. Parsonsfield.
'35d	Brown, James......	Mass. line...	Private....	74	York........	('20).
'35c	Brown, James......	Mass. line...	Private....	74	Lincoln......	Died Jan. 28, 1827.
'35c	Brown, James, 2d...	Va. line.....	Private....	74	York........	('20).
'35d	Brown, Jeremiah...	Mass. mil....	Private....	74	Kennebec....	
'40				79	Kennebec....	Res. Winthrop.
'35c	Brown, Jesse......	Mass. line...	Private....	70	Cumberland	('20).
'35d	Brown, John......	Mass. state..	Private....	77	York........	('20).
'35c	Brown, John......	Mass. line...	Private....	74	Kennebec....	Died Oct. 22, 1822.

List.	Name.	Service.	Rank.	Age.	County.	Remarks.
'35d	Brown, Jonathan...	Mass. line...	Matross...	82	Lincoln.....	
'40	Brown, Jonathan...			68	Lincoln......	Res. Bowdoinham.
'40	*Brown, Mary*.....			73	Kennebec...	Res. Monmouth.
'35c	Brown, Moody.....	Mass. line...	Private....	70	Oxford......	('20).
'40	Brown, Moody.....			75	York........	Res. Cornish.
'28	Brown, Peter Wyer.		Ensign...			
'35c	Brown, Peter W....	Mass. line..	Ensign...	80	Cumberland	('20) d.Feb. 28, 1830
'35d	Brown, Samuel.....	Mass. line...	Private....	66	Oxford......	('20).
'40	————			72	Oxford......	Res. Oxford.
'25d	Brown, Thaddeus...	Mass. mil....	Private....	73	Oxford......	
'40	————			79	Oxford......	Res. Waterford.
'35c	Brown, Thomas....	Cont. navy..	Mariner...	68	York........	('20,"Dean" frigate)
'35c	Brown, William....	Mass.line...	Private....	79	Lincoln......	('20).
'40	Brown, William....			80	Lincoln.....	Res. Bath.
'35c	Brownwell, Ichabod	Mass. line...	Private....	85	Kennebec....	Died 1823.
'35d	Bruckett, James....	Mass. line...	Pvt. of Art.	79	Cumberland	
'28	Bryan Joseph......		2d Lieut.			Invalided.
'35d	Bryant, Abijah.....	Mass. state..	Private....	74	Oxford......	
'40	Bryant, Abijah.....			79	Oxford......	Res. Hartford.
'35c	Bryant, Daniel.....	Mass. line...	Private.,..	75	York........	('20).
'35d	Bryant, John......	Mass. mil...	Pvt of Art.	69	Washington..	.('31a).
'35d	Bryant, Joseph.....	Mass. mil...	Priv'te and Q. M.	75	Cumberland	
'40	————			83	Cumberland	Res. Baldwin.
'35c	Bryant, Stephen....	Mass. line...	Private....	67	York........	('20) d. 1823.
'31a	Buck, Moses.......		Private....			Deserted.
'35c	Buman, John......	Mass. line...	Private....	70	Kennebec....	Same as Bceman ?
'20	Bumfries, Morris...	Mass......	Private....			Same as Bompus,M?
'40	Bumps, Shubal....			81	Waldo......	Same as Bumpus, S. Res. Thorndike.
'40	*Bumpus, Hannah*..			76	Oxford......	Res. Hebron.
'40	*Bumpus, Huldah*...			78	Oxford......	Res. Paris.
'35c	Bumpus, Shubael...	Mass. line...	Fifer......	75	Waldo......	('20) same as Bumps S.
'35d	Burbank, Eleazer...	Mass. line...	Musician..	69	Kennebec....	('20, '31b as Ebenezer.)
'35d	Burbank, John.....	Mass.st. navy Mass. state..	Mariner, Sergt. and Master at Arms	83	York........	('20 Ship "Good Richard" '31b.)
'40	————			88	York........	Res. Lyman.
'35c	Burdeen, Timothy..	Mass. line...	Private....	70	York........	('20) Same as Berdens, T.
'40	*Burgese, Keziah*....			80	Kennebec....	Res. Wayne.
'35d	Burgess, David.....	Mass. line...	Private....	72	Somerset....	('20, '31b) d. Nov. 11, 1832.
'35c	Burgess, Edward...	Mass. line...	Private....	85	Kennebec....	('20) d. Jan. 12, 1831
'35d	Burgess, Jonathan..	Mass. line...	Priv'te and Sgt. Maj.	75 & 73	Kennebec....	('20).
'40	————			81	Kennebec....	Res. Vassalborough.
'35c	Burkman, Thomas..	Mass. line...	Lieut......	82	Hancock....	Same as following ? d. May, 1826
'20	Burkmar, Thomas..	Conn......	Lieut......			Same as preceding ?
'35c	Burnell, John......	Mass. line...	Private....	75	Somerset....	('20) d. Jan. 14, 1823
'40	Burnheimer, Jacob..			75	Lincoln.....	Same as Bornhumen. Res. Waldoboro.
'35d	Burr, Daniel.......	Mass. line...	Private....	72	Kennebec....	('20) d. Mar. 15, 1834.
'31b	Burr, David.......		Private....			Same as preceding.
'35c	Burr, Joseph!......	Mass. line...	Private....	84	Kennebec....	('20).
'35d	Burrell, Humphrey	Mass. line...	Pvt. Gunner & Corp.	81	Somerset....	('20).
'35c	Burrell, John......	Mass. line...	Private....	82	Penobscot...	('20).
'40	Burrill, John.......			83	Piscataquis..	Res. Sangerville.
'35d	Burrill, Noah......	Mass. line...	Sergeant..	73	Somerset....	('20 as Burrell).
'35d	Burton, Thomas....	Mass. mil...	Pvt. Corp. & Lieut.	92	Lincoln.....	
'35d	Burton, William....	Mass. state...	Private....	77	Lincoln......	
'40	————			83	Lincoln......	Res. Cushing.
'40	Bussel, Isaac.......			84	Washington..	('20) same as Bussell, I. ? Res. Columbia.
'35c	Bussell, Isaac......	Mass. line...	Private....	63	Washington..	Same as Bussel, I. ?
'35e	Bussell, Isaac......	Mass. line...	Private....		Washington..	
'35d	Bussell, Jonathan...	Mass. mil...	Private....	73	Kennebec...	
'35d	Butland, Jesse.....	Mass. mil...	Private....	77	York........	
'35c	Butland, Nathaniel.	Mass. line...	Private....	84	York........	('20 as Nathan) d. Feb. 18, 1834.

List	Name	Service	Rank	Age	County	Remarks
'35d	Butler, Moses	Mass. state	Private	78	Hancock	
'35c	Butler, Nathaniel	Mass. line	Private	90	Cumberland	Died May 21, 1824.
'35d	Butler, Nathaniel	Mass. mil	Private	76	York	
'35c	Butler, Phineas	Mass. line	Private	75	Lincoln	('20).
'40	————			82	Lincoln	Res. Thomaston.
'35c	Butman, Benjamin	Mass. line	Private	78	Penobscot	('20) ('35d).
'35d	Butterfield, Jesse	Mass. line	Corp. and Sgt.at arms	82	Kennebec	
'40	Butterfield, Jesse			88	Franklin	Res. Farmington.
'35d	Buxton, William	Mass. mil	Private	71	Cumberland	
'35d	Buzzell, James	Mass. mil	Drummer	76	York	
'35d	Byram, Ebenezer	Mass. line	Private	79	Kennebec	('31b) d. Nov. ,27 1832.
'35d	Byram, Jonathan	Mass. line	Private	80	Cumberland	('20).
'35c	Byram, Melzar	Mass. line	Private	61	Cumberland	('20).

WILLIAM HUTCHINS of Penobscot.
Revolutionary. (See page 53.)

List.	Name.	Service.	Rank.	Age.	County.	Remarks.
'35c	Cain, David	Mass. line	Private	67	York	('20). d. March 1825.
'35c	Cain, Nicholas	Mass. line	Private	72	Lincoln	Transf. from Suffolk Co., Mass. 1820. d. Sept. 4, 1826.
'35d	Calderwood, John	Cont. navy	Marine	81	Waldo	
'40				88	Waldo	Res. Lincolnville.
'35c	Calderwood, Thos	Mass. line	Private	81	Lincoln	d. Dec. 12, 1831.
'40	Calvin, Jotham			80	Kennebec	Res. China.
'35c	Cammett, Samuel	N. H. line	Private	64	York	('20, '31b.)
'35c	Campbell, Alexander	Mass. line	Private	72	Cumberland	('20) d. Feb. 15, 1827.
'35d	Campbell, James	Mass. state	Pvt. of art.	79	Lincoln.	
'35d	Campbell, James	N. H. line	Pvt. and drum maj	77	Kennebec	('20 as musician).
'40				81	Kennebec	Res. Wales.
'40	Campbell, William			42	Cumberland	Res. Minot.
'35c	Campernell, William	Mass. line	Private	95	York.	
'40	Campnell, William			80	York	Res. Parsonsfield.
'40	Card, Thurston			48	Lincoln	Res. Woolwich, Smith or Fairfield.
35d	Carey, Luther	Mass. state	Musician	73	Oxford	Same as Cary, L.
'35c	Carey, Simeon	Mass. line	Private	70	Lincoln	('20) d. May, 1825
	Carl, Ebenezer,	see Carll.				
35c	Carl, John	Mass. line	Sergeant	77	Kennebec	('20) d. Sept. 17, 1832.
35d	Carl, Joseph	Mass. mil	Private	81	Waldo	
'35d	Carle, John	Mass. line	Private	75	York.	
'40	Carle, William			77	Franklin	Res. Salem; same as Carll, W.?
'40	Carleton, Jonathan			79	Kennebec	Res. Vassalboro', same as Carlton J.
35c	Carleton, Samuel	Mass. line	Private	80	Lincoln	Same as Carlton, S
'35d	Carlisle, James	Mass. mil	Private	76	York.	
35c	Carlisle, John	N. H. line	Private	78	York	('20).
'35d	Carlisle, Joseph	Mass. mil	Private	73	Lincoln.	
'35c	Carll, Ebenezer	Mass. line	Private	78	Lincoln	('20 as Carl) all given Carroll.
'40	Carll, Ebenezer			82	York	Res. Hollis.
'35d	Carll, William	Mass. mil	Private	70	Somerset	Same as Carle W.?
'35c	Carlton, Ezra	N. H. line	Private	69	Oxford	('20).
'40	Carlton, Ezra			76	Franklin	Res. Letter E.
'35c	Carlton, John	Mass. line	Private	73	Kennebec	('20).
'40	Carlton, John, 2d			59	Waldo	Res. Frankfort.
'35c	Carlton, Jonathan	Mass. line	Private	73	Kennebec	('20) Same as Carleton J.
'20	Carlton, Samuel	Mass. line	Private			SameasCarleton S
35d	Carpenter, Thomas	N. H. state	Private	71	York	
'40				76	York	Res. Waterboro'.
'35c	Carr, William	Mass. line	Private	78	Waldo	('20).
'40				84	Waldo	Res. Frankfort.
'35d	Carrell, Benjamin	Mass. state	Private	73	Kennebec.	
	Carroll, Ebenezer,	see Carll.				
'35c	Carson, James	Del. line	Private	79	Washington	d. Oct. 28, 1832.

25

List.	Name.	Service.	Rank.	Age.	County.	Remarks.
'35d	Carter, Abijah	Mass. mil	Private	72	Cumberland.	
'40	Carter, Abijah			78	Oxford	Res. Waterford.
'35c	Carter Edward	N. H. line	Private	84	Hancock	('20) d. Apr. 1827.
'35c	Carter, John	N. H. line	Private	63	York	d. Mar. 1822.
'35c	Carter, Thaddeus	Mass. line	Private	83	Kennebec	('20 as Thadeus) d. June 16, 1828
'40	Carter, Thomas			63	Waldo	Res. Montville.
'35d	Carthill, Pelutiah	Mass. state	Private	87	Waldo.	
'40	*Carvill, Mercy*			82	Lincoln	Res. Lewiston.
'40	Cary, Luther			79	Oxford	Res. Turner; same as Carey, L.
'35d	Caryell, David	Mass. mil	Priv'te and Sergeant.	80	Waldo.	
'35d	Case, Isaac	R. I. mil	Private	74	Kennebec	
'40				79	Kennebec	Res. Readfield.
'35c	Casewell, Simeon	Mass. line	Private	71	Cumberland	Same as Caswell?
'35d	Cash, John	Mass. line	Private	82	Cumberland	('20).
'35c	Cash, John	Mass. line	Private	73	York.	
'35c	Cash, Samuel	Mass. line	Private	74	Cumberland	('20) d. Aug. 4, 1818.
'40	Cashman, Andrew			79	Kennebec	Res. Leeds; same as Cushman, A.?
1792	Cass, Moses	3d N. H. line	Private			Maimed at Valley Forge.
1794						Res. Hallowell.
'35c	Cass, Moses	N. H. line	Private	78	Somerset	('20).
'40				82	Somerset	Res. Cornville.
'40	Caswell, Simeon			77	Cumberland	Res. Harrison. Same as Casewell S?
'35c	Caswell, Squire	Mass. line	Private	66	Oxford	('20) d. August 13 1821.
'40	Causland, Robert M			82	Somerset	Res. Pittsfield.
'35d	Cay, John	Mass. line	Private	86	Cumberland.	
1794	Chadbourn, Levi	Wigglesworth's regiment.	Private	—	York	Wounded in R. I., Aug. 1778.
'40				82	York	Res. Parsonsfield.
'40	Chadbourn, Seammon			85	York	Res. S. Berwick.
'40	Chadbourn, Simeon			91	York	Res. Lyman; same as Chadbourne, S.
'35d	Chadbourne, Cummon.	Mass. mil	Private	79	York	Same as Chadbourn, Seamon?
'35c	Chadbourne, Silas	Mass. line	Lieutenant	71	Cumberland	('20 as Chadbourn) d. June 15, 1823.
'35d	Chadbourne, Simeon	Mass. mil	Sergeant	84	York	Same as Chadbourn, S.
'35c	Chadwick, James	Mass. line	Private	71	Kennebec	('20) d. Oct. 25, 1826.
'35c	Chamberlain, Aaron	Mass. line	Private	79	Cumberland	d. Sept. 11, 1831
'35c	Chamberlain, Ephraim.	Mass. line	Private	71	Oxford	d. Nov. 1827.
'35d	Chamberlain, Ephraim.	Mass. mil	Private	70	Cumberland	d. Dec. 23, 1832.
'35c	Chamberlain, Jeremiah.	Conn. line	Private	71	Lincoln	('20) d. Oct. 26, 1831.
'35d	Chamberlain, John	Mass. mil	Private	84	Cumberland.	
'40	Chamberlain, John			90to100	York	Res. Buxton.
'35c	Chamberlain, Moses	Mass. line	Private	73	Kennebec	(20).
'40	*Chambertin, Mary*			80	York	Res. So. Berwick.
'40	*Chandler, Hannah*			75	Kennebec	Res. Winthrop.
'35d	Chandler, John	R. I. line	Private	79	Kennebec	('20).
'35d	Chandler, John	Mass. line	Private	75	Cumberland.	
'40				82	Cumberland	Res. Minot.
'40	Chandler, John			78	Kennebec	Res. Augusta.
'35e	Chandler, Moses	Mass. line	Corporal	—	Kennebec	d. June 1, 1828.
35c	Chandler, Moses	Mass. line	Corporal	70	Kennebec	('20).
'35c	Chandler, Moses	N. H. line	Private	55	Oxford	('20).
'35d	Chandler, Nathaniel	Mass. line	Private	74	Cumberland	
'40				80	Cumberland	Res. Minot.
'35c	Chaney, John	Mass. line	Private	76	Lincoln	('20) d. Sept. 11, 1827.
'35c	Chaney, John	Mass. line	Private	61	Kennebec	Same as Cheney, J.
'20	Chaplin, Daniel	Mass. line	Private			

List.	Name.	Service.	Rank.	Age.	County.	Remarks.
'35c	Chaplin, David	Mass. line	Private	60	Oxford	('20) Age probably incorrectly given.
'35d	Chaplin, David	Mass. line	Private	80	Oxford	
'35d	Chaplin, John	Mass. state	Private	—	Cumberland.	
'40	*Chaplin, Lydia*			78	Oxford	Res. Waterford
'35d	Chapman, Benjamin	Mass. mil	Private	74	Kennebec.	
'40	Chapman, Benjamin			80	Lincoln	Res. Nobleboro'.
'35c	Chapman, Nathaniel	Mass. line	Private	60	Somerset	('20) d. Jan. 2, 1819.
'35c	Chase, Benjamin	N. H. line	Private	61	Kennebec	('20).
'35d	Chase, Ebenezer	Mass. mil	Private of artillery.	70	Lincoln.	
'40				74	Lincoln	Res. Edgecomb.
'35c	Chase, Ezekiel	R. I. line	Private	62	Penobscot	('20, '31b).
'35e	Chase, Ezekiel	Mass. line	Private	—	Penobscot.	
'40	Chase, Ezekiel			77	Piscataquis	Res. Sebec.
'35d	Chase, Isaac	Mass. mil	Private	77	Cumberland.	
'40				82	Cumberland	Res. Standish.
35d	Chase, Isaac	Mass. state	Private	75	Lincoln.	
'40				80	Lincoln	Res. Bowdoin.
'35d	Chase, Nathaniel	Mass. mil	Private	73	Oxford.	
'40				78	Oxford	Res. Buckfield.
'35c	Chase, Robert	N. H. line	Private	73	Lincoln	('20).
'40				79	Lincoln	Res. Georgetown.
'35d	Chase, Thomas	Cont. navy	Mariner & Private.	78	Oxford	('20, ship "Alliance") ('31b).
'40				84	Oxford	Res. Livermore.
'31b	Cheats, Ebenezer		Private	—		Perhaps same as Choate, E.
'20	Cheney, John	Mass. line	Private	—		Same as Chaney.
'35c	Chesley, Sawyer	N. H. line	Private	71	Kennebec	d. May 29, 1823.
'35d	Chick, Isaac	Mass. mil	Private	74	York.	
'40				81	York	Res. York.
'35c	Chick, John	Mass. line	Private	75	Lincoln	('20) d. June 23, 1826.
'35d	Child, Amos	Mass. line	Musician & Mus. of art.	70	Kennebec	('20).
'40	Childs, Amos			75	Kennebec	Res. Vassalboro'.
'28	'hilds, Ebenezer		Captain		Kennebec	Invalid. ('35a)
'40	Childs, Ebenezer			52	Franklin	Res. Farmington.
'35d	Childs, Enoch	Mass. mil	Private	75	Somerset	d. Jan. 7, 1834.
35d	Chipman, William	Mass. line	Private	70	Oxford	(20).
'40				77	Oxford	Res. Oxford.
35d	Choate, Ebenezer	Mass. line and state.	Private	70	Cumberland	('20).
'40				75	Cumberland	Res. Bridgton.
'40	Church, Amos			84	Kennebec	Res. Augusta.
35d	Church, Charles	Mass. line	Private	72	Somerset	('20, '31b).
'40	Church, Charles			78	Franklin	Res. Phillips.
'35d	Church, John	Mass. mil	Pvt., Drummer and Corp.	81	Somerset.	
'35d	Church, Samuel	Mass. mil	Private	78	Kennebec.	
'40	*Church, Susannah*			84	Somerset	Res. Mercer.
'40	Churchell, Jabez			80	Oxford	Res. Buckfield, same as Churchill, Jabish?
'35c	Churchill, Jabez	Mass. line	Sergeant	80	Oxford	('20).
'40				86	Oxford	Res. Hartford.
'35c	Churchill, Jabish	Mass. line	Private	75	Oxford	('20 as Jabesh) Same as Churchell, J.?
'35c	Churchill, James	Mass. line	Private	73	Kennebec	('20).
'35d	Churchill, Joseph	Mass. mil	Private	73	Waldo.	
'35c	Churchill, Joshua	Mass. line	Private	92	Oxford	('20).
'35d	Churchill, Josiah	Mass. state	Sergeant	77	Cumberland	d. Jan. 30, 1833.
'35d	Churchill, William	Mass. state	Private	71	Kennebec.	
'40	Churchill, William			75	Oxford	Res. Livermore.
'35a	Chute, Josiah	Mass. mil	Sergeant	—	Cumberland	Pensioned July 11, 1776.
'35d	Chute, Josiah	Mass. line	Pvt., Corp. and Serg.	75	Cumberland	('20).
'35c	Clark, Bunker	N. H. line	Private	74	Kennebec	('20) d. May 10, 1819.
'35d	Clark, Charles	Mass. mil	Private	74	Kennebec.	
'40				78	Kennebec	Res. Augusta.

List.	Name.	Service.	Rank.	Age.	County.	Remarks.
'35d	Clark, Charles G...	Mass. mil.....	Private....	70	York.	
'40	—	....	....	75	York........	Res. Berwick.
'35c	Clark, David......	Mass. line.....	Private....	73	Cumberland .	('20).
'35e	Clark, David......	3d regt. Mass. line.	Private....	—	Cumberland .	('29) d. Mar. 18, 1831.
'35d	Clark, Ebenezer....	Mass. mil.....	Private....	82	York.	
'35c	Clark, Ebenezer....	N. H. line.....	Private....	75	York........	d. Dec. 25, 1831.
'20	Clark, Eleazer......	N. H. line.....	Private....			Prob. same as Ebenezer.
'31b	Clark, Ephraim....	....	Private....	—		
'35d	Clark, Ephraim....	Cont. navy...	Mariner...	78	York........	('20, ship "Alliance").
'40	—	....	....	84	York........	Res. Limington.
'35c	Clark, Hanson.....	Mass. line.....	Private....	78	Kennebec.	
'35c	Clark, James.......	Mass. line.....	Private....	73	Penobscot..	('20) ('31b, as James 2d.)
'40	—	....	....	77	Penobscot...	Res. Newport.
'40	Clark, James......	....	....	51	Waldo......	('20 as James 2d) Res. Frankfort.
'35d	Clark, John........	Mass. state....	Private....	79	York.	
'35d	Clark, John........	N. H. line.....	Ensign....	78	Somerset.	d. Sept. 2, 1832.
'20	Clark, Jonathan....	Mass. line.....	Lieutenant	—	....	('31b).
'35c	Clark, Joseph......	Mass. line.....	Private....	70	Lincoln.....	('20).
'40	—	....	....	74	Lincoln.....	Res. Wiscasset.
'35d	Clark, Josiah......	N. H. line.....	Private....	70	York........	('20).
'40,	Clark, Patience.....	....	....	88	York........	Res. Lebanon.
'35c	Clark, Thomas.....	Mass. line.....	Private ..	81	Lincoln.....	('20) d. 1821.
'35d	Clark, William......	N. H. mil.....	Private....	82	York.	
'40	—	....	....	88	York........	Res. Lyman.
'35c	Clay, Benjamin....	Mass. line.....	Private....	67	York........	('20, '31b).
'35d	Cleaves, Abraham..	Mass. mil.....	Private....	71	Kennebec.	
'40	—	....	....	76	Kennebec....	Res. Windsor.
'35c	Cleaves, Edmund..	Mass. line.....	Private....	78	Cumberland .	('20) d. June 29, 1828.
'35c	Cleaves, William...	Mass. line.....	Private....	79	Cumberland .	('20).
'40	Cleaves, William...	....	....	80	Cumberland .	Res. Cumberland.
'35c	Clewley, Isaac......	Mass. line.....	Private....	80	Penobscot...	('20 as Clewly).
'35c	Clifford, David.....	N. H. line.....	Private....	65	Lincoln.....	('20). H
'31b	Clough, Benjamin..	....	Private.....	—		
'35d	Clough, Benjamin..	Mass. line.....	Pvt. and drummer	70	Cumberland.	
'35d	Clough, Benjamin..	Mass. line.....	Private....	70 & 79	Kennebec ...	('20).
'40	—	....	....	75	Kennebec ...	Res. Monmouth.
'35c	Clough, John......	N. H. line.....	Private....	74	Somerset	('20).
'40	Clough, John......	....	....	80	Franklin....	Res. Phillips.
1794	Clough, Noah......	Arnold's regt.	Private....		....	Wounded at Quebec, Dec. 31, 1775. Res. Arundel.
'35c	Cluff, Noah........	Mass. line.....	Private....	70	York........	('20) Prob. identical with preceeding. Transf. from Mass.1819 d. Sept. 1824.
'35c	Coambs, John......	N. H. line.....	Private....	78	Kennebec ...	Same as Coombs? Transf. from Merrimac Co., N. H. 1826.
'35d	Cobb, Daniel.......	Mass. mil......	Pri. of art.	72	Cumberland.	
'40	—	....	....	79	Cumberland .	Res. Portland. Transf. to Bristol Co., Mass.
'29	Cobb, David.......	Mass.........	Capt.of art			
'35e	Cobb, David.......	5 regt., Mass. line.	Lieut. Col.	—	Hancock.....	Transf. to Bristol Co., Mass.
'35c	Cobb, Ebenezer....	Mass. line.....	Private....	67	Oxford......	('20) d. May 9, 1826.
'35d	Cobb, Mallatiah...	Mass. line.....	Pvt.& Serg.	79	Somerset	('20 as Milatiah).
'35d	Cobb, Nathaniel ...	Mass. line.....	Pvt.&Corp.	85	Cumberland.	
'35c	Cobb, Roland......	Mass. line.....	Private....	78	Lincoln.....	('20).
'40	Cobb, Rowland.....	....	....	82	Lincoln.....	Res. Warren.
'35c	Cobb, Silvanus.....	Mass. line.....	Private....	72	Cumberland .	('20).
'35d	Cobb, William.....	Mass. state....	Private....	70	Oxford.	
'40	—	....	....	75	Oxford......	Res. Hebron.
'35d	Coblidge, Joseph...	Mass. line.....	Private....	72	Oxford......	Same as Coolidge?
'35c	Coburn, Jeptha....	Mass. line.....	Private....	72	Kennebec ...	Transf. from Middlesex Co., Mass. 1828.

List.	Name.	Service.	Rank.	Age.	County.	Remarks.
'40	Coburn, Jephthah..			81	Franklin	Res. New Sharon.
'35c	Coburn, Moses	Mass. line	Private	69	Oxford	Transf. from Middlesex,Co.,Mass 1824.
'35d	Coffin, Isaac	Mass. mil	Private	78	York.	
'40	———			84	York	Res. Lyman.
'35c	Coffin, Nathaniel	Mass. line	Lieutenant	84	Waldo	d. July 23, 1823.
'35c	Coffin, Nicholas	N. H. line	Private	69	Waldo	('20).
'35c	Coffin, Peter	N. H. line	Private	76	Oxford	('20).
'35d	Coffren, Robert	N. H. line	Private	79	Kennebec.	
'40	Cofren, Robert			75	Kennebec	('20 N. H. line) Res. Vienna. ('31b).
'35d	Cogswell, Northend.	Mass. mil	Private	72	York.	
'35c	Coker, William	Cont. navy	Private	74	Lincoln	('20 Mariner, ship "Boston") d. 1824.
'40	Colbath, Leighton			45	Penobscot	Res. Exeter.
'35d	Colbeth, Peter	Mass. mil	Pvt. of art.	83	Washington.	
'40	Colbey, Benjamin			89	Somerset	Res. Embden. Same as Colby?
'40	Colborn, Thomas			82	Franklin	Res. Wilton. Same as Colburn, T?
'35d	Colbroth, Lemuel	Mass. mil	Private	71	Kennebec	See also Coolbroth
'35d	Colburn, Ebenezer	Mass. state	Private	73	Waldo.	
'40	Colburn, Henry			79	Waldo	Res. Knox.
'35c	Colburn, Thomas	N. H. line	Private	76	Kennebec	Same as Colborn? Transf. from Stafford Co., N. H. 1822.
'35d	Colburn, William	Mass. mil	Private	74	Penobscot.	
'40	—. ———			79	Penobscot	Res. Orono.
'35d	Colby, Benjamin	Mass. mil	Sergeant	84	Kennebec	Same as Colbey?
'35d	Colby, Ebenezer	N. H. state	Private	74	York.	
'40	———			81	York	Res. Newfield.
'35d	Colby, James	Mass. mil	Private	71	Kennebec.	
'40	Colby, James			76	Lincoln	Res.Webster.
'35c	Colby, Samuel,2d	Mass. line	Private	72	Lincoln	('20).
'40	Colby, Samuel			79	Lincoln	Res. Westport.
'20	Colby, Samuel	Mass. line	Private			
'40	Colby, Samuel			78	Cumberland	Res. Portland.
'35c	Colby, Sylvanus	Mass. line	Private	70	Lincoln	('20) d. Feb. 2, 1833.
'35d	Colcord, Josiah	N. H. line	Private	79	York.	
'35d	Cole, Abel	Mass. state	Private	82	Lincoln.	
'35d	Cole, Abijah	Mass. line	Private	72	Hancock.	
'35c	Cole, Barnet	Mass. line	Private	73	Kennebec	('20).
'35d	Cole, Benjamin	Mass. mil	Private	74	Kennebec.	
'40	Cole, Edward			59	Waldo	Res. Frankfort.
'35d	Cole, Eleazer	Mass. state	Sergeant	87	Oxford	d. Aug. 4, 1833.
'35d	Cole, Eli	Mass. line	Private	74	York	('20) d. Dec. 16, 1832.
'28	Cole, Henry		2d Lieut.			Invalid.
'35c	Cole, Issiah	Mass. line	Private	79	Lincoln.	
'35c	Cole, John	Mass. line	Private	77	Kennebec	(20,'31b) See also Cool.
'40	*Cole, Mary C*			81	Lincoln	Res. Waldoboro'
'35c	Cole, Samuel	Mass. line	Private	78	Lincoln	('20).
'40	———			83	Lincoln	Res. Lewiston.
'35d	Colley, Richard	Mass. line	Private	78	Cumberland	
'40	———			80	Cumberland	Res. Cumberland.
'40	Colley, William			89	Cumberland	Res. Falmouth. Same as Culley?
'40	Collings, Daniel			84	Franklin	Res. Industry. See also Collins D.
'40	Collings, Lemuel			83	Franklin	Res. Industry. See also Collins, L.
'35c	Collins, Benjamin	Mass. line	Private	68	Somerset	('20).
'40	———			73	Somerset	Res. St. Albans.
'20	Collins, Daniel	Mass. line	Private	—		('31b)
'35d	Collins, Daniel	N. H. line	Private	76	Somerset	Same as Collings, D.
'35d	Collins, David	R. I. line	Pvt. and Marine.	79	Somerset	(31 b) Ship "Alfred". See also Collings.

29

List.	Name.	Service.	Rank.	Age.	County.	Remarks.
'35c	Collins, Daniel	Cont. navy	Mariner	79	Somerset	(31b).
'35d	Collins, Joseph	Mass. mil	Private	74	Cumberland	
'40	Collins, Joseph			80	Kennebec	Res. Gardiner.
'35d	Collins, Lemuel	Mass. line	Pvt. and Pvt. of artillery.	77	Kennebec	('20) see also Collings.
'35d	Collins, Philemon	Mass. mil	Private	74	Somerset.	
'35d	Collins, Richard	Mass. line	Private	81	Washington.	
'35c	Collins, Solomon	Mass. line	Private	72	Hancock.	
'40	Collins, Solomon			77	Waldo	Res. Frankfort
'20	Colson, David	Mass. line	Private	—		
'35c	Colson, Hateevil	Mass. line	Private	84	Hancock	d. June 26, 1821.
'35c	Combs, Hezekiah	Mass. line	Private	73	Lincoln	('20) d. June 19, 1830.
'20	Combs, Hosea	Mass. line	Private	—		Prob. same as Corms, H.
'35d	Combs, William	Mass. line	Private	81	Cumberland	Same as Coombs, W.
'35d	Conant, Benjamin	Mass. line	Private	78	Oxford	('20, '31b).
'40	Conant, Sylvia,			84	Oxford	Res. Turner.
	Conch, John	see Couch, John				
'40	Condon, John			65	Hancock	Res. Penobscot.
'40	Condra, Ephraim M			48	Aroostook	Res.Houlton.
'35c	Cone, Elijah	Mass. line	Private	69	Oxford.	
'35c	Cone, Samuel	Conn. line	Private	80	Penobscot	('20).
'40				89	Penobscot	Res. Hampden.
'35d	Coney, Daniel	Mass. mil	Pvt. and Lieut.	82	Kennebec	Same as Cony.
'35c	Conn, Jonathan	Mass. line	Corporal	80	Oxford	('20).
'40	Cony, Daniel			87	Kennebec	Res. Augusta. Same as Coney.
'35c	Cook, David	Mass. line	Captain	73	Cumberland	('20) Invalid, pensioner under act of 1791.d. Oct. 27, 1823.
'35d	Cook, Eli	Mass. line	Private	76	Cumberland	('20).
'35c	Cook, Joseph	Mass. line	Private	72	Kennebec	('20).
'40	Cook, Sarah			87	York	Res. Lebanon.
'35c	Cook, Saul	Mass. line	Private	77	Somerset.	
'40	Cook, Saul			82	Kennebec	('20). Res. Litchfield.
'35c	Cookson, Reuben	Mass. line	Private	84	Kennebec	('20) d. Feb. 14, 1829.
'35d	Cool, John	Mass. line	Private	79	Kennebec	('20, 31b).
'40				83	Kennebec	Res. Waterville.
'35c	Coolbroth, Daniel	Mass. line	Private	80	Oxford	See also Colbroth.
'40	Coolidge, Joseph			79	Oxford	Res. Canton.Same as Coblidge?
'20	Coolidge, Silas	N. H. line	Private	—		
'35c	Coolidge, Silas	Mass. line	Private	78	Hancock.	
'35d	Coombs, John	Mass. line	Private	78	Cumberland	See also Coambs.
'40	Coombs, John			77	Cumberland	Res. Harpswell.
'35d	Coombs, Joseph S	Mass. line	Private	77	Cumberland	('20, 31b).
'40	Coombs, Rachel			79	Lincoln	Res. Bowdoinham
'40	Coombs, William			86	Cumberland	Res. Harpswell. Same as Combs, W.
'35c	Cooms, Samuel C	Mass. line	Private	75	Lincoln	('20) d. Oct. 31, 1826.
'35c	Cooper, Alexander	Mass. line	Private	90	York	('20).
'35c	Corms, Hosea	Mass. line	Private	68	Hancock	Prob. same as Combs, H., d. June 14, 1824.
'35c	Cornish, John	Mass. line	Private	79	Cumberland	('20).
'40				84	Cumberland	Res. Brunswick.
'35c	Cotton, John	Mass. line	Private	97	Lincoln	('20, quartermaster serg.) d.May 20, 1824.
'35c	Couch, John	Mass. line	Private	68	Kennebec	('20) d. Sept. 5, 1825.
'40	Couch, John			54	Kennebec	Res. Hallowell.
'35c	Cousens, Ebenezer	Mass. line	Private	56	York	('20), ('31b, as Cousins).
'35d	Cousins, Nathaniel	Mass. state	Corp. and Lieut.	89	York	d. Aug. 13, 1832.
'35c	Cousins, Samuel	Mass. line	Private	74	Waldo	('20).
'35d	Covall, Judah	Mass. mil	Pvt. and Serg.	76	Waldo	

List.	Name	Service	Rank	Age	County	Remarks
'40	Covill, Judah....			87	Hancock....	Res. Deer Isle.
'40	*Cowan, Elizabeth*...			77	Kennebec...	Res. Sidney.
'35c	Cowan, Isaac....	Mass. line.....	Private....	67	Kennebec...	('20) d. Mar. 3, 1830.
'40	*Cowan, Jane*......			75	Kennebec...	Res. Vassalboro'.
'35c	Cowan, William....	N. H. line.....	Private....	75	Kennebec...	('20).
'35c	Cowing, Calvin....	Mass. line.....	Private....	82	Lincoln......	('20).
'40	——			88	Lincoln......	Res. Lisbon.
'35c	Cox, Benjamin....'..	Mass. line.....	Private....	82	Oxford......	('20) d. Jan. 14, 1832.
'35c	Cox, Bray.........	Cont.navy....	Seaman...	64	York........	('20, frigate "Dean") d.Jan. 14, 1821.
'35d	Cox, Hugh........	Mass. state....	Private....	75	Kennebec.	
'35d	Crafts, Samuel.....	Mass. mil......	Private....	72	York.	
'40	Crafts, Samuel.....			77	Oxford......	Res. Hebron.
'35d	Craig, Elias........	Mass. line.....	Private....	78	Kennebec...	('20, '31b).
'35d	Craig, Enoch......	Mass. state....	Pvt. and Matross.	76	Kennebec.	
'35d	Craig, Samuel......	Mass. mil......	Private....	76	Penobscot.	
'35c	Cram, John S......	Mass. line.....	Drummer.	70	York........	('20) d. Jan. 3, 1824.
'35c	Cram, Tristram....	N. H. line.....	Private....	77	Waldo......	('20).
'40	Crammer, John....			76	Lincoln......	Res. Waldoboro. See also Creamer
'35d	Crane, Abijah.....	Mass. line.....	Private....	73	Kennebec...	('20, 1b).
'35d	Crane, Rufus......	Mass. mil......	Private....	75	Lincoln.	
40	——			83	Lincoln.....	Res. Warren.
'35d	Crary, Joseph......	Mass. line.....	Pvt. and Sergeant	78	Waldo......	('31b).
'40	——			83	Waldo......	Res. Jackson.
'35d	Crawford, Thomas.	Mass. line.....	P v t. a n d Pvt. of art.	78 & 79	Lincoln.....	('20, '31b).
'35d	Crawford, William.	Mass. state....	Pvt. of art.	74	Kennebec.	
'40	——			82	Kennebec...	Res. Gardiner.
'35d	Creamer, John.....	Mass. mil......	Private....	77	Lincoln.....	See also Crammer.
'35d	Cree, Asa.........	Mass. line.....	P v t. a n d Pvt. of art.	83	Lincoln......	('20) d. Oct. 30, 1833.
'20	Creech, Richard...:	Mass. line.....	Musician..			Same as Cruch.
'40	Creesey, Benjamin.			83	Cumberland.	Res. Falmouth. Same as Cresy, B.
'35c	Cresy, Benjamin...	Mass. line.....	Private....	78	Cumberland.	('20 as Cresey) Same as Creesey
'40	Crips, Michael.....			58	Lincoln......	Res Bowdoinham.
'35c	Crocker, Benjamin.	Mass. line.....	Private....	82	Penobscot..	('20).
'31a	Crockett, Benjamin.			—	....	Rejected as serving in reg't not on Cont. establishment.
'35d	Crockett, Ephraim.	Mass. line.....	Private....	79	Cumberland.	
'35c	Crockett, Samuel...	Mass. line.....	Private....	73	Cumberland.	('20).
'40	——			79	Cumberland.	Res. Cape Elizabeth.
'35c	Cromelt, Jeremiah..	Mass. line.....	Sergeant..	82	Lincoln.....	('20 as Cromett) d. Jan. 1828.
'35c	Cromwell, Joseph...	Mass. line.....	Private....	91	Lincoln......	('20) d. May 12, 1831.
'35c	Crooker, Joshua....	Mass. line.....	Private....	—	Cumberland.	('20).
'40	*Crooker, Ruth*.......			80	Cumberland.	Res. Minot.
'35c	Crosby, Charles....	R. I. line......	Private....	80	Penobscot...	('20).
'35d	Crosby, Eben......	Mass. mil......	Private....	74	Penobscot.	
'35c	Crosby, Stephen....	Mass. line.....	Private....	70	Kennebec...	('20) d. May 5, 1830.
'35d	Cross, Caleb.......	Mass. mil......	Private....	81	Kennebec.	
'35c	Cross, Joseph......	Mass. line.....	Musician..	69	Cumberland.	('20) d. May 2, 1822.
'35c	Crossman, Joseph A	Cont. navy....	Mariner...	82	Cumberland.	d. July 22, 1831.
'35c	Crowell, Enoch.....	Mass. line.....	Private....	63	Kennebec...	('20 as Enock) d. Apr. 4, 1823.
'35d	Crowell, Manoah...	Mass. mil......	Private....	71	Kennebec.	
'40	——			78	Kennebec...	Res. Waterville.
'35c	Crowell, Michael...	Mass. line.....	Private....	78	Kennebec...	('20).
'40	——			83	Kennebec...	Res. China.
'35c	Croxford, John.....	Mass. line.....	Private....	67	Penobscot...	('20) d. Dec. 15 1820.

31

List.	Name.	Service.	Rank.	Age.	County.	Remarks.
'35c	Cruch, Richard	Mass. line	Private	—	Kennebec	Same as Creech,, d, June 13,1819.
1794	Crummitt, James	2d. N. H. regt.	Private			Wounded on retreat from Ticonderoga, July 7, 1777. Res. Washington.
'35d	Culley, William	Mass. line	Private	82	Cumberland	Same as Colley, W?
'35d	Cummings, Asa	Mass. mil	Private	73	Oxford	
'35d	Cummings, Josiah	Mass. mil	P v t. a n d Corp.	79	Cumberland	
'35d	Cummings, Richard	Mass. line	Pvt.of art.	84	Lincoln	
'40	Cummings, Richard			45	Waldo	Res. Hope.
'35c	Cummings, Thomas	Mass. line	Private	79	Cumberland	
'35c	Cumings, Thomas	Mass. line	Lieutenant	83	Cumberland	('20) d. Oct. 24, 1825.
'35d	Cunningham, Sam'l.	Mass. state	Private	74	Lincoln	
'35c	Cunningham, Thos.	N. H. line	Private	79	Lincoln	('20).
'35d	Cunningham, Timothy.	Mass. state	P v t. a n d Seaman.	79	Lincoln	
'35d	Currier, Abraham	Mass. line	Private	75	York	
'40	———			81	York	Res. Kennebunkport.
'40	Curtis, Benjamin			83	Waldo	Res.Monroe; same as Curtiss, B.
'35c	Curtis, Caleb	Mass. line	Private	75	Lincoln	
'40	———			82	Lincoln	Res. Topsham.
'35c	Curtis, Charles	Mass. line	Private	74	Lincoln	('20 as Curtiss) d. Aug. 27, 1819.
'35c	Curtis, Joseph	Mass. line	Private	77	York	('20 as Curtiss) d. Dec. 11, 1823.
'35c	Curtiss, Benjamin	Cont.navy	Mariner	79	Waldo	Same as Curtis,B.
'35c	Curtiss, David	Mass. line	Private	80	Somerset	d. Dec. 1827.
'35c	Curtiss, Stephen	Mass. line	Private	79	Oxford	('20).
'35c	Cushing, Loring	Mass. line	Private	68	Cumberland	('20) d.Apr.,1820.
'35d	Cushman, Andrew	Mass. line	Private	73	Kennebec	('20, '31b). Same as Cashman?
'35d	Cushman, Caleb	Mass. line	P v t. a n d Sergeant	83	Oxford	d. Mar. 16, 1833.
'35d	Cushman, Caleb	Mass. mil	P v t. a n d Fifer.	78	Oxford	
'35d	Cushman, Gideon	Mass. mil	Private	83	Oxford	SameasCushmon.
'35d	Cushman, Isaac	Mass. mil	Private	90	Oxford	
'35d	Cushman, Isaiah	Mass. line	Private	74 & 77	Cumberland	('20). ?
'35d	Cushman, Isaiah	Mass. line	Private	74	Oxford	Same as preceding
'40	Cushman, Isiah			84	Oxford	Res. Sumner.
'31a	Cushman, Job		Private	—		Rejected on account of am't. of his property.
'35d	Cushman, John	Mass. line	Private	73	Kennebec	d. Jan. 27, 1834.
'35d	Cushman, Jonathan	Mass. line	Sergeant	79	Oxford	Res. Norway.
'40	Cushman, Margaret.			73	Oxford	Res. Oxford.
'40	Cushman, Sarah			78	Lincoln	
'35d	Cushman, Silvanus	Mass. mil	Private	70	Oxford	
'35d	Cushman, William	Mass. mil	Private	75	Oxford	Res. Hartford.
'40	———			71	Oxford	
'35c	Cushman, Zebedee	Cont. navy	Mariner			('20, ship "Providence.")
'40	Cushmon, Gideon			89	Oxford	Res. Hebron, same as Cushman, G.

List.	Name.	Service.	Rank.	Age.	County.	Remarks.
'35c	Dacy, John	Mass. line	Private	75	Cumberland	('20) d. July 4, 1830
'40	Dacy, Mehitable			94	Cumberland	Res. Poland.
'35c	Daggett, Tristram	Mass. line	Private	76	Somerset	('20), ('29 & '31 b. Tristam.)
'35e	Daggett, Tristram	Mass. line, 7th regt.	Private	—	Somerset	
'40	Daggtt, Trustum			80	Franklin	Res. Industry.
'35d	Dailly, Nezer	Mass. mil.	Private	72	Washington	
'35d	Dain, John	Mass. line	Sergeant	81	Lincoln	('20).
'35c	Dakin, Thomas	Mass. line	Private	71	Washington	('20) d. Jan. 29, 1828.
'40	Dalino, Ruth			85	Somerset	Res. Starks. See also Delano.
'35c	Dalliver, Peter	Mass. line	Private	73	Hancock	d. Apr. 4, 1828, Same as Dolliver?
'35d	Damans, Abiah	Mass. state	Pvt. of art.	73	Washington	See also Demons.
'35d	Dame, Jonathan	Mass. mil	Pvt.&Corp.	83	York	
'35c	Dana, Luther	Cont. navy	Midsh'p'n.	69	Cumberland	d. Feb. 19, 1832.
'35c	Danforth, Abner	Mass. line	Private	74	Lincoln	('20).
'40	Danforth, Abner			75	Kennebec	Res. Litchfield.
'35d	Davenport, Ephraim	Mass. mil	Private	72	Oxford	
'35d	Davenport, Thomas	Mass. mil	Private	70	Kennebec	
'35c[1]	Davidson, Alexander	Mass. line	Private	80	Lincoln	('20).
'35d	Davis, Aaron	Mass. line	Private	74	Oxford	('31 b.)
'35d	Davis, Aaron	Mass. line	Private	72	Lincoln	
'40	Davis, Aaron			79	Lincoln	Res. Warren.
'35d	Davis, Allen	Mass. line	Private	78	Cumberland	('20).
'35c	Davis, Benjamin	Mass. line	Private	—	Waldo	Transf. from Essex Co., Mass., Mar. 4, 1826.
'35d	Davis, Cyrus	Mass. mil	Pvt. & Serg	83	Waldo	
'35d	Davis, David	Mass. line	Private	75	Somerset	
'20	Davis, Ezra	R. I.	Private			
'35c	Davis, Ezra	Mass. line	Private	71	Kennebec	d. Sept. 9, 1826.
'40	Davis, Gashum			81	Oxford	Res. Buckfield. Same as following?
'35d	Davis, Gersham	Mass. mil	Private	75	Oxford	
'35c	Davis, Isaac	Mass. line	Private	77	Cumberland	('20).
'40	Davis, Isaac			82	Cumberland	Res. Durham.
'35d	Davis, Jesse	N. H. line	Private	70	Hancock	
'20	Davis, John	R. I.	Private			
'35d	Davis, John	{ Mass. line.. Mass. mil	Private Drummer	78	Kennebec	('20).
'35c	Davis, John	Mass. line	Musician	78	Washington	
'35c	Davis, Joshua	Mass. line	Private	76	Oxford	('20).
'40				81	Oxford	Res. Canton.
'35d	Davis, Josiah	Mass. mil	Private	84	York	
'40				90	York	Res. Parsonsfield.
'35c	Davis, Michael	Mass. line	Private	83	Lincoln	('20) d. Feb. 11, 1825.
'35c	Davis, Michael	Mass. line	Private	74	Kennebec	('20 as Micah) d. Jan. 7, 1822.
'20	Davis, Moses	N. H.	Private			
'35c	Davis, Moses	Mass. line	Private	61	Kennebec	d. Mar. 6, 1822.
'35c	Davis, Nicholas	Mass. line	Private	79	York	('20) d. Jan. 14, 1832.

List.	Name.	Service.	Rank.	Age.	County.	Remarks.
35d	Davis, Philip	Mass. line	Pvt. &Pvt. of art	76	Kennebec	('20).
40	"			82	Kennebec.	Res. Fayette.
35d	Davis, Robert	Mass. state	Private	74	York.	
35c	Davis, Samuel	N. H. line	Lieutenant	83	Kennebec	('20), ('28) ('31b) d, Mar. 6, 1826.
35d	Davis, Samuel	Mass. line	Private	78 or 72	Cumberland	('20).
'40	Davis, Samuel			78	Cumberland	Res. Standish.
'35c	Davis, Sanford	Mass. line	Private	73	Kennebec	('20 as Sandford).
'35c	Davis, Thomas, 2d	Cont. navy	Seaman	76	Hancock	('20, ship "Ranger") d. Feb. 20, 1831.
'35d	Davis, Thomas, 1st.	Mass. line	Private	74 or 75	York	('20, also '35c)
'35c	Davis, William, 4th.	N. Y. line	Private	89	Somerset.	
'35c	Davis, William, 2d	Mass. line	Private	79	Lincoln	('20).
'40	Davis, William			83	Waldo	Res. Palermo.
'35c	Davis, William	Mass. line	Corporal	72	Oxford	('20) d. Nov. 18, 1823.
'35c	Davis, William, 3d	Mass. line	Private	71	Penobscot	('20).
'40	Davis, William			78	Penobscot	Res. Eddington.
'35d	Davis, Zebulon	Mass. mil	Drummer	79	Cumberland	
'35d	Day, Abraham	Mass. mil	Private	71	Lincoln	
'40	"			77	Lincoln	Res. Phipsburg.
'40	Day, Mehitable			87	York	Res. Kennebunk.
'35c	Day, Nathaniel, 2d.	Mass. line	Private	79	York	('20).
'35c	Day, Nathaniel	Mass. line	Private	71	Oxford	('20).
,40	"			77	Oxford	Res. Lovell.
'40	Deab, George			89	Lincoln	Res. Waldoboro.
'35c	Deal, George	Sheldon's dragoons.	Private	79	Waldo	('20, from Conn.) Same as preceding?
'35d	Dean, Abraham	Mass. state	Pvt.& Serg.	72	Oxford.	
'40	Dean, Ebenezer			80	Somerset	Res. Madison.
'35d	Dean, Edmond	Mass. line	Private	74	Oxford	('20, as Edmund).
'40	Dean, Edmund			81	Oxford	Res. Paris.
'35d	Dean, Gideon	Mass. mil	Private	77	Washington.	
'40	"			80	Washington	Res. Robbinston.
'35d	Dean, John	Mass. line	Pvt.&Corp. & Matross	73	Waldo.	
'40	Dean, John			81	Waldo	Res. Palermo.
'29	Dearborn, Henry	N. H.	Capt.of Art & L't Col.			
'35e	"	N. H. line	Lieut. Col.	—	Kennebec	d. June 6, 1828.
'35d	Dearborn, Levi	Mass. line	Pvt.&Corp.	86	Kennebec	
'40	Dearborn, Simon			77	Kennebec	Res. Greene.
'35c	Dearbourn, Simeon, Jr.	N. H. line	Private	73	Kennebec	('20 as Dearborn, Simeon, Jr.) Prob. same as preceding.
'35d	DeBasse, Joshua	Mass. state	Pvt. & Mus	76	Oxford.	
'35c	Decker, Thomas	Mass. line	Private	72	Lincoln	Same as Dicker.
'35c	Decker, Thomas	Mass. line	Private	68	Lincoln.	
'40	Decker, Thomas			86	Lincoln	Res. Boothbay.
'35d	Decker, William	Mass. line	Private	88	Lincoln.	
'35c	Dedston, Benjamin	Mass. line	Private	74	Somerset	Same as Didston?
'35c	Delaney, Nathan	Mass. line	Private	62	Kennebec	d. Mar. 5, 1827. Same as Delay?
'35c	Delano, Alpheus	Mass. line	Private	90	Lincoln	('20).
	Delano, Amasa, see Dilano.					
'35d	Delano, Amaziah	Mass. mil	Private	75	Kennebec.	
'35c	Delano, Jabez	Mass. line	Private	75	Oxford	('20).
'40	"			79	Oxford	Res. Livermore.
'35c	Delano, Jonathan	Mass. line	Private	75	Lincoln	('20).
'40	Delano, Peggy			88	Lincoln	Res. Warren.
1794	Delano, Seth	10th Mass. regt.	Sergeant	—		Res. Winthrop. Enl. 8 Jan.,1777 wounded at Tarrytown, 1779.
'35d	Delano, Seth	Mass. line	Sergeant	82	Somerset	('20). See also Dalino.
'31a	Delano, Thomas		Private	—		Rejected as serving only 6 mos.
'20	Delay, Nathan	Mass.	Private			Same as Delaney?

List.	Name.	Service.	Rank.	Age.	County.	Remarks.
'35d	Delesdernier, Lewis F.	Mass. state	Lieutenant	82	Washington	('31a).
'35d	Demons, Gamaliel	Mass. line	Private	80	Washington	See also Damans
'20	Dennet, Ebenezer	N. H.	Private.			
'35d	Dennett, Ebenezer	Mass. line & mil.	Private	72	Kennebec.	
'35d	Dennett, Joseph	Mass. mil	Private	79	York	('20) ('31b).
'35d	Dennison, David	Mass. line	Private	74	Cumberland	('20).
'40]				79	Cumberland	Res. Freeport.
'35d	Dennison, Robert	Mass. line	Private	88	Kennebec.	
'35c	Deshon, James	Mass. line	Private	72	York.	
'35d	Deshon, Moses	Mass. mil	Private	71	York.	
'40				76	York	Res. Waterborough.
'35c	Dexter, Thomas	Mass. line	Ensign	85	Washington	('20, '28).
'20	Dicker, Thomas	Mass	Private	—		Same as Decker.
'20	Dickey, Eleazer	R. I.	Private.			
'35c	Dickey, Eleazer	Mass. line	Private	76	Waldo.	
'40	Dickey, Eleazer B.			80	Waldo	Res. Monroe.
'20	Didston, Benjamin	Mass.	Private	—		Same as Dedston?
'40	Dilano, Amasa			82	Cumberland	Res. Gray.
'35c	Dillingham, John	Mass. line	Private	—	Cumberland	d. July 1, 1819.
'35d	Dillingham, John	Mass. mil.	Private	71	Cumberland	('20).
'40				77	Cumberland	Res. Minot.
'35d	Dillingham, Lemuel.	Cont. navy	Seaman	76	Waldo.	
'40				82	Waldo	Res. Belfast.
'35d	Dingley, Levi	Mass. line	Private	78	Cumberland.	
'40				84	Cumberland	Res. Harpswell.
'40	Dix, Abigail			90	Penobscot	Res. Bangor.
'35c	Dix, William	Mass. line	Sergeant	83	Kennebec	('20).
'35c	Doane, Amos	Mass. line	Private	76	Penobscot	('20).
'40				82	Penobscot	Res. Hampden.
35d	Doane, Oliver	Mass. state	Private & Seaman	80	Penobscot.	
'40				85	Penobscot	Res. Orrington.
'40	Dobbin, James			88	Cumberland	Res. Falmouth.
'35c	Dobbins, James	S. C. line	Private	80	Cumberland	('20).
'35c	Dodd, Stephen	Mass. line	Private	74	Lincoln	('20, '31b).
'35c	Dodge, Abner	Mass. line	Sergeant	77	Cumberland	('20)d.Jan.28,1833
'40	Dodge, Be'sey			75	Waldo	Res. Burnham.
'35c	Dodge, Nicholas	N. H. line	Private	75	Kennebec	('20)d. Dec. 10, 1827.
35c	Dodge, Paul	Mass. line	Lieutenant	65	Lincoln	('20) ('31b as Dodger).
'40	Doe, Henry			73	Kennebec	Res. Augusta.
35c	Doe, James	Mass. line	Private	82	Waldo.	
'40	Doe, Olive			87	Waldo	Res. Burnham.
'35c	Doe, Sampson	Mass. line	Private	76	Kennebec	('20) d. Dec. 25, 1828.
'35c	Doe, Simon	Mass. line	Private	—	Somerset	('20).
'40				81	Somerset	Res. Fairfield.
'35c	Dolbear, Benjamin	Mass. line	Private	63	Somerset	('20).
'35c	Dole, Amos	Mass. line	Private	76	Penobscot	('20)d. July 20, 1832.
'40	Dole, Matilda			75	Penobscot	Res. Orrington.
'35c	Dole, Richard	Mass. line	Corporal	87	Oxford	('20) d. Dec. 4, 1824.
'35c	Dolliff, Noah	N. H. line	Private	74	Waldo.	
'20	Dolliver, Peter	Mass	Private	—		Same as Dalliver?
'40	Dolloff, Richard			85	Oxford	Res. Rumford.
'35d	Doloff, Richard	N. H. state	Private	79	Oxford	Same as preceding
'40	Donnell, Abigail			79	York	Res. York. See also Dunnell.
'35c	Donnell, Jotham	Mass. line	Sergeant	70	York	('20, '31b).
'35c	Donnell, Obadiah	Cont. navy	Marine	69	York	('20, ship "Ranger"), ('31b).
'35d	Dorman, Israel	Mass. line	Private	92	York	('20, '31 b).
'35c	Dorman, John	Mass. line	Private	82	York	('20) d. July 26, 1827.
'35c	Dorr, William	Mass. line	Private	77	Kennebec.	
'40				84	Kennebec	Res. Augusta.
'35d	Doten, Samuel	Mass. navy	Mariner	76	Cumberland.	
'40				83	Cumberland	Res. N. Yarmouth
'35c	Doty, John	Mass. line	Private	65	Cumberland	('20)d.Oct. 5,1827.
'35d	Doughty, Benjamin.	Mass. line	Private	92	Cumberland	d. Apr. 12, 1833.
'35c	Doughty, Ichabod	Mass. line	Private	80	Cumberland	('20).
'40				86	Cumberland	Res. Brunswick.

List.	Name.	Service.	Rank.	Age	County.	Remarks.
'35d	Doughty, James....	Mass. line.....	Private....	69	Cumberland.	('20, '31b)('35c as James, 2d.
'40	Doughty, James....			76	Cumberland.	Res. Harpswell.
'35c	Doughty, James....	Mass. line.....	Private....	67	Lincoln.....	('20)d. Jan. 30, 1820.
	Doughty, John.....	See Doty.....		—		
'35d	Doughty, Joseph...	Mass. line.....	Private....	78	Cumberland.	
'35c	Doughty, Nathaniel	Mass. line.....	Private....	72	Cumberland.	('20). Also given Doty.
'40	Douglass, Elisha ...			71	Waldo......	Res. Burnham.
'35c	Douglass, John.....	Mass. line.....	Private....	73	Oxford......	('20).
'40	———			80	Oxford......	Res. Denmark.
'35c	Dow, Henry.......	Mass. line,....	Private....	83	Lincoln.....	Transferred from Hillsboro Co.,N. H., 1824. d. June 9, 1828.
'35c	Dowlf, Ellis........	Mass. line.....	Private....	82	Lincoln.....	('20).
'40	Downe, Mary H....			68	Penobscot...	Res. Bangor.
'35c	Downing, John.....	Mass. line.....	Private....	71	Hancock....	('20).
'40	Downing, John.....			74	Cumberland.	Res. Minot.
'35c	Downing, Samuel ..	Mass. line.....	Private....	69	Cumberland.	('20).
'40				75	Cumberland.	Res. Minot.
'40	Downs, Aaron.....			79	York........	Res. Berwick.
'35d	Downs, Paul.......	Mass. mil......	Private....	77	York.	
'35c	Doyen, Jacob......	N. H. line.....	Private....	70	Somerset....	('20) d. April 13, 1830.
'35c	Doyle, James......	Mass. line.....	Private....	81	Penobscot...	('20).
'35d	Doyle, Michael.....	Mass. mil......	Corporal...	73	Kennebec.	
'31a	Doyne, Samuel.....		Private....	—		Claim rejected as he did not serve 9 mos. in Cont. army.
'35c	Drake, Ebenezer...	Mass. line.....	Private....	74	Oxford......	('20) o. Dec. 14, 1829.
'35d	Drake, John.......	Mass. mil......	Private....	76	Oxford.	
'35c	Drake, Oliver......	Mass. line.....	Private....	67	Kennebec ...	('20) d. March 3, 1828.
'35d	Dresser, Aaron.....	Mass. state....	Private....	76	Cumberland.	
'40	———			81	Cumberland..	Res. Danville.
'35d	Dresser, Elijah.....	Mass. line.....	Private....	83	Oxford.	
'40	———			89	Oxford......	Res. Turner.
'35d	Dresser, Joseph....	Mass. mil......	Private....	86	Cumberland.	
'35d	Dresser, Levi......	Mass. state....	Pvt.&Corp.	72	Oxford.	
'40				79	Oxford......	Res. Lovell.
'35c	Dresser, Richard...	Mass. line.....	Private....	76	York........	('20).
'40				81	York........	Res. Buxton.
'40	Drew, Jerusha.....			83	Oxford......	Res. Buckfield.
'35c	Drown, Moses.....	Mass. line.....	Private....	79	York........	('20) d. 1825.
'35c	Drown, Stephen....	Mass. line.....	Private....	75	York........	('20).
'35c	Dudley, Nathan....	Mass. line.....	Private....	76	Cumberland.	
'35d	Dudley, Nathan....	Mass. line.....	Pvt. & Pvt. of art...	74 or 76	Oxford......	('20).
'35d	Dummer, Jeremiah.	Mass. mil......	Private....	70	Kennebec.	
'35d	Dummer, Richard..	Mass. mil......	Private....	77	Kennebec ...	d. Sept. 2, 1832.
'40	Dun, Joshua.......			81	Oxford......	Res. Andover, No. Surplus;same as Dunn, J.?
'35c	Dunbar, David.....	Mass. line.....	Private....	—	Hancock....	('20).
'35d	Dunbar, David.....	Mass. line.....	Private....	77	Hancock....	Same as preceding
'40				83	Hancock....	Res. Penobscot.
'35d	Dunbar, Elijah.....	Mass. mil......	Private....	79	Lincoln.	
'40				85	Lincoln.....	Res. Nobleboro'.
'35d	Dunbar, Jacob.....	Mass. mil......	Private....	93	Oxford.	
'40	Dunbar, Jacob.....			98	Washington.	Res. Pembroke.
'35d	Dunbar, Obed.....	Mass. mil......	Private....	90	Washington.	
'35c	Dunfee, Cornelius..	Mass. line.....	Private....	92	Kennebec ...	('20).
'35c	Dunham, Ammi ...	Mass. line.....	Private....	70	Cumberland.	('20).
'40	Dunham, Ammi....			75	Lincoln.....	Res. Jefferson.
'35d	Dunham, Moses ...	Mass. line.....	Private....	77	Oxford......	('20).
'40				84	Oxford......	Res. Hartford.
'40	Dunlap, Dorcas.....			76	Lincoln.....	Res. Topsham.
'35c	Dunlap, James.....	Mass. line.....	Private....	82	Lincoln.....	('20).
'40	Dunlap, James.....			88	Kennebec ...	Res. Litchfield.
'35c	Dunlap, John......	Mass. line.....	Private....	64	Lincoln.....	('20) d. Oct. 25, 1818.
'35d	Dunn, Christopher.	Mass. line.....	Private....	74	Kennebec ...	('20).

List.	Name.	Service.	Rank.	Age.	County.	Remarks.
'35c	Dunn, Joshua	Mass. line	Private	73	Cumberland	Same as Dun, J.?
'35a	Dunnells, John		Private	—	York	See also Donnell.
'31a	Dunnells, Oliver		Private	—		Claim rejected as regt. was not on Cont. establishment.
'35d	Dunning, John	Mass. mil	Pvt. & Serg	81	Cumberland	
'20	Durell, Benjamin	Mass	Private	—		Same as Durrill?
'35c	Durell, Peter	Mass. line	Private	65	Oxford	('20)d. July 24, 1823.
'35d	Durgen, John	Mass. line	Private	84	York.	
'35c	Durow, William	Mass. line	Private	77	Lincoln	('20 as Duron) d. Oct. 21, 1832.
'35d	Durrell, David	Mass. state	Serg	87	York	d. May 9, 1833.
'35c	Durrill, Benjamin	Mass. line	Private	92	Kennebec	d. Jan. 4, 1820. Same as Durell?
'35c	Dwelley, Allen	Mass. line	Private	—	Penobscot	('20).
'40				78	Penobscot	Res. West half Township No.6.
'35d	Dwelly, John	Mass. mil	Seaman	68	Waldo.	
'40				74	Waldo	Res. Frankfort.
'35c	Dyer, Bickford	Mass. line	Private	87	Cumberland	('20 as Rickford)d. May 5, 1828.
'35c	Dyer, Ephraim	Mass. line	Private	77	Hancock	('20).
'40	Dyer, Hannah			77	Cumberland	Res. Cape Elizabeth.
'35d	Dyer, Isaac	Mass. line	Pvt. & Pvt. of art	74	York	('20, '31b,Isaac 2d)
'40	Dyer, Isaac			82	York	Res. Limington.
'35c	Dyer, Isaac, 1st	Mass. line	Drummer	71	Lincoln	('20)d. Feb. 10, 1820.
'40	Dyer, James			86	Franklin	Res. New Sharon.
'40	Dyer, Mary			76	Cumberland	Res. Harpswell.
'35c	Dyer, Paul	Mass. line	Private	67	Cumberland	('20) d. April 13, 1827.

37

List.	Name.	Service.	Rank.	Age.	County.	Remarks.
'35c	Eames, Ebenezer...	Mass. line.....	Private....	80	Oxford......	('20) d. Aug. 19, 1833.
'35d	Eames, James......	Mass. line.....	Private....	71	Oxford......	
'40		....	....	78	Oxford......	Res. Newry.
'35d	Eames, Samuel.....	Mass. line.....	Private....	72	Kennebec...	
'35d	Eastman, Daniel...	Mass. mil.....	Private....	78	York........	
'40		....	....	83	York........	Res. Cornish.
'35d	Eastman, Daniel...	Mass. state....	Private....	68	Oxford......	
'35c	Eastman, Jacob....	N. H. line.....	Musician..	72	York........	('20).
'40		....	....	77	York........	Res. Parsonsfield.
'35d	Eastman, James....	N. H. line.....	Private....	81	Oxford......	d. Nov. 13, 1833.
'35c	Eastman, John......	N. H. line.....	Private....	65	Oxford......	('20) d. Sept. 6, 1827.
'35c	Eastman, Zachariah.	Mass. line.....	Private....	78	Cumberland.	('20).
'40	Eastman, Zechariah	....	....	95	Cumberland.	Res. Scarborough.
'40	Eastmon, Sarah....	....	....	78	Oxford......	Res. Fryeburg.
'35d	Eaton, Benjamin...	Mass. mil.....	Private....	73	Somerset....	
'35d	Eaton, Ebenezer....	Mass. line and N. H. line.	Private....	68	Kennebec...	('20).
'35d	Eaton, Eliab.......	Mass. line.,...	Corp. and Serg.	70	Somerset....	('20).
'40	Eaton, Eliab.......	....	....	77	Franklin....	Res. Strong.
'35c	Eaton, Eliah........	Mass. line.....	Private....	70	Somerset....	
'35c	Eaton, Samuel.....	Mass. line.....	Private....	75	Cumberland.	('20) d. Aug. 4, 1830.
'35d	Eaton, William.....	Mass. line.....	Sergeant..	78	York........	('20, '31b).
'40		....	....	85	York........	Res. Wells.
'20	Eaton, William.....	Mass.........	Private....	—		
'40	Eddy, Celia........	....	....	78	Penobscot...	Res. Eddington.
'35d	Edes, Thomas......	Mass. mil.....	Private....	70	Cumberland.	
'40		....	....	78	Cumberland.	Res. Otisfield.
'35d	Edgecomb, James..	Mass. line.....	Private....	77	Cumberland.	('20, Edgcomb).
'35d	Edgerly, Richard...	N. H. mil......	Private....	85	York........	('31a.)
'40	Edgerly, Richard...	....	....	79	York........	Res. Limington.
'35c	Edminster, Noaha..	Mass. line.....	Private....	73	Penobscot...	('20, Noah).
'35d	Edmonds, Asa.....	Mass. line.....	Pvt. & Serg	77	Waldo......	
'40	Edmuns, Eunice....	....	....	83	Waldo......	Res. Belfast.
'35c	Edwards, Joshua...	Mass. line.....	Sergeant..	83	Kennebec...	('20).
'35c	Edwards, Nathaniel.	Mass. line.....	Private...	79	York........	('20).
'35d	Edwards, Samuel...	Mass. state....	Artificer...	82	York........	
'35c	Edwards, Stephen..	Mass. line.....	Sergeant..	70	York........	('20) d. Feb. 12, 1825.
'35d	Elden, Gibeon.....	Mass. line.....	Private....	—	York........	
'35d	Elden, Gibeon.....	Mass. line.....	Private....	73	York........	('20).
'35d	Elder, Joshua......	Mass line.....	Private....	70	Kennebec...	
'40	Elder, Joshua......	....	....	76	Penobscot...	Res. Dexter.
'35c	Eldridge, Daniel....	Mass. line.....	Private....	73	York........	('20) d. June 10, 1832.
'35d	Elliott, Jacob......	Mass. mil.....	Private....	70	Cumberland.	
'40		....	....	77	Cumberland.	Res. Falmouth.
'35d	Elliott, Jedediah...	Mass. line.....	Private....	73	Cumberland.	('20, '31b).
'40		....	....	79	Cumberland.	Res. Windham.

List.	Name.	Service.	Rank.	Age.	County.	Remarks.
'35c	Ellis, Atkins	Mass. line	Private	83	Somerset	('20) d. Oct. 18, 1833.
'35c	Ellis, Edward	N. H. line	Private	75	Kennebec	
'20	Ellis, Robert	Mass.	Private	69	Kennebec	
'35c	Ellis, Robert	N. H. line	Private	74	Kennebec	Res. Sidney.
'40						
'35c	Ellis, Samuel	Mass. line	Non. com. officer	80	Washington	('20).
'40	Elwell, Jeremiah			50	Cumberland	Res. Poland.
'35d	Emerson, Samuel	N. H. state	Fifer & Fife major	79	York	
'40	Emerson, Samuel			76	York	Res. Kennebunk.
'40	Emery, Abigail			80	Somerset	Res. Fairfield.
'35c	Emery, Daniel	Mass. line	Private	75	Kennebec	d. Nov. 18, 1830.
'35c	Emery, Daniel	Mass. line	Private	76	York	
'20	Emery, Daniel	N. H.	Private			
'20	Emery, David	Mass.	Private			
'35d	Emery, Isaac	Mass. mil	Private	77	York	
'35c	Emery, Jacob	Mass. line	Private	77	York	('20).
'35d	Emery, James	Mass. line	Private	78	York	d. Sept. 12, 1832.
'35d	Emery, James	Mass. mil	Private	70	York	
'35d	Emery, Job	Mass. line	Private	87	York	('20, '31b). d. July 27,1832.
'35c	Emery, John	Mass. line	Private	80	Somerset	('20).
'40				87	Somerset	Res. Bloomfield.
'40	Emery, Joseph			63	Waldo	Res. Montville.
'35c	Emery, Joshua	Mass. line	Private	71	Cumberland	d. April 6, 1827.
'35c	Emery, Nathaniel	Mass. line	Private	77	Somerset	('20) d. May 6, 1824.
'35c	Emery, Ralph	Mass. line	Private	70	York	('20) d. in 1830.
'35d	Emery, Samuel	Mass. line	Sergeant	79	Somerset	('20).
'35d	Emmons, Pendleton	Mass. mil	Private	89	York	
'35d	F-skine, David	Mass. mil	Private	75	Lincoln	
'35d	Esty, Edward	Mass. mil	Pvt. &Serg.	80	Kennebec	
'35c	Eustice, Jacob	Mass. line	Private	71	Hancock	
'35d	Evans, Benjamin	Mass. mil	Pvt.of art.	84	York	
'40	Evans, James P			68	Kennebec	Res. Gardiner.
'35d	Evans, James Pratt	Mass. state	Private	79	Penobscot	d. March 14, 1833.
'35d	Evans, John	Mass. mil	Private	82	Somerset	
'35c	Evans, Joseph	Mass. line	Private	86	Kennebec	('20) d. April 15, 1826.
'35c	Evans, Nathaniel	Mass. line	Private	72	Hancock	('20) d. June 14, 1819.
'35d	Evans, William	Mass. mil	Private	69	Oxford	
'40	Eveans, William			75	Oxford	Res. Fryeburg.
'35d	Eveleth, Isaac	Mass. mil	Private	73	Cumberland	
'35d	Eveleth, James (widow)	Mass. line	Pvt.&Corp. of cav.	82	Kennebec	d. Jan. 22, 1834.
'35c	Everett, Josiah	Mass. line	Private	74	Somerset	('20).
'40				80	Somerset	Res.New Portl'd.
'35c	Everton, Zephariah	Mass. line	Private	70	Lincoln	('20).
'35c	Ewer, Jonathan	Mass. line	Private	75	Kennebec	('20) d. Jan. 29, 1829.
'35c	Fairbank, John	Mass. line	Private	80	Lincoln	Transf. from Middlesex County, Mass., 1826, d, July 10, 1830.
'35d	Fairbank, Nathaniel	Mass. line	Private	80	Kennebec	
'35d	Fairbanks, Elijah	Mass. mil	Private	78	Kennebec	
'40	Fairbanks, Lydia			74	Kennebec	Res. Wayne.
'35c	Fairfield, John	Mass. line	Private	77	York	('20).
'35c	Fairfield, William	Mass. line	Private	66	York	('20).
'35c	Fall, George	N. H. line	Sergeant	66	Kennebec	('20, '31b).
'35e		N. H. regt.	Sergeant	—	York	('29 as Falls).
'40	Fanin, John			80	Lincoln	Res. Bath. Same as Farrin?
'40	Fannington, ohn			83	Penobscot	Res.Brewer. Same as Farrington.
'40	Farnham. Dorcas			85	Lincoln	Res. Boothbay.
'35c	Farnham, Jonathan	Mass. line	Private	81	York	('20).
'35c	Farnham, Jonathan	Mass. line	Private	68	York	d. May 29, 1823.
'35c	Farnham, Nathaniel	Mass. line	Private	77	Oxford	('20, N. H. line).
'40	Farnham, Nathaniel			83	Somerset	Res. Mercer.
'40	Farnham, Ralph			84	York	Res. Acton. Same as Furnham?
'40	Farnsworth, Abigail			90	Lincoln	Res. Waldoboro.
'35d	Farnsworth, Robert	Mass. navy	Pvt. & Seaman.	70	Lincoln	
'35d	Farnsworth, W lliam	N. H. line	Private & Lieut.	81	Lincoln	

List.	Name.	Service.	Rank.	Age.	County.	Remarks.
'20	Farnum, Jonathan	Mass.	Private	—		Same as Farnham?
'35d	Farnum, Simeon	Mass. line	Private	78	Penobscot	
'40				85	Penobscot	Res. Newburg.
'35d	Far.and, William	Mass. mil	Private & Drum	72	Somerset	
'20	Farrin, John	Mass	Private	—		Same as Fanin?
'35c	Farrington, Abner	Mass. line	Private	82	Lincoln	
'40				88	Lincoln	Res. Warren.
'35d	Farrington, Ithamar	Mass. line	Pvt.& Serg.	78	Oxford	
'40	Farrington, Ithamas			84	Oxford	Res. Livermore.
'35d	Farrington, John	Mass. mil	Private	76	Penobscot	Same as Fannington, J?
'35d	Farrington, William	Mass. line	Serg. maj. & Adj.	72	Cumberland	d. Aug. 11, 1832.
'35d	Farris, William	Mass. line	Private	78	Kennebec	
'40	Farris, William			81	Kennebec	Res. China.
'35d	Farrow, John	Mass. line	Private	77	Lincoln	('20, '31b).
'35d	Fassett, Richard	Mass. mil	Private & Drum.	85	Somerset	
'35c	Faxon, John	Mass. line	Private	53	Washington	('20).
'35d	Fay, Silas	Mass. line	Pvt.&Corp	84	Waldo	
'35c	Felker, Joseph	N. H. line	Private	74	Somerset	('20).
'40				80	Somerset	Res. Embden.
'35c	Fenderson, John	Mass. line	Private	78	York	('20).
'35d	Fenderson, Pelatiah	Mass line	Private	75	Cumberland	('20, '31b).
'40	Fennin, Richard			79	Kennebec	Res. Litchfield, Same as Ferrin.
'35d	Fernald, Dennis	Mass. mil	Private	76	York	('20, '31b).
'40	Fernald, Elizabeth			79	York	Res. Elliott.
'35d	Fernald, Hercules	Mass. line	Private	84	York	
	Fernald, Nicholas	See Furnald.				
'35c	Fernald, Tobias	Mass. line	Private	71	York	('20) d. Jan. 1828.
'35c	Ferren, Jonathan	Mass. line	Private	65	York	('20).
'35c	Ferrin, John	Mass line	Private	78	Lincoln	
'35c	Ferrin, Richard	Mass. line	Private	73	Lincoln	('20). Same as Fennin.
'35d	Fessenden, Ebenezer	Mass. mil	Private	77	Oxford	('31a).
'40	Fickett, Lucy			88	Cumberland	Res. Cape Elizabeth.
'35c	Fickett, Nathaniel	Mass. line	Private	74	Cumberland	('20) d. May 23, 1832.
'35c	Fickett, Vinson	Mass. line	Private	77	Cumberland	('20).
'40	Fickett, Zebulon			81	Washington	Res. Harrington.
'40	Field, Rachel			88	Oxford	Res. Greenwood.
'40	Field, Luty			81	Oxford	Res. Paris.
'35d	Fields, Thomas	Mass. state	G'n'rs'm'te	84	Kennebec	
'40	Fields, Thomas			90	Franklin	Res. New Sharon.
'35c	Fii eld, John	Cont. navy	Serg.ofmar.	81	York	Transf.from Stratford Co., N. H. 1826.
'35e	Fifield, ohn	Crane's art	Matross	—	Oxford	('20 Mass. line, '29).
'40				78	Oxford	Res. Fryeburg.
'35c	Fifield, John	Mass. line	Private	58	Oxford	
'35d	Files, Ebenezer	Mass. line	Private	76	Cumberland	('20 & '31b as File)
'40	Files, Esther			70 to80	Cumberland	Res. Gorham.
'35d	Files, Samuel	Mass. line	Private	74	Cumberland	('20 & '31b as File)
'35d	Files, William	Mass. mil	Private	73	Cumberland	
'35d	Fillebrown, James	Mass. mil	Pvt.&Corp.	77	Kennebec	
'35d	Fillebrown, Thomas	Mass. state	Matross	71	Kennebec	
'40				76	Kennebec	Res. Winthrop.
'35c	Fish, David	Mass. line	Private	73	Kennebec	d. Jan. 28, 1823; Same as Fisk?
'35d	Fish, Jacob	Mass. mil	Private	83	Oxford	
'35c	Fish, Simeon	N. H. line	Private	78	Lincoln	
'40	Fish, Simeon			68	Lincoln	Res. Patricktown Plant.
'35d	Fisher, Ebenezer	Mass. line	Private	75	Penobscot	('20, '31b).
'35c	Fisher, Elijah	Mass. line	Private	78	Oxford	('20).
'40				82	Oxford	Res. Livermore.
'35d	Fisher, Jacob	Mass. line	Private	74	York	('20).
'40				78	York	Res. Kennebunk.
'35d	Fisk, Abner	Mass. mil	Pvt.& Serg.	78	York	
'20	Fisk, David	Mass	Private	—		Same as Fish?
'40	Fitts, Abigail			89	Kennebec	Res. Litchfield.
35d	Fitts, Samuel	Mass. mil	Private	72	Cumberland	

List.	Name.	Service.	Rank.	Age.	County.	Remarks.
'35c	Fitz, Abraham	R. I. line	Private	67	Kennebec	('20).
'35c	Fitzgerald, David	Mass. line	Private	60	York	('20, '31b).
'35c	Fitzgerald, John	Mass. line	Private	83	Lincoln	('20, '31b).
'35c	Flagg, Asa	N. H. line	Private	66	Penobscot	d. Sept., 1822.
'35d	Flagg, Isaac	N. H. line	Private	86	Waldo	
'35c	Flagg, Samuel A.	Mass. line	Drummer	70	Lincoln	('20).
'40				78	Lincoln	Res. Nobleboro.
'35c	Flamming, James	Mass. line	Sergeant	95	Kennebec	('20) d. Aug. 18, 1827.
'35c	Flanders, John	Mass. line	Private	76	Kennebec	('20, '31b).
'35c	Flanders, Philip	N. H. line	Private	77	Waldo	('20).
'40				82	Waldo	Res. Freedom.
'40	Fletcher, Elizabeth			68	Oxford	Res. Summer.
'35d	Fletcher, Jeremiah	Mass. line	Corporal	78	Kennebec	
'35d	Fletcher, John	Mass. line	Private	72	Oxford	('20).
'40	Flint, Levi			86	Kennebec	Res. Clinton.
'35c	Flint, Thomas	Cont. navy	Mariner	67	Cumberland	('20 ship "Hancock", '31b).
'35c	Flood, Henry	Mass. line	Private	79	York	('20).
'35c	Flood, James	Mass. line	Private	71	Cumberland	('20) d. Sept. 22, 1825
'35d	Fly, William	Mass. state	Private	83	Lincoln	
'35c	Fobs, Jonah	Mass. line	Private	85	Oxford	('20, Fobes) d. 1826.
'35c	Fogg, Aaron	Mass. line	Private	60	York	('20) d. Feb. 5, 1832.
'35d	Fogg, Caleb	Mass. mil	Private	73	Kennebec	
'35c	Fogg, Charles	Mass. line	Private	71	Oxford	('20).
'35d	Fogg, George	Mass. line	Private	72	Lincoln	('20, '31b).
'40	Fogg, George			73	Kennebec	Res. Wales
'40	Fogg, Hannah			60	Cumberland	Res. Gorham.
'35d	Fogg, Samuel	Mass. mil	Private & Drum.	to70 78	Somerset	
'40				83	Somerset	Res. Cornville.
'20	Folron, John	Mass.	Private	—		Same as Folson.
'35d	Folsom, Moses	N. H. state	Private	82	York	
'35c	Folson, John	Mass. line	Private	75	Oxford	Same as Folron, d. May 23, 1830.
'35c	Forbes, William	Mass. line	Private	72	Penobscot	('20).
'40				78	Penobscot	Res. Bangor.
'35d	Ford, Caleb	Mass. mil	Private	79	York	
'35d	Ford, Charles	Mass. state	Private	77	Oxford	
'40				82	Oxford	Res. Sumner.
'35d	Ford, Joshua	Mass. line	Private	74	Oxford	
'35c	Ford, Miles	Mass. line	Private	68	Kennebec	('20) d. Aug. 15, 1830.
'35d	Ford, Nathaniel	Mass. line	Pvt.&Corp. & Serg...	75	Kennebec	
40	Foss, Elias			74	York	Same as Fosse. Res. Limington.
'35d	Foss, Isaiah	Mass. mil	Private & Drum.	79	Somerset	
'35d	Foss, James	Mass. mil	Private	85	Cumberland	
'35d	Foss, John	Mass. mil	Corporal	84	York	
'35c	Foss, Joseph	Mass. line	Private	74	Oxford	
'40				81	Oxford	Res. Dixfield or Peru.
'40	Foss, Susannah			85	York	Res. Limington.
'35d	Foss, Zachariah			74	Cumberland	('20, '31b).
'35d	Fosse, Elias	Mass. line	Private	68	York	('20, '31b). Same as Foss.
'35d	Foster, Benan	Mass. state	Private	74	York	
'35c	Foster, David	R. I. line	Private	82	Kennebec	('20) d. April 7, 1825.
'35c	Foster, Jonathan	Mass. line	Private	85	Hancock	('20).
'35c	Foster, Parker	Mass. line	Sergeant	73	York	('20).
'40				79	York	Res. Elliot.
'35c	Foster, Samuel	R. I. line	Private	82	Kennebec	('20, Corp.) d. April 7, 1825.
'35d	Foster, Stephen	Mass. mil	Private	78	Kennebec	
'40	Foster, Stephen			74	Kennebec	Res. Leeds.
'35d	Foster, William	Mass. state	Sergeant	84	Lincoln	
'35c	Fowle, Phineas	R. I. mil	Sergeant	77	York	('20) d. Sept. 12, 1819.
'35d	Fowler, John	Mass. mil	Private	80	Cumberland	d. Aug. 25, 1832.
'35c	Fowler, Matthew	Mass. line	Private	70	Waldo	('20).
'40				77	Waldo	Res. Unity.

41

List.	NAME.	Service.	Rank.	Age.	County.	Remarks.
'35d	Fox, John........	Mass. mil......	Private....	73	Oxford......	
'35c	Foy, James........	N. H. line.....	Private....	75	York......	('20)d. Jan. 1,1828
'35d	Foy, John.........	Mass. line.....	Private....	75	Kennebec...	
'35d	Foy, Moses........	Mass. mil.....	Private....	74	York........	
'40	Foye, Moses,......	....	....	79	York........	Res. Berwick.
'35d	Frank, James......	Mass. line.....	Private....	82	Cumberland.	
'35c	Frank, Thomas....	Mass. line.....	Private....	75	Cumberland.	('20) d. Oct. 11, 1831.
'35c	Frederick, Joseph ..	Cont. navy....	Mariner...	80	Somerset....	('20, ship "Alliance"). d. March, 1822.
'35c	Freeman, John 1st.	Mass. line.....	Private....	74	Kennebec ...	('20).
'35c	Freeman, John, 2d.	Mass. line.....	Private....	86	York........	('20) d. 1822.
'40	Freeman, John.....	....	....	80	Kennebec ...	Res. Monmouth.
'35d	Freeman, John.....	Mass. mil.....	Private....	74	Lincoln.....	
'40	Freeman, Sampson .	....	....	75	Kennebec ...	Res. Waterville.
'20	Freethey, Joseph...	Mass........	Private....	—	....	Same as Fruthy.
'35d	French, Ebenezer...	N. H. line.....	Private....	79	Kennebec ...	
'40	French, Mary......	....	....	82	Franklin....	Res. Jay.
'35d	French, Obadiah...	Mass. state....	Private....	76	Kennebec ...	
'40	French, Sarah......	....	....	93	Oxford......	Res. Turner.
'40	French, William....	....	....	78	Oxford......	Res. Canton.
'35d	French,'William....	Mass. mil....	Private....	72	York........	
'35d	Frost, Elliott......	Mass. line.....	Private....	73	York........	('20). (as Flliot).
'40	—	....	....	79	York........	Res. Elliot.
'35d	Frost, Jacob.......	Mass. mil.....	Pvt.& Serg.	82	Oxford......	Invalid pensioner, 1785.
'35c	Frost, John........	Cont. navy....	Midsh'p'n.	83	Washington..	('20, Mariner, ship "Raleigh")
'35c	Frost, Mark.......	Mass. line.....	Private....	87	Kennebec....	('20, '31b)
'35d	Frost, Moses.......	Mass. mil....	Private....	73	Oxford.....	
'35c	Frost, Nathaniel ..	Mass. line.....	Private....	75	York........	d. Feb. 17, 1829.
'20	Frost, Nathaniel ..	Mass........	Sergeant ..	—	....	
'40	Frost, Phinehas....	....	....	46	Oxford......	Res. Bethel.
'35c	Frost, Samuel......	Mass. line.....	Sergeant ..	70	Kennebec ...	('20)d. Oct. 27, 1823.
'40	Frost, Sarah.......	....	....	76	York........	Res. Elliot.
'35c	Frost, Stephen.....	Cont. navy....	Marine....	82	York........	('20 ship 'Raleigh") d. Oct. 8, 1824.......
'35c	Frost, William.....	Mass. line.....	Lieut.....	80	York........	('20) d. June 2, 1827.
'35c	Fruthy, Joseph.....	Mass. line.....	Private....	80	Hancock....	Same as Freethey.
'35c	Frye, Ebenezer.....	N. H. line.....	Captain...	83	Hancock....	('20, '28). d. March 9, 1825.
'35c	Frye, Nathaniel,Sr.	Mass. line.....	Lieut.....	75	Hancock....	('20, '28, '29) Relinquished benefit of act of 1818 for that of 1828. d. Apr. 17,1833; Dolly Frye, widow.
'35e	Frye, Nathaniel....	Mass. line, 8th regt.	Lieut.....	—	Oxford......	
'35d	Fuller, Aaron.......	Mass. line.....	Private....	78	Oxford......	
'40	Fuller, Aaron......	....	....	83	Cumberland.	Res. Otisfield.
'35c	Fuller, Andrew.....	Mass. line.....	Private....	78	Lincoln......	('20) d. Jan. 31, 1820.
'35e	Fuller, Barzilla.....	Mass. line, 8th regt.	Corporal ..	—	Oxford......	('29) d. Aug. 8, 1833; Mary Fuller, widow.
'35c	Fuller, Barzilla.....	Mass. line.....	Private....	69	Oxford......	('20, Barzillia, '31b).
'35c	Fuller, Enoch......	Mass. line.....	Private....	79	Kennebec ...	('20).
'40		....	....	85	Kennebec ...	Res. Winslow.
'40	Fuller, Hannah....	....	....	85	Lincoln......	Res. Cushing.
'35c	Fuller, Isaac.......	Mass. line.....	Private....	72	Kennebec ...	('20) d. Apr. 27, 1833.
'40	Fuller, Mary.......	....	....	89	Oxford......	Res. Hebron.
'35c	Fuller, Robert.....	Mass. line.....:	Private....	77	Oxford.....	('20) d. March 18, 1829.
'35d	Fuller, William.....	Mass. line.....	Pvt.&Corp.	73	Kennebec ...	
'40		....	....	79	Kennebec ...	Res. Gardiner.
'35c	Furbush, Benjamin.	N. H. line.....	Private....	75	Kennebec ...	
'35c	Furnald, Nicholas..	Mass. line.....	Private....	72	Oxford......	('20)d. May 25, 1822.
'35d	Furnham, Ralph...	Mass. mil.....	Pvt. and Serg.	78	York........	Same asFarnham?

List.	Name.	Service.	Rank.	Age.	County.	Remarks.
'35d	Gage, Amos.......	N. H. line......	Private ...	74	Oxford......	('20,'31b). d. Aug. 29, 1833.
'35d	Gage, Daniel.......	N. H........	Sergeant ..	73 or 74	Oxford......	('20).
'40	———			79	Oxford......	Res. Bethel.
'40	Gage, Louis........	....	....	81	Oxford......	Res. Waterford.
'35c	Gaitskill, William...	Mass. line.....	Private ...	70	Kennebec ...	('20) d. July 29, 1820.
'35d	Gale, Daniel.......	Mass. line.....	Private ...	73	Somerset....	('20).
'35d	Gamage, Joshua....	Mass. state....	Sergeant ..	79	Oxford.	
'35d	Gammon, David...	Mass. mil.....	Private ...	79	Oxford.	
'35d	Gammon, Joseph...	Mass. state....	Private ...	73	Oxford......	Same as Gammond?
'35d	Gammon, Joshua...	Mass. mil.....	Private ...	71	Penobscot.	
'40	Gammon, Joshua...	....	....	78	Cumberland.	Res. Cape Elizabeth.
'35d	Gammon, Moses...	Mass. line.....	Pvt. & Serg.	84	Oxford......	('20, also '35c).
'35d	Gammon, Samuel..	Mass. line.....	Private ...	79	Oxford.	
'40	Gammond, Joseph..	....	....	76	Oxford......	Res. Norway. Same as Gammon, J.?
'35c	Gardiner, Charles ..	Mass. line.....	Private ...	61	Lincoln.....	('20)d. in 1824.
'35c	Gardiner, Elijah....	Mass. line.....	Bomb'dier	82	Washington..	('20).
'35c	Gardiner, John.....	Cont. navy....	Seaman...	75	Oxford......	Same as Gardner, J.?
'40	Gardner, John.....	....	....	79	Oxford......	Res. Oxford. Same as Gardiner, J.?
'35d	Gardner, Jonathan.	Mass. line.....	Private ...	74	Oxford.	
'40	*Gardner, Sarah*	....	....	73	Oxford......	Res. Buckfield.
'35c	Garland, James....	Mass. line.....	Private ...	83	Penobscot.	
'35c	Garnett, Daniel....	Mass. line.....	Private ...	69	Washington.	('20) d. Oct. 19, 1819.
'35c	Gatchell, Benjamin.	Mass. line.....	Private ...	68	Cumberland.	('20) d. Jan. 5, 1827.
'40	Gatchell, William			84	Cumberland.	Res. Brunswick. Same as Gattchell, W.
'35d	Gattchell, Nathaniel	Mass. mil.....	Private ...	79	Cumberland.	d. Jan. 12, 1833. See also Gettchell, Gitchel & Gaitskill.
'35d	Gattchell, William..	Mass. mil....'.	Private ...	77	Cumberland.	Same as Gatcheil, W.
'40	*Gawen, Mary*......	....	....	73	York........	Res. Wells.
'35c	Gedding, Samuel...	N. H. line.....	Private ...	74	Oxford......	('20).
'35d	Genthner, Andrew..	Mass. mil.,...	Private ...	76	Lincoln.....	Same as following.
40	Gentner, Andrew...	....	....	81	Lincoln.....	Res. Waldoboro.
'35c	George, Francis....	Mass. line.....	Private ...	76	Kennebec ...	('20).
'40	George, Francis....	....	....	77	Kennebec ...	Res. Leeds.
'40	*George, Margaret*...	....	....	78	Lincoln.....	Res. Thomaston.
'20	George, Thomas....	N. H. line.....	Private ...			
'35c	George, Thomas....	Mass. line.....	Private ...	80	Penobscot.	

List.	Name.	Service.	Rank.	Age.	County.	Remarks.
'35d	Gerrish, Timothy...	Mass. state....	Pvt.& Seaman.	70	York.	
'40	Getchell, Sarah.....			84	Washington.	Res. Machias.
'35c	Getchell, Seth......	Mass. line.....	Private...	80	Kennebec...	('20) See also Gaitskill, Gatchell and Gitchel.
'40				86	Kennebec...	Res. Waterville.
'35d	Gettchell, Joseph...	Mass. state....	Pvt. of art.	77	Washington.	
'35d	Gettchell, Nathaniel	Mass. mil.....	Private...	72	Waldo.	
'35d	Gibbs, Elisha......	Mass. line.....	Private...	81	Penobscot.	
'35d	Gibbs, Pelatiah....	Mass. line.....	Private...	76	Oxford.	
'40				83	Oxford......	Res. Livermore.
'35c	Gibson, James.....	Mass. line.....	Private...	81	Penobscot.	
'35d	Gibson, John......	Mass. mil.....	Private...	71	Washington.	
	Gidding, Samuel...	See Gedding....				
'35d	Gilbert, Samuel...	Mass. line.....	Private...	75	Oxford.	
'40	Gilbert, Samuel....			78	Oxford......	Res. Buckfield.
'40	Gilbreth, Benjamin.			56	Kennebec...	Res. Augusta.
'35c	Gilchrist, Samuel...	R. I. line......	Private...	80	Lincoln.....	('20).
'35c	Giles, John........	Mass. line.....	Private ...	76	York........	d. in 1825.
'35c	Giles, Joseph......	N. H. line.....	Private...	77	York........	('20) d. Sept. 3, 1823.
'35c	Gilford, John Jr....	Mass. line.....	Private...	70	York........	Same as Guilford.
'40	Gilford, John......			76	York........	Res. Hollis.
'35c	Gilkey, James......	Mass. line.....	Private...	—	York........	('20).
'35c	Gillman, Ezekiel...	N. H. line.....	Private...	89	Somerset.	
'35d	Gillpatrick, James...	Mass. line.....	Private...	75	York........	('20).
'35d	Gillpatrick, Joseph .	Mass. line.....	Private...	70	York........	('20, '31 b).
'40				77	York........	Res. Kennebunk.
'35d	Gillpatrick, Joshua .	Mass. mil.....	Private...	76	York........	Same as Gilpatrick, J.
'35d	Gillpatrick, N'th'iel	Mass. line.....	Private...	73	York.	
'40	Gilman, David.....			75	Penobscot...	Res. Newburg.
'35d	Gilman, Jonathan..	N. H. line.....	Private...	84	Waldo.	
'35d	Gilman,Peter widow.	N. H. line.....	Private...	83	Lincoln.	
'35d	Gilman, Peter......	Mass. mil.....	Private...	80	Somerset.	
'40	Gilman, Sarah.....			82	Kennebec...	Res. Waterville. See also Gillman.
'35d	Gilmore, Samuel ...	Mass. line.....	Private...	69	Penobscot...	('20).
'40				77	Penobscot...	Res. Brewer.
'40	Gilpatrick, Joshua...			82	York........	Res. Lyman. Same as Gillpatrick,J.
'35c	Gilpatrick, N'th'iel	Mass. line.....	Private...	79	Lincoln.....	('20 Gillpatrick).
'40	Ginings, Eliphatet..			75	Franklin ...	Res. Farmington.
'40	Gitchel, Nathaniel..			79	Waldo......	Res. Northport See also Gaitskill, Gatchell & Getchell.
'35d	Given, John.......	Mass. line.....	Pvt. &Serg.	80 or 81	Cumberland.	('20).
'35c	Glass, Consider....	Mass. line.....	Private...	72	Penobscot.	('20).
'40	Glass, Consider....			81	Piscataquis..	Res. Guilford.
'20	Glass, John........	Mass. line.....	Private.			
'35d	Gledden, Andrew..	Mass. line.....	Pvt.&Serg.	84	Waldo......	
'35c	Glidden, Arnold....	Mass. line.....	Private...	79	Penobscot...	('20).
'40	Glidden, Arnold....			87	Penobscot...	Res. Howland.
'35c	Glidden, Gideon...	N. H. line.....	Private...	79	Kennebec...	('20). See also Gledden.
'35d	Glines, Israel......	Mass. mil.....	Private...	81	Oxford.	
'35c	Goddard, Josiah....	Mass. line.....	Private...	—	Lincoln.....	('20) d. June 5, 1821.
'40	Godding, Samuel...			80	Cumberland.	Res. Poland.
'35c	Goding, Spencer....	Mass. line.....	Private...	67	Kennebec...	('20) d. April 4, 1819.
'35d	Goff, James........	Mass. line.....	Pvt., Corp. & Serg.	74	Cumberland.	('20).
'40				80	Cumberland.	Res. Minot.
'20	Gold, Noah M.....	Mass. line.....	Private...			Same as Gould.
'35c	Goldthwait, Philip .	Mass. line.....	Private...	67	York........	('20 '31b Goldthwait '29).
'35e	Goldthwait. Philip .	2d dragoons ...	Dragoon...		York........	d. Nov. 25, 1832.- M. Goldthwait, widow. See also Zouldthwait.
'40	Goldthwait, Tim'thy			78	Kennebec...	('20). Res. Augusta.

List.	Name.	Service.	Rank.	Age.	County.	Remarks.
'35d	Goldthwaithe, Timothy	Mass. line Mass. mil	Private Pvt. of art.	72	Kennebec	('31bGoldthwaite)
'35d	Gooch, Jedediah	Mass. line	Private	81	York	('20) d. Aug. 22, 1832.
'35c	Goodale, Zachariah	Mass. line	Private	92	York	d. Sept. 2, 1825.
'35d	Goodenow, John	N, H. line	Private	82	Oxford	
'40	Goodin, John			77	Oxford	Res. Hebron. Same as Goodwin, J.
'40	Goodmon, John			89	Oxford	Res. Hiram.
'35c	Goodridge, Benj	Mass. line	Private	76	York	('20) d. Sept. 4, 1832.
'35c	Goodwin, Aaron	Cont. navy	Mariner	73	York	d. Sept. 28, 1827.
'35d	Goodwin, Adam	Mass. line	Private	76	York	('20, '31b).
'35d	Goodwin, Amaziah	N. H. line	Private	75	York	
'40	Goodwin, Amaziah			77	York	Res. Lyman.
'35d	Goodwin, Amos	Mass. mil	Private	79	York	
'35d	Goodwin, Benjamin	Mass. state		80	York	
'35c	Goodwin, Benjamin	Mass. line	Private	66	York	('20, '31b).
'40	Goodwin, Eunice			72	York	Res. Sanford.
'35c	Goodwin, George	Mass. line	Private	75	Kennebec	('20).
'40	Goodwin, George			77	Franklin	Res. Avon.
'35c	Goodwin, Jacob	Mass. line	Private	80	Lincoln	Transf. from Middlesex Co., Mass., 1832.
'35d	Goodwin, John	Mass. mil	Private	68	Oxford	Same as Goodin?
'35d	Goodwin, Joseph	Mass. mil	Private	82	Somerset	
'40	Goodwin, Mary			76	York	Res. Lebanon.
'35c	Goodwin, Paul	Mass. line	Private	87	York	('20).
'35d	Goodwin, Reuben	Mass. line	Private	72	York	('20,'35c, Reuben, jr.).
'40				79	York	Res. Lebanon.
'35c	Goodwin, Reuben	Mass. line	Private	60	York	('20).
'35d	Goodwin, Richard	Mass. line	Corporal	80	Cumberland	
'40	Goodwin, Ruth			74	York	Res. Lebanon.
'35d	Goodwin, Simeon	Mass. line	Private	71	York	('20).
'35d	Googins, David	N. H. mil	Private	74	York	
'35c	Googins, Stephen	Mass. line	Private	80	York	('20).
'40				86	York	Res. Saco.
'35e	Gookin, Daniel	N. H. line	Lieutenant	—	York	('29) d. Sept. 24, 1831. Abigail Gookin, widow.
'40	Goold, Alexander			88	York	Res. Elliot ('20, mariner and "Raleigh") Same as Gould, A.
'35c	Goold, Daniel	Mass. line	Private	76	York	Also given Gould. ('20) d. Dec. 31, 1825.
'40	Goold, John			85	York	Res. Elliot. Same as Gould, J.
'35d	Goold, Joseph	Mass. line	Private	83	Cumberland	
'31b	Gorden, Joseph		Private			Same as Gordon,J?
'40	Gordin, Josiah			83	Franklin	Res. Industry.
'35c	Gordon, Benjamin	R. I. line	Private	77	Waldo	('20).
'35c	Gordon, Caleb	Mass. line	Private	68	Kennebec	('20) d. July 8, 1833.
'20	Gordon, James	N. H. line	Private			
'35c	Gordon, James	Mass. line	Private	86	Kennebec	
'35e	Gordon, Joseph	N. H. line 2d regt.		—	Waldo	
'40				81	Waldo	Res. Belfast.
'35c	Gordon, Joseph	N. H. line	Private	61	Hancock	('20, '29 Corp.).
'35d	Gordon, Josiah	Mass. line	Pvt. of art.	77	Kennebec	Same as Gordin,J?
'35c	Gore, Jacob	Mass. line	Private	70	Washington	
'35c	Gorham, Josiah	Mass. line	Fifer	74	Lincoln	('20).
'40				80	Lincoln	Res. Edgecomb.
'20	Goss, Ebenezer H	N. H.	Surgeon			Same as Gross.
'35d	Gould, Alexander	Cont. navy	Mariner & seaman.	82	York	('31b) Same as Goold, A.
'35d	Gould, Daniel	Mass. line	Private	80	Oxford	See also Gould.
'40				86	Oxford	Res. Rumford.
'35d	Gould, Daniel	Mass. mil	Pvt. of art.	68	Kennebec	('20).
'35c	Gould, Jabez	Mass. line	Private	80	Kennebec	('20) d. Jan. 28, 1825.
'35d	Gould, Jesse	Mass. mil	Pvt. of art.	78	Kennebec	

List.	Name.	Service.	Rank.	Age.	County.	Remarks.
'35c	Gould, John	Mass. line	Private	80	York	('20). Same as Gould, J.
'35c	Gould, Jonas	Mass. line	Private	65	Somerset	('20) d. June 22, 1819.
'40	Gould, Levi			54	Penobscot	Res. Charleston.
'40	Gould, Lucy			79	Somerset	Res. Norridgewock.
'35c	Gould, Moriah	Mass. line	Private	—	Somerset	('20) d. June,1827.
'35c	Gould, Noah M	Mass. line	Private	72	Kennebec	d Sept. 1, 1830. Same as Gold.
'35c	Gould, Silas	Conn. line	Corporal	75	Kennebec	('20).
'40	Gould, Silas			83	Franklin	Res. Wilton.
	Gouldthwait, Elizabeth	See Zouldthwait Elizabeth				
'20	Gove, Jacob	Mass	Private			Same as Gore?
'40	Gove, Lois			70	York	Res. Limington.
'40	Gove, Martha			69	Washington	Res. Lubec.
'35d	Gowell, Benjamin	Mass. mil.	Private	84	York	('31c).
'40	Gowell, Susan			—	York	Res. Lebanon.
'40	Grace, Huldah			78	Lincoln	Res. Bath.
'35d	Grace, John	Mass. state	Private	73	York	
'40				79	York	Res. Saco.
'35c	Grace, Patrick	Mass. line	Private	62	Lincoln	('20, '31b).
'40	Graffam, Sarah			81	Cumberland	Res. Brunswick.
'35c	Graffham, Enoch	Mass. line	Private	74	Cumberland	('20) d. Aug. 28, 1827.
'31a	Graffom, Uriah		Private			Deserter.
'40	Granger, Daniel			78	Washington	Res. Eastport.
'40	Grant, Abigail			94	York	Res. York.
'35c	Grant, Edmund	N. H. line	Private	80	York	Transf. from Essex Co., Mass., 1819.
'20	Grant, Edward	N. H.	Private.			
'35c	Grant, John	Mass. line	Quartermaster.	80	York	('20) d. Nov.1825
'35c	Grant, Joshua	Mass. line	Private	89	York	('20).
'35c	Grant, Martin	Mass. line	Private	86	Lincoln	('20).
'35d	Grant, Peter	Mass. line	Private	77	York	
'35d	Grant, Silas	Mass. mil	Private	81	York	
'40d				86	York	Res. Lyman.
'35c	Grant, Thomas	Mass. line	Sergeant	75	Lincoln	('20) d. in 1827.
'35c	Grant, William	N. H. line	Private	80	Waldo	('20) d. in 1825.
'35d	Grant, William	N. H. line	Private	78	York	
'35c	Graves, Samuel	N. H. line	Private	80	Lincoln	('20).
'35c	Gray, Aaron	Mass. line	Private	87	York	('20).
'35d	Gray, Alexander	Mass. mil	Pvt. of art.	83	Kennebec	
'35c	Gray, John	Mass. line	Private	73	Lincoln	('20) d. Dec. 25, 1825.
'35d	Greely, Noah	N. H. line	Private	74	Kennebec	('20, Greeley).
'35c	Green, Benjamin	Mass. line	Private	79	Cumberland	('20) d. Aug. 4, 1824.
'35d	Green, Daniel	Mass. line	Private	78	Cumberland	d. Jan. 20, 1833.
'35c	Green, Daniel	Mass. line	Private	70	Kennebec	('20).
'35c	Green, Jonathan	Mass. line	Private	73	Waldo	('20).
'35c	Green, Joseph	Cont. navy	Mids'pm'n	83	Lincoln	('20 mariner, ship "Ranger") d. May 28, 1822.
'35c	Greenlaw, John	Mass. line	Private	70	Oxford	('20).
'4d				74	Oxford	Res. Brownfield.
'35c	Greenleaf, Benjamin	Mass. line	Private	74	Lincoln	('20).
'40				80	Lincoln	Res. Wiscasset.
'35c	Greenleaf, Daniel	Mass. line	Private	80	Oxford	('20).
'35c	Greenleaf, Enoch	Mass. line	Private	81	Lincoln	('20).
'35d	Greenleaf, John	Mass. line	Private	79	Somerset	('20, '31b).
'40				84	Somerset	Res. Starks.
'35c	Greenough, Jonathan	Mass. line	Private	64	Somerset	d. Sept. 25, 1818.
'35c	Greer, James	N. H. line	Private	—	Waldo	
'40				81	Waldo	Res. Belmont.
'35d	Gregg, David	Mass. state	Corp. & Serg.	82	Waldo	
'40	Gregory, Luther			60	Waldo	Res. Montville.
'35c	Grindle, William	R. I. line	Private	71	Hancock	('20) d. Jan. 31, 1820.
'35d	Grinnell, Bailey	R. I. state	Pvt., Corp. & Serg.	74	Lincoln	
'35d	Grinnell, Royall	R. I. mil	Private	79	Lincoln	
'35d	Groat, William	Mass. line	Private	80	Waldo	

List.	Name.	Service.	Rank.	Age.	County.	Remarks.
'35d	Gross, Benjamin....	Mass. line.....	Private...	75	Hancock....	('20).
'40	Gross, Benjamin...			85	Hancock....	Res. Bucksport.
'35c	Gross, David......	Mass. mil.....	Private...	68	Cumberland.	
'35c	Gross, Ebenezer H..	N. H. line.....	Surgeon...	80	Oxford......	Same as Goss.
'20	Grouse, George.....	Mass.........	Private.			
'40	*Grover, Elizabeth*...			85	Franklin....	Res. Weld.
'20	Guilford, John, 1st.	Mass.........	Private...	—	....	Same as Gilford.
'20	Guilford, John, Sr..	Mass.........	Private...			
'35c	Gunnison, Josiah...	Mass. state....	Private...	74	York.	
'35d	Gurney, Eliab......	Mass. line.....	Private...	77	Cumberland.	('20) d. Nov. 5, 1818.
'35d	Gurney, Jacob.....	Mass. line.....	Private...	—	Oxford.	
'40				76	Oxford......	Res. Hebron.
'35c	Gurney, Jonathan..	Mass. line.....	Private...	—	Oxford......	('20) d. June 25, 1818.
'35d	Gurney, Lemuel....	Mass. mil.....	Pvt. & marine.	70	Cumberland.	
'40	Gurney, Samuel....			76	Cumberland.	Res. Cumberland.
'35c	Gustin, Thomas....	Mass. line.....	Private...	78	Cumberland.	('20) d. Sept. 4, 1818.
'35c	Hackett, Elijah....	Mass. line.....	Private....	69	Cumberland.	('20).
'35c	Hackett, Ezekiel...	Mass. line.....	Private....	72	Kennebec...	('20 Hacket)
'35c	Hackett, Judah....	N. H. line.....	Private....	62	Somerset....	('20, '31b Hacket)
'20	Hagens, Edmund...	Mass.........	Private....			Same as Higgins and Hugens?
'35d	Hager, Ezekiel.....	Mass. mil.....	Private....	77	Lincoln.	d. Mar. 17, 1833.
'35c	Haines, Samuel....	Mass. line.....	Private....	81	Kennebec...	('20)d Dec. 29, 1821. See also Haynes.
'20	Haines, Simeon....	N. H. line.....	Private.			
'40	Halbrook, David...			75	Waldo......	Res. Prospect. Same as Holbrook, D.?
'35d	Hale, Benjamin....	Mass. line.....	Private....	71	Cumberland.	('20, '31b).
'40	Hale, Benjamin....			77	Oxford......	Res. Waterford.
'35d	Hale, Israel........	Mass. line.....	Private....	75	Oxford......	('20, '31b)
'40				80	Oxford......	Res. Waterford.
'40	Hale, Oliver.......			79	Oxford......	Res. Waterford.
'35d	Haley, Joseph......	Mass. mil.....	Private....	75	York.	
'35c	Haley, Richard.....	Mass. line.....	Private....	88	York.......	('20) d. Jan. 25, 1829.
'35d	Hall, Calvin.......	Mass. mil.....	Pvt.& Serg.	75	Kennebec.	
'35c	Hall, Charles.......	Mass. line.....	Private....	75	Cumberland.	('20)
'40	Hall, Charles.......			85	Cumberland.	Res. Baldwin.
'35d	Hall, David........	Mass. state....	Pvt.& Serg.	81	York.	
'40	*Hall, Elizabeth*.....			70	Cumberland.	Res. Brunswick.
'35d	Hall, Enoch........	Mass. mil.....	Private....	81	Somerset....	('20)
'35d	Hall, Enoch........	Mass. line.....	Private....	74	Oxford.	
'40	*Hall, Hannah*.....			77	Kennebec...	Res. China.
'35d	Hall, Isaac.........	Mass. mil.....	Private....	87	Lincoln.	
'40				94	Lincoln.....	Res. Georgetown.
'35d	Hall, Isaac........	Mass. line.....	Pvt.& Corp	77	Waldo.	
'40	Hall, Isaac........			86	Waldo......	Res. Knox.
'35c	Hall, Jabez........	Mass. line.....	Private....	68	Kennebec...	('20)
'35c	Hall, Job..........	Mass. line.....	Private...,	76	Kennebec...	('20) d. May 22, 1823.
'35d	Hall, John.........	Mass. mil.....	Surg's m'te	80	Kennebec.	
'20	Hall, Joseph.......	N. H.........	Private.			
'35c	Hall, Joseph.......	Mass. line.....	Private....	71	Kennebec.	
'35c	Hall, Levi.........	Mass. line.....	Private....	76	Lincoln.....	('20)
'40				—	Lincoln.....	Res. Washington.
'35c	Hall, Luther.......	Mass. line....	Private....	69	Cumberland.	('20) d. Nov. 1826
'35d	Hall, Noah........	Mass. state....	L't.& Corp.	92	Hancock.	
'35d	Hall, Oliver.......	Mass. mil.....	Private....	73	Oxford.	
'40	*Hall, Rhoda*........			70	Waldo......	Res. Belfast.
'35c	Hall, William......	Mass. line.....	Private....	75	Lincoln.....	('20) d. July 31, 1819.
'35c	Hall, William......	Mass. line.....	Private....	64	York.......	d. July 31, 1819.
'40	Hallet, Elisha.....			82	Kennebec...	Res. Waterville.
'35c '35d	} Hallet, Solomon..	{ Mass. line.... Mass. mil...	Private.... Pvt.& Mas. at arms.	66 & 80 66	Kennebec. Kennebec...	('20, '31b Hallett)
'40			...\......	86	Kennebec...	Res. Waterville
'35c	Halloway, William..	Mass. line.....	Sergeant...	84	Kennebec...	('20)d. May 10, 1831.
'40	*Hallowell, Mary*....			85	Kennebec...	Res. Windsor.
'35c	Ham, John........	N. H. line.....	Private....	70	Kennebec...	('20)
'40	Ham, John........			81	Kennebec...	Res. Leeds.

List.	Name.	Service.	Rank.	Age.	County.	Remarks.
'35d	Ham, Nathaniel....	Mass. line.....	Private....	79	Cumberland .	
'40	———	....	....	85	Cumberland .	Res. Brunswick.
'35d	Hamblin, America..	Mass. line.....	Private....	72	Oxford......	Same as Hamlin, A
'35c	Hamblin, William ..	Conn. line.....	Private....	73	Lincoln.....	Same as Hamlin, W.
'35c	Hames, Simeon....	N. H. line.....	Private....	79	Waldo.	
'35d	Hamilton, John....	Mass. mil.....	Private....	74	York.	
'40	Hamilton, John....	....	....	75	York........	Res. Waterbor'h.
'20	Hamilton, Jonathan	Mass.........	Private.			
'40	Hamilton, Jonathan	....	....	85	York........	Res. N. Berwick.
'35c	Hamilton, Richard .	N. H. line.....	Private....	74	Waldo......	('20)
'35d	Hamilton, William .	Mass. line.....	Private....	72	Cumberland .	('20, '31b)
'40	———	....	....	78	Cumberland .	Res. N. Yarmouth
'20	Hamlin, America...	Mass.........	Private....		....	Same as Hamblin.
'35c	Hamlin, Prince.....	Mass. line.....	Private....	77	Cumberland .	('20)
'20	Hamlin, Seth......	Mass.........	Private.			
'20	Hamlin, William...	Conn.........	Private....			Same as Hambli.n
'40	Hammon, Josiah...	....	....	79	Penobscot...	Res. Corinna.
'35d	Hammond, Moses..	Mass. line.....	Private....	72	Hancock.	
'35c	Hammond, Paulipus	Mass. line....	Private....	73	Kennebec ...	('20)
'35d	Hammond, Roger ..	Mass. state...	Private....	74	York.	
'35d	Hammonds, Edmo'd	Mass. state...	Private....	83	York.	
'20	Hancock, John Lane	R. I.........	Private.			
'35c	Hancock, Nathan...	Mass. line.....	Fifer......	64	Lincoln.....	('20) d. Sept. 1823
'35c	Hancock, William..	Mass. line.....	Private....	73	York........	('20)
'35c	Hands, James......	Mass. line.....	Private....	63	Cumberland .	d. Oct. 6, 1825
'35d	Handy, Benjamin ..	Mass. state...	Marine....	74	Oxford.	
'35c	Handy, Elnathan...	Mass. line.....	Private....	73	Hancock....	('20)
'40	Handy, Lucy......	....	....	77	Franklin....	Res. Berlin.
'35d	Haney, Daniel.....	Mass. line.....	Private....	79	Cumberland .	
'40	Haney, Daniel.....	....	....	86	Oxford......	Res. Greenwood.
'35c	Hankerson, William.	R. I. line......	Private....	70	Kennebec ...	('20) d. March 3, 1830.
'35c	Hannewell, William.	Cont. navy....	Marine....	73	Somerset....	d. Aug. 23, 1820. Same as Hunnewell?
'20	Hans, James.......	Mass.........	Private.			
'35c	Hans, William.....	Mass. line.....	Private....	73	Cumberland .	('20) d. Sept. 8, 1831.
'35c	Hanscom, Gideon ..	Mass. line.....	Private....	69	York........	('20) d. in 1825.
'35d	Hanscom, Humphrey	Mass. line.....	Pvt.& Corp	82	Cumberland .	
'35d	Hanscom, Nathan..	Mass. mil.....	Pvt. of art.	84	Kennebec.	
'40	Hanscom, Nathan..	....	....	93	Franklin....	Res. Avon.
'35c	Hanscom, Reuben..	Mass. line.....	Private....	66	York........	('20)
'40	Hanscom, Robert...	....	....	77	York........	Res. Kennebunkport. Same as Hansicum?
'35c	Hanscomb, John 1st.	Mass. line.....	Private....	77	York........	('20)d. in 1827.
'35c	Hanscomb, John 2d.	Mass. line.....	Private....	70	Lincoln.....	('20)
'35c	Hanscomb, Nathan'l	Mass. line.....	Private....	73	York........	('20) d. April 1, 1830.
'40	Hanscomb, Uriah ..	....	....	59	York........	Res. Lyman.
'35c	Hansicum, Robert..	Mass. line.....	Private....	73	York........	Same as Hanscom, R.?
'35c	Hanson, Jonathan..	Mass. line.....	Private....	64	York........	('20, '31b)
'40	Harden, I hebe.....	....	....	83	Waldo......	Res. Unity.
'35c	Harding, David....	Mass. line.....	Private....	96	Cumberland .	('20) d. March 1, 1828.
'35c	Harding, Hezekiah .	Mass. line.....	Lieut nant.	80	Cumberland .	d. May 1, 1825.
'35d	Harding, Seth......	Mass. mil.....	Private....	80	Waldo.	
'35c	Hardison, Stephen..	Mass. line.....	Private....	70	Waldo.	
'35c	Hardison, Stephen..	Mass. line.....	Private....	69	York........	('20, '31b)
'35c	Hardy, William....	Mass. line.....	Private....	79	Kennebec ...	('20)
'40	Harkness, Elizabeth	....	....	76	Waldo......	Res. Camden.
'35c	Harlow, Josiah.....	Mass. line.....	Private....	74	Lincoln.....	('20) d. in 1825.
'35c	Harlow, Nathaniel .	Mass. line.....	Private....	80	Penobscot...	('20)
'35d	Harlow, Sylvanus...	Mass. mil.....	Private....	72	Penobscot.	
'40	———	....	....	79	Penobscot...	Res. Plymouth.
'35d	Harman, Pelatiah ..	Mass. line.....	Private....	62	Strafford Co., N. H.	Paid at Portland agency. Apparently same as Harmon, P.
'35d	Harman, Thomas ..	Mass. line.....	Private....	78	Oxford......	('20) ('31b Harmon)
'35c	Harman, William...	Mass. line.....	Fifer......	70	Cumberland .	Same as Harmon, W.?
'35c	Harmon, Abner....	Mass. line.....	Ser-major..	78	York........	('20)
'35d	Harmon, Joel......	Mass. mil.....	Private....	72	York.	

List.	Name.	Service.	Rank.	Age.	County.	Remarks.
'35c	Harmon, Josiah....	Mass. line.....	Musician..	71	Waldo......	('20)
'35c	Harmon, Pelatiah..	Mass. line.....	Private....	62	Oxford......	('20) Same as Harman.
'35c	Harmon, Samuel...	Mass. line.....	Corporal..	82	Penobscot...	('20, Harman)
'20	Harmon, William...	Mass........	Fifer......			('31b) Same as Harman, W.?
'40	Harmon, William...			78	Cumberland.	Res. Standish.
'35c	Harriman, Joab....	Mass. line.....	Private....	74	Kennebec...	('20)
'35d	Harriman, Simon...	Mass. mil.....	Private....	70	Penobscot.	
'35c	Harrington, Abiel...	Mass. line.....	Private....	74	Kennebec...	('20) See also Herrington.
'35c	Harris, Charles.....	Mass. line.....	Private....	74	Kennebec...	('20, '31b) d.July 1, 1832.
'35c	Harris, John.......	Mass. line.....	Private....	58	Lincoln. .	
'40	Harris, John.......			75	Lincoln.....	Res. Bowdoin.
'35c	Hart, Jacob........	Mass. line.....	Private....	73	Penobscot...	('20) d. Nov. 4, 1833.
'35c	Hart, James.......	Mass. line.....	Lieutenant.	78	York........	('20) d. May 1825.
'35d	Hart, John.........	N. H. line.....	Private....	70	Penobscot...	('20)
'35c	Hart, John, 2d.....	Conn. line.....	Private....	69	Somerset....	d. Jan. 7, 1826.
'40	Hart, John.........			78	Piscataquis..	Res. Atkinson.
'35d.	Hartwell, Edward..	Mass. line.....	Private....	86	Kennebec.	
'40				93	Somerset....	Res. St. Albans.
'35c	Hartwell, Oliver....	Mass. line.....	Private....	79	Penobscot...	('20)
'40	Hartwell, Oliver....			80	Penobscot...	Res. Stetson.
'35c	Harvest, John A....	Mass. line.....	Private....	78	Waldo......	Trans.from Providence Co., R. I., 1833.
'35d	Harvey, James.....	N. H. line.....	Pvt.& Corp	72 or 74	Penobscot.	
'40				78	Penobscot...	Res. Bradford.
'40	Harvey, Libby.....			76	York........	Res. Limington.
'31a	Harvey, Thomas...		Private....			Did not serve 9 mos. on Cont. estab.
'35d	Harvey, William...	Mass. line.....	Pvt.& Serg.	74	York........	('20, '31b)
'35d	Hasey, Ebenezer...	Mass. mil......	Private....	76	Penobscot...	See also Hersey.
'40	Hasgatt, Davis.....			89	Hancock....	Res. Mt. Desert.
'40	Haskell, Josiah.....			80	Lincoln.....	('20) Res. Thomaston. Same as Haskill, J.
'35c	Haskell, Stephen...	Mass. line.....	Private....	76	Oxford......	('20) d. Dec. 3, 1830.
'35c	Haskell, Stephen...	Mass. line.....	Private....	65	Cumberland.	d. Dec. 3, 1830.
'20	Haskell, Ward.....	Mass. line.....	Private.			
'35c	Haskell, William...	Mass. line.....	Private....	61	Kennebec...	('20, '31b)
'35c	Haskll, Josiah.....	Mass. line.....	Private....	73	Lincoln.....	Same as Haskell, J
'40	Haskill, Mary......			83	Waldo......	Res. Knox.
'35e	Hastings, John.....	Mass. line 9th regt.......	Captain....	—	Hancock.....	('29) Transf. to Middlesex Co., Mass.
'35d	Hasty, David......	Mass. mil......	Private....	72	Cumberland.	
'35d	Hasty, Samuel.....	Mass. mil.....	Pvt.& Serg.	91	York.......	
'35c	Hasty, William.....	Mass. line.....	Lieutenant.	78	Cumberland.	('20, '28) d. Dec. 23, 1831.
'40	Hatch, Ann........			84	Oxford......	Res. Fryeburg.
'35d	Hatch, David......	Mass. mil.....	Private....	70	York.......	
'40	Hatch, David......			79	York.......	Res. Wells.
'35c	Hatch, Eliakim....	Mass. line.....	Private....	57	Somerset....	('20) d. Dec. 14, 1829.
'35d	Hatch, Elihu......	Mass. mil.....	Private....	80	Kennebec.	
'35c	Hatch, Elijah......	Mass. line.....	Private....	78	York.......	('20)
'35d	Hatch, Ezekiel.....	Mass. state....	Private....	79	York.	
'35d	Hatch, Philip......	Mass. mil.....	Private....	78	Lincoln.	
'40	Hatch, Philip......			86	Lincoln.....	Res. Bristol.
'35c	Hatch, Samuel.....	Mass. line.....	Private....	77	Cumberland.	('20)
'40				84	Cumberland.	Res. Minot.
'35d	Hatch, Samuel.....	Mass. mil.....	Private....	73	York.	
'35d	Hatch, Sylvanus...	Mass. line.....	Private....	74	Waldo.	
'35d	Hatch, Walter.....	Mass. mil.....	Corp.of art.	75	Waldo.	
'40				82	Waldo......	Res. Belfast.
'35d	Hatch, Zaccheus...	Mass. line.....	Private....	84	Lincoln.....	d. Apr. 23, 1833.
'35d	Hathaway, Ephraim	Mass. line.....	Private & Artificer	77	Oxford......	('20, '31b)
'35d	Hathorn, Nathaniel.	Mass. state....	Private....	79	Lincoln.	
'35c	Havenor, Charles...	Mass. line.....	Private....	75	Lincoln.....	Same as Heavenor Heavner and Hevenor.

List.	Name.	Service.	Rank.	Age.	County.	Remarks.
'35d	Hawawas, Nicholas	Mass. state	Lieutenant.	90	Washington.	
'35d	Hawes, Abijah	Mass. state	Private	82	Lincoln.	
'35c	Hawes, Jonathan	Mass. line	Private	76	Kennebec	('20) d. Nov. 10, 1823.
'35c	Haws, Joseph	Mass. line	Private	79	Cumberland	('20, Hawes)
'40	Haws, Joseph			87	Cumberland	Res. Minot.
'40	Hayden, Jonathan			77	Somerset	Res. Madison. Same as Haydon?
'35c	Hayden, Josiah	Mass. line	Major	83	Kennebec	('20) d. Sept. 2, 1818.
'35d	Haydon, Jonathan	Mass. mil	Private	71	Kennebec	Same as Hayden?
'35d	Hayens, Walter	Mass. mil	Private	79	York.	
'40	Hayes, Amos M			85	Cumberland	Res. N. Yarmouth Same as Hays, A. M.
'35d	Hayford, William	Mass. mil	Private	72	Oxford.	
'40				78	Oxford	Res. Hartford.
'35c	Haynes, Ephraim	Mass. line	Private	93	Hancock	('20) See also Haines.
'35c	Haynes, James	Mass. line	Private	67	Lincoln	('20) d. June 1824
'35c	Haynes, Parley	Mass. line	Drummer	77	Hancock	('20, Perley)
'40	Haynes, Simeon			82	Waldo	Res. Swanville See also Hayens
'35d	Hays, Amos M	Mass. line	Private	79	Cumberland	Same as Hayes, A. M.
'35d	Hayward, Edward	Mass. mil	Private	73	Kennebec	
'35c	Hayward, Isaiah	Mass. line	Private	79	Kennebec	('20)
'40	Hayward, Susanna			65	Kennebec	Res. Sidney
'40	Hazen, Hann			65	Kennebec	Res. Gardiner.
'35c	Hazen, Jacob	Mass. line	Private	72	Cumberland	('20)
'40				78	Cumberland	Res. Bridgton.
'35c	Head, James	Mass. line	Private	85	York	d. March 31, 1832.
'35d	Head, James	Mass. mil	Private	75	Oxford	Reported dead in 1835.
'40	Head, James W			74	Lincoln	Res. Warren.
'35c	Head, Moses	N. H. line	Private	72	Penobscot.	
'35c	Heald, Oliver	Mass. line	Corporal	77	Somerset	('20)
'35d	Heald, Thomas	Mass. mil	Private	70	Kennebec.	
'35d	Healey, Eliphaz, widow	Mass. line	Private	80	Lincoln.	
'40	Heall, Levi			83	Lincoln	Res. Nobleboro'h.
'20	Heard, James	Mass	Private			Same as Head?
'35d	Heard, Tristram	N. H. state	Corporal	86	Somerset.	
'35d	Hearl, John	Mass. mil	Private	79	York.	
'40				85	York	Res. S. Berwick.
'35d	Hearsay, James	Mass. line	Pvt.& Corp & Serg.	76	Oxford	Same as Hursey.
'35d	Hearsay, Noah	Mass. state	Private	71	Lincoln.	
'35d	Hearsay, Zadock	Mass. mil	Private	83	Washington	Same as Hersey.
'20	Heath, Benjamin	Penn	Private.			
'35d	Heath, Isaac	Mass. mil	Private	77	Lincoln.	
'40				83	Lincoln	Res. Whitefield.
'20	Heath, Richard		Private.			
'35a	Heath, William	N. H. Scammell s regt.	Private			('20, '31b, '35e)
'40				76	Hancock	Res. Mt. Desert.

List.	Name.	Service.	Rank.	Age.	County.	Remarks.
'35d	Heavenor, Charles..	Mass. line	Private	75	Lincoln	Same as Havenor, Hevenor & Heavner.
'40	Heavner, Charles			81	Lincoln	Res. Waldoboro. Same as preceding.?
'35c	Hebberd, John	Mass. line	Private	76	Oxford	('20) d. Feb. 27, 1820. See also Hibbert.
'35c	Helmershausen, Henry F.	Conn. line	Private	84	Lincoln	('20) d. July 2, 1831.
'35d	Hemmenwrey, Asa..	Mass. mil.	Fifer	71	Kennebec.	
'35d	Henderson, Benj'm'n	Mass. mil.	Sergeant	78	Lincoln.	
'40				86	Lincoln	Res. Webster.
'40	Henick, Sarah			76	Cumberland	Res. Portland.
'35d	Herri k, Jacob	Mass. state	Pvt.&Lieut	76	Cumberland	d. Dec. 16, 1832.
'40	Herriock, Oliver			57	Lincoln	Res. Lewiston.
'35d	Herring, Daniel	Mass. mil.	Private	96	Penobscot.	
'20	Herrington, Joseph	R. I.	Private.			
'40	Hersey, Zadok			88	Washington	Res. Pembroke. Same as Hearsay. See also Hasey, Hursey.
'40	Hersom, Samuel			77	York	Res. Lebanon. Same as Horsum?
'40	Heselton, Elizabeth			85	Kennebec	Res. Winthrop.
'20	Hevenor, Charles	Mass.	Private.			
'35c	Hewit, William	N. (H?) line	Private	75	Lincoln	d. April 27, 1826.
'40	Heyer, Cornelius			88	Lincoln	Res. Waldoboro. See also Hyer.
'35c	Hibbert, Jonathan..	Penn. line	Private	79	Somerset	See also Hebberd.
'35d	Hicks, Samuel	Mass. line	Corporal	80	Cumberland	('20, '31b, '35c)
'40	Higgins, Edmund			83	Cumberland	Res. Scarborough. Same as Hagens and Hugens?
'35d	Higgins, Philip	Mass. mil.	Private	75	Lincoln.	
'40	Higgins, Walter			75	York	Res. Limington.
'40	Hilborn, Lucy			89	Cumberland	Res. Minot.
'35d	Hilborn, Robert	Mass. line	Pvt. of art.	94	Cumberlan	d. Jan. 8, 1834.
'20	Hill, Daniel		Mariner			Ship "Ranger"
'35d	Hill, Daniel	Mass. line	Ens.& Serg	79	Cumberland	('20, '31b)
'35c	Hill, Jeremiah	Mass. line	Captain	72	York	('20) d. June 11, 1820.
'40	Hill, Noah			50 to 60	York	Res. Hollis.
'40	Hill, Rebecca			76	York	Res. Elliot.
'35c	Hill, Samuel	Cont. navy	Marine	63	York	d. June 4, 1824.
'35d	Hilton, Dudley	Mass. mil.	Private	81	York.	
'20	Hilton, Ebenezer, 2d	Mass.	Private			('31b)
'35d	Hilton, Ebenezer	Mass. line	Private	70 or 68	York	d. July 23, 1832.
'35c	Hilton, Ebenezer	Mass. line	Private	66	Somerset	('20 Ebenezer 1st)
'35d	Hilton, Edward	Mass. line	Private	69	York	('20, '31b)d. Apr. 27, 1833.
'31a	Hilton, Isaac		Seaman			Served less than 9 months.
'35d	Hilton, Isaac	Mass. line	Dr. & Mar.	73	Cumberland	
'35d	Hilton, Joseph	Mass. line	Private	81	York	('20, '31b)
'40				85	York	Res. Wells.
'20	Hilton, Morral	R. I.	Private.			
'35c	Hilton, Morrill	Mass. line	Private	79	Lincoln.	
'35d	H lton, William, 1st.	Mass. line	Private	75	Somerset	('20, '31b)
'35d	H lton, William, 2d.	Mass. line	Pvt. & Mar	75	Somerset	('20, '31b)
'40	H lton, William			81	Somerset	Res. Solon.
'40	Hilton, William H..			80	Somerset	Res. Cornville.
'40	Hinckley, Edith			74	Hancock	Res. Bluehill.
'35d	Hinckley, Nehemiah	Mass. line	Private	71	Hancock	Same as Hinkley, N.
'31a	Hind, Joshua		Private			Served only 8 months.
'35c	Hinds, Benjamin	Mass. line	Private	79	Somerset	('20)
'35d	Hinds, Nimrod	Mass. mil.	Private	76	Somerset.	
'35c	Hinds, Samuel	Mass. line	Private	75	Lincoln	('20)
'40				80	Lincoln	Res. St. George.
'35d	Hine, Richard	Mass. line	Pvt.& Serg	78 & 87	Oxford	('20)
'20	Hinkley, Nehemiah.	Mass.	Private			Same as Hinckley, N.
'35c	Hobbey, William	Mass. line	Sergeant	65	Cumberland	('20 Hobby) d. Mar. 10, 1831.

List.	Name.	Service.	Rank.	Age.	County.	Remarks.
'40	Hobbs, Abigail......	....	....	72	York........	Res. Wells.
'35d	Hobbs, Josiah......	Mass. line....	Sergeant..	71	Cumberland..	('20)
'40	————	....	....	77	Cumberland.	Res. Falmouth.
'35c	Hobbs, Morrell.....	Mass. line.....	Private....	81	Cumberland.	('20) d. Oct. 20, 1826.
'35c	Hobson, William...	Mass. line.....	Private....	97	York........	('20) d. Sept.,1827
'40	Hodgdon, Caleb....	....	....	87	Lincoln.....	Res. Westport. Same as Hogsdon, C.?
'35c	Hodgdon, Jeremiah.	Mass. line.....	Private....	87	Oxford......	('20 Hogdon) d. Aug. 24, 1823.
'40	Hodgdon, Stephen..	....	....	82	Oxford......	Res. Gilead.
'35c	Hodges, Ezra......	Mass. line.....	Private....	73	Kennebec...	('20)
'40	Hodgkins, Abigail..	....	....	80	Lincoln.....	Res. Bath.
'35c	Hodkins, Thomas, 2d.	Mass. line.....	Private....	84	Oxford......	('20) d. Feb. 25, 1821.
'35c	Hodgman, John....	Mass. line.....	Private....	79	Lincoln.....	('20) d. Feb. 24, 1634.
'35c	Hodkins, Thomas,. 1st.	Mass. line.....	Sergeant..	81	Lincoln.....	('20) d. Mar. 7, 1827.
'20	Hodsdon, Benjamin.	Mass.........	Private....	...	....	Same as Hogsdon, B.
'40	————	....	....	83	Cumberland.	Res. Falmouth.
'35c	Hodsdon, Samuel...	N. H. line.....	Private....	70	York........	('20) d. Aug. 31, 1825.
'35c	Hodsdon, Stephen..	Mass. line.....	Private....	76	Oxford......	('20)
'35d	Hody, Josiah.......	Mass. mil.....	Private....	72	Somerset.	
'40	Hoffses, Margaret...	....	....	88	Waldo.......	Res. Waldoboro. See also Hoofses.
'35d	Hogdon, Caleb.....	Mass. mil.....	Private....	76	Lincoln.....	Same as Hodgdon, C.?
'35c	Hogsdon, Benjamin	Mass. line.....	Private....	77	Cumberland.	Same as Hodsdon, B.
'40	Hoit, Nathaniel....	....	....	45	Penobscot...	Res. Edinburg. See also Hoyt.
'35d	Holbrook, David...	N. H. mil.....	Private....	68	Penobscot...	Same as Halbrook?
'35d	Holbrook, John....	Mass. state....	Private....	72	Lincoln.	
'35d	Holbrook, Peter....	Mass. mil.....	Private....	82	Somerset.	
'35c	Holbrook, Silas.....	Mass. line.....	Private....	72	Cumberland.	('20) d. Sept. 16, 1828.
'35c	Holden, Daniel.....	Mass. line.....	Private....	57	Oxford......	('20) ('29 bombardier. '35e Crane's art.)
'40	Holden, Daniel.....	....	....	76	Oxford......	Res. Sweden.
'35c	Holden, John......	Mass. line.....	Private....	74	Cumberland.	('20)
'35c	Holden, Samuel....	Mass. line.....	Private....	72	Penobscot...	('20)
'35d	Holland, Joseph....	Mass. line.....	Pvt.& Corp	73	Kennebec.	
'40	————	....	....	79	Kennebec...	Res. Vienna.
'35c	Holland, Park......	Mass. line.....	Lieutenant	75	Penobscot...	('20, '28, '29) Relinquished act of 1818 for that of 1828. ('35e, 5th regt.)
'40	Holland, Park......	....	....	87	Penobscot...	Res. Eddington.
'35c	Hollis, Stephen.....:	Mass. line.....	Private....	66	Kennebec ...	('20) ('31b, Holles)
	Holloway.........	See Halloway...	....	...	....	....
'35d	Holman, Stephen..;	Mass. mil.....	Private....	76	Somerset.	
'40	Holmes, Gersham ..	....	....	75	Cumberland.	Res. Minot.
'35d	Holmes, Gershom ..	Mass. mil.....	Private....	69	Cumberland.	Same as preceding.
'35c	Holmes, Jonathan..	Mass. line.....	Private....	—	Oxford......	('20) ('29 Serg.) ('35e, 5th regt.)
'40	Holmes, Mercy.....	....	....	70	Oxford......	Res. Hartford.
'35d	Holmes, Thomas...	Mass. state....	Private....	75	Kennebec.	
'35c	Holt, Darius.......	Mass. line.....	Private....	69	Oxford......	('20)
'40	————	....	....	76	Oxford......	Res. Norway.
'35c	Holt, John.........	Mass. line.....	Private....	65	Oxford......	('20) d. July 16, 1830.
'35d	Holt, Jonathan.....	Mass. line.....	Pvt.& Serg.	79	Somerset....	d. Dec. 12, 1832.
'40	Holt, Lydia........	....	....	76	Oxford......	Res. Bethel.
'35d	Holt, William......	Mass. line.....	Private....	69	Penobscot.	
'35c	Holt, William...,...	Mass. line.....	Fifer.....	68	Oxford......	('20) d.Sept.,1827.
'35c	Honnewell, Thomas.	Mass. line.....	Private....	73	Somerset....	d. April 22, 1829- See also Hunnewell.
'35c	Hood, Daniel......	Mass. line.....	Private....	97	Lincoln.	

List.	Name.	Service.	Rank.	Age.	County.	Remarks.
'35c	Hood, Robert	Mass. line	Private	84	Somerset	('20) d. Jan. 29, 1826.
'35d	Hoofses, Christian	Mass. line	Private	65 & 80	Lincoln	('20) d. Feb. 19, 1833. See also Hoffses.
'35c	Hooper, Casper	Cont. navy	Mariner	74	Somerset	('20, ship "Warren") d. Sept. 1822.
'35d	Hooper, David	Mass. mil	Private	90	Cumberland	
'40	Hooper, Rachael			89	Cumberland	Res. Freeport.
'40	Hopkins, Martha			69	Waldo	Res. Camden.
'35c	Hopkins, Solomon	Cont. navy	Private	82	York	('20, ship "Ranger").
'35c	Hopkins, Solomon	Mass. line	Private	81	York	('20) d. Mar., 1832
'40	Hopkins, Solomon			85	York	Res. Biddeford.
'20	Hopkins, Theophilus	Mass	Private.			
'35d	Hopkinson, Caleb	Mass. mil	Private	87	York.	
'40				94	York	Res. Limington.
'35d	Horn, Benjamin	N. H. line	Private	81	York.	
'35c	Horn, Daniel	N. H. line	Private	79	York.	
'40				88	York	Res. Acton.
'35c	Horn, Jonathan	Cont. navy	Marine	70	Somerset	('20, ship "Dean")
'40	Horn, Jonathan			85	York	Res. Shapleigh.
'35d	Hornden, Richard	Mass. mil	Lieutenant	80	Lincoln.	
'40	Horsaw, Jonathan			83	York	Res. Berwick. Same as Hosum?
'35c	Horsom, Benjamin	Mass. line	Private	80	York	('20 Horsum)
'35c	Horsom, Jacob	N. H. line	Private	87	York	('20 Horsum.) d. Aug. 8, 1823.
'35d	Horsum, David	N. H. state	Pvt. & Mar.	74	York	('20, '31b)
'35d	Horsum, Samuel	N. H. state	Pvt. & Seaman.	74	York.	Same as Hersom?
'35d	Hosmer, Daniel	Mass. line	Corporal	86	Kennebec.	
'35d	Hosum, Jonathan	Mass. state	Private	76	York	Same as Horsaw?
'35c	Houghton, Jonathan	Mass. line	Private	74	Oxford	('20)
'20	House, Nathaniel	Mass	Private.			
'35c	House, Nathaniel	Cont. navy	Mariner	78	Kennebec.	
'40	House, Thomas			65	Cumberland	Res. Brunswick.
'35d	Houston, Samuel	N. H. line	Pvt. & Corp of art.	81	Waldo	('20, '31b)
'35d	Howard, Amos	N. H. line	Private	82	Oxford.	
'35d	Howard, Joseph	Mass. line	Private	79	Oxford	('20)
'40	Howard, Joseph			81	Oxford	Res. Brownfield.
'35c	Howard, Samuel	Mass. line	Private	89	Oxford	('20)
'35d	Howard, Uriah	N. H. state	Private	70	Somerset.	
'40	Howard, Uriah			77	Franklin	Res. Phillips.
'35c	Howe, Jacob	Mass. line	Private	70	Oxford	('20) d. Jan. 30, 1830.
'40	Howe, Mary			81	Franklin	Res. Temple.
'35c	Howe, William	Mass. line	Private	89	Lincoln	('20) d. Dec. 1827.
'35d	Howell, Silas	Mass. line	Private	87	Cumberland.	
'35d	Howes, Lemuel	Mass. mil	Private	82	Somerset.	
'35d	Howes, Sylvanus	Mass. mil	Private	72	Penobscot	Same as Hows?
'35d	Howland, Abraham	Mass. line	Private	73	Lincoln.	
'40	Hows, Sylvenus			77	Kennebec	Res. Vassalborough. Same as Howes, S?
'35c	Hoyt, John	Mass. line	Private	84	Cumberland	('20, Hoit) d. Feb. 6, 1829. See also Hoit.
'35c	Hubbard, Daniel	Mass. line	Private	72	York	('20) d. Feb. 2, 1825.
'35d	Hubbard, Francis	Mass. mil	Private	73	Kennebec.	
'35d	Hubbard, Jonathan	Mass. mil	Private	73	York.	
'40				78	York	Res. Acton.
'35d	Hubbard, Levi	Mass. line	Private	69	Oxford.	
'40	Hubbard, Mary			75	Oxford	Res. Paris.
'40	Hubbard, Mehitable			85	Penobscot	Res. Corinna.
'35d	Hubbard, Richard	Mass. state	Private	74	York.	
'35c	Hudson, Timothy	R. I. line	Private	87	Kennebec	('20)
'35d	Huff, Daniel	Mass. mil	Private	81	York	('20)
'40				86	York.	Res. Kennebunkport.
'35c	Huff, Daniel	Mass. line	Private	74	Lincoln.	
'40				80	Lincoln	Res. Edgecomb.
'35d	Huff, Israel	Mass. mil	Private	79	York.	
'35d	Huff, John	Mass. mil	Private	74	York.	
'35d	Huff, Moses	Mass. mil	Pvt. & Seaman.	73	Lincoln.	

List.	Name.	Service.	Rank.	Age.	County.	Remarks.
'40	————	....	....	76	Lincoln.....	Res. Edgécomb.
'35d	Hugens, Edmund...	Mass. line.....	Private....	75	Cumberland.	Same as Hagens and Higgins?
'35c	Hull, John........	N. H. line.....	Private....	79	Washington.	
'35c	Humewell, Richard.	Mass. line.....	Lieutenant.	66	Cumberland.	d. May 14, 1823. Same as Hunewell?
'35c	Humphrey, Jesse...	Mass. line.....	Private....	82	Lincoln.....	d. June, 1831.
'20	Hunewell, Richard.	N. Y.........	Lieutenant.		....	Same as Humewell?
'40	*Hunnewell, Abig il* .	....	....	78	Cumberland.	Res. Standish See also Honnewell.
'20	Hunnewell, Thomas.	Mass.........	Private.			
'20	Hunnewell, William.	....	Mariner...		....	Ship "Hancock" Same as Hannewell?
'20	Hunsuim, Robert...	Mass.........	Private.			
'35c	Hunt, Ichabod.....	Mass. line.....	Private....	63	Kennebec ...	('20, 31b)
'35d	Hunt, John........	Conn. state....	Private....	76	Penobscot...	
'35c	Hunt, Oliver.......	Mass. line.....	Lieutenant.	67	Cumberland.	('20) d. March 24, 1822.
'40	Hunter, Thomas ...	....	....	69	Kennebec ...	Res. Clinton Gore.
'35d	Hunter, William ...	Mass. mil.....	Private....	67	Lincoln.	
'40	Hunter, William ...	....	....	76	Lincoln.....	Res. Topsham.
'20	Huntoon, Jonathan.	Mass.........	Private.			
'40	Hursey, James.....	....	....	82	Oxford......	Res. Sumner. Same as Hearsay.
'40	Hurton, John......	....	....	77	York........	Res. Sanford. Same as Huston
'35c	Huston, John, Jr...	Mass. line.....	Private....	73	York........	('20)
'40	*Hutchens, Abigail*...	....	....	87	York.......	Res. Waterborough.
'35c	Hutcheons, Simeon.	Mass. line.....	Private.....	81	York........	Same as Hutchins, S.
'35c	Hutchings, Benj'm'n	Cont. navy ...	Marine....	76	Lincoln.....	('20 ship "Hancock")
'35c	Hutchings, Eastman	Mass. line.....	Sergeant ..	68	York.	
'35c	Hutchings, John ...	N. H. line.....	Private....	77	Kennebec ...	('20) d. Sept. 5, 1824.
'35d	Hutchings, Thomas.	Mass. mil.....	Private....	75	Lincoln.	
'40	Hutchings, William.	....	....	75	Hancock....	Res. Penobscot. Same as Hutchins, W.
'35c	Hutchins, Enoch...	Mass. line.....	Sergeant ..	74	York........	('20 Enock) d Feb. 1832.
'35c	Hutchins, Joseph...	Mass. line.....	Private....	71	Oxford.....	('20)
'35c	Hutchins, Levi.....	Mass. line.....	Private....	86	York........	('20)
'35d	Hutchins, Moses...	Mass. state....	Private.....	68	Oxford.	
'35c	Hutchins, Nathaniel	N. H. line.....	Captain...	83	Oxford......	('20, '28, '29) Relinquished act of 1818 for 1828. ('35e, d. Jan. 10 1832.)
'20	Hutchins, Simeon ..	Mass.........	Private....		....	Same as Hutcheons, S.
'35d	Hutchins, William..	Mass. state....	Private....	70	Hancock....	Same as Hutchings, W.
'35d	Hutchinson, Asa....	N. H. mil	Private....	75	Kennebec.	
'40	Hutchinson, Asa ...	....	....	89	Kennebec ...	Res. Fayette.
'35d	Hutchinson, Israel...	N. H. line.....	Pvt. of art.	70	Kennebec ...	('20, '31b)
'40	*Hutchinson, Mary* ..	....	....	81	Kennebec ...	Res. Litchfield.
'35c	Hutchinson, Nehemiah.	N. H. line.....	Sergeant ..	81	Lincoln.....	('20, private)
'35c	Hutchinson, Samuel.	Mass. line.....	Private....	85	Lincoln.....	('20)
'35c	Hutchinson, Stephen	Mass. line.....	Private....	85	Cumberland.	('20, Hutchison) d. Dec. 9, 1826.
'35c	Hutchkins, Edmund	N. H. line.....	Private....	65	York........	d. Mar. 1, 1825.
'35c	Hyer, Conrad......	Mass. line.....	Private....	81	Lincoln.....	('20) See also Heyer.
'35d	Ingalls, Nathan....	Mass. mil.....	Private....	79	Cumberland.	
'40	*Ingalls, Phebe*.....	....	....	—	Hancock....	Res. Mercer.
'35d	Ingalls, Phineas....	Mass. line.....	Artificer...	77	Cumberland.	
'40	....	....	....	82	Cumberland.	Res. Bridgton.
'35d	Ingbe, Ebenezer....	Mass. line.....	Private....	70	Washington.	Same as Inglee?
'35d	Ingersoll, Nathaniel Widow of.	Mass. mil.....	Private....	81	Cumberland.	April 20, 1834.
'35c	Ingerson, Richard..	N. H. line.....	Private....	75	York........	('20).

List.	Name.	Service.	Rank.	Age.	County.	Remarks.
'35d	Ingham, Daniel....	Mass. state....	Private....	74	Kennebec.	
'35c	Ingham, David.....	Conn. line.....	Private....	75	York........	(20).
'35c	Inghram, David....	Conn. line.....	Private....	78	Kennebec.	
'40	Inglee, Ebenezer ...			76	Washington .	Res. Machias. Same as Ingbe?
'35d	Ingraham, Job.....	Mass. mil.....	Private....	79	Lincoln.	
'40	Ireland, Joel.......			49	Oxford.......	Res, Canton.
'35d	Irish, Isaac........	Mass. mil.....	Private....	71	Cumberland .	d. Feb. 10, 1834.
'35d	Irish, Thomas......	Mass. line.....	Pvt. & Serg	95	Cumberland .	d. Aug. 16, 1832.
'35c	Jack, Robert.......	Mass. line.....	Private....	79	Lincoln.....	(20) d. July 9,1831
'35c	Jackman, Richard..	Mass. line.....	Private....	75	Kennebec ...	(20).
'40				84	Kennebec ...	Res. Fayette.
'35c	Jackson, Barnabas .	Mass. line.....	Private....	—	Somerset....	(20) d. Jan. 2, 1819.
'35d	Jackson, Bart h o l- omew.	Mass. mil.....	Private....	85	Lincoln.	
'35c	Jackson, Eli.......	Mass. line.....	Private....	69	Cumberland .	('20 Eli) d. Nov. 30, 1825.
'35d	Jackson, Enoch....	Mass. mil.....	Pvt. & Mar	80	Somerset....	d. Dec. 20, 1833.
'35d	Jackson, Isaac.....	Mass. mil.....	Private....	76	Oxford.	
'35d	Jackson, John......	Mass. mil.....	Private....	71	Kennebec ...	d. Aug. 15, 1833.
'35c	Jackson, Joseph....	Mass. line.....	Private....	81	Oxford......	('20).
'35c	Jackson, Joseph, 2d	N. H. line.....	Private....	75	Lincoln.....	('20).
'35c	Jackson, Nathaniel.	Mass. line.....	Private....	65	Oxford......	('20, '31b).
'35d	Jackson, Samuel....	Mass. mil.....	Private....	70	Oxford.	
'35d	Jackson, Thomas...	Mass. line.....	Serg.& Qtr- master.	82	Kennebec ...	('20) d. Aug. 6, 1833.
'35c	Jacobs, George.....	Mass. line.....	Lieutenant	80	York........	('20,'28) d. June 4, 1831.
'40	Jacobs, Herribeth...			85	York........	Res. Sanford.
'35c	Jacobs, John.......	Mass. line.....	Private....	77	Kennebec ...	('20)..
'40	Jacobs, John.......			85	Kennebec ..	Res. Mt. Vernon.
'35c	James, John.......	Mass. line.....	Private....	80	Kennebec ...	('20).
'35c	Jaques, Richard.....	N. H. line.....	Private....	77	Hancock....	('20 Jacques).
'40				85	Hancock....	Res. Castine.
'40	Jay, Lydia.........			92	York........	Res. S. Berwick.
'35d	Jefferd, Samuel M. .	Mass. state....	Private....	71	York.	
'40				77	York........	Res. Wells.
'35c	Jenkins, John......	Cont. navy....	Marine....	—	York........	d. Mar. 1827. Same as Junkins
'20	Jenkins, Josiah.....	Mass.........	Captain...	76		('28).
'35d	Jenkins, Lemuel....	Mass. line.....	Pvt. & Sap.	72	Lincoln.....	('20, '35c).
'40	Jenkins, Lemuel....			76	Kennebec ...	Res. Clinton.
'35d	Jenkins, Samuel....	Mass. line.....	Sergeant ..	76	Oxford......	('20) d. Nov. 15, 1832.
'35c	Jennings, Eliphalet .	Mass line.....	Private....	68	Kennebec ...	('20).
'35c	Jennison, Samuel...	Mass. line.....	Lieutenant	67	Lincoln.....	('20) d. Sept. 1, 1826.
'40	Jepson, Bradbury T.			54	Lincoln.....	Res. Lewiston.
'35c	Jewell, John, 1st ...	N. H. line.....	Private....	69	York.......	('20) d. Apr. 22, 1831.
'35c	Jewell, John 2d....	Mass. line.....	Private....	72 or 70	YorkorOxford	d. Aug. 5, 1827.
'35d	Jewell. Samuel.....	Mass. mil.....	Private....	75	Oxford.	
'35c	Jewet, Moses.......	Mass. line.....	Private....	60	Lincoln.	
'40	Jewett, Mary......			76	Somerset....	Res. St. Albans.
'35d	Jewitt, David......	Mass. mil.....	Private....	80	Somerset.	
'35d	Jewitt, John.......	Mass. mil.....	Private....	94	Kennebec.	
'35d	Jewitt, Noah.......	Mass. line.....	Private....	76	York.	
'35c	Johnson, Andrew...	N. H. line.....	Private....	75	Oxford......	('20).
'35d	Johnson, Asa......	Mass. mil.....	Private....	73	Cumberland .	d. Nov. 16, 1833.
'35c	Johnson, Benjamin .	Mass. line.....	Private....	71	Waldo.	
'40				75	Waldo......	Res. Knox.
'20	Johnson, Benjamin .	N. H.........	Private.			
'35c	Johnson, Daniel....	N. H. line.....	Private....	70	Waldo......	('20) d. Dec. 27, 1832.
'40	Johnson, Daniel....			76	Waldo	Res. Belfast.
'35c	Johnson, Dennis ...	Mass. line.....	Private....	79	York.	
'35c	Johnson, James....	Mass. line.....	Captain...	96	Kennebec ...	('20, '28) d. June 1830.
'35c	Johnson, Jonathan .	Mass. line.....	Private....	74	Cumberland .	('20) d. Dec. 17, 1832.
'35d	Johnson, Joseph....	Mass. line.....	Private....	76	Cumberland .	
'40	Johnson, Joseph....			77	Cumberland .	Res. Poland.
'35c	Johnson, Nathan...	Mass. line.....	Private....	88	Cumberland .	('20) d. Oct. 30, 1831.
'35c	Johnson, Thomas ..	Mass. line.....	Private....	75	Kennebec ...	('20) d. Oct. 22, 1818.

List.	Name.	Service.	Rank.	Age.	County.	Remarks.
'35c	Johnson, William...	Mass. line.....	Private....	82	York........	('20) d. April 10 1830.
'35d	Johnston, David...	Mass. mil.....	Private....	77	Cumberland.	
'35d	Johnston, James ...	Mass. mil.....	Seaman & Matross.	75	Cumberland.	
'35d	Johnston, John.....	N. Y. state....	Private....	92	Washington.	
'40	———	....	....	97	Washington..	Res. Perry.
'35d	Johnston, John.....	Cont. navy....	Serg.& Mar	70	Penobscot.	
'40	Johnstone, Ruth....	....	....	88	Penobscot...	Res. Milford.
'35c	Johonnet, Gabriel ..	Mass. line.....	Lieut. Col.	76	Penobscot...	('20 Johonnot). d. Oct. 9, 1820.
'35c	Jones, Amos.......	Mass. line.....	Private....	72	Waldo.	
'40	———	....	....	78	Waldo......	Res. Unity.
'35d	Jones, Cornelius....	Mass. state....	Pvt. & Sea.	72	Oxford.	
'40	———	....	....	77	Oxford......	Res. Turner.
'35c	Jones, David.......	Mass. line.....	Surgeon...	86	Cumberland.	('20, '31 b.).
'40	Jones, Elizabeth ...	....	....	79	Cumberland.	Res. N. Yarmouth
'35d	Jones, Isaac.......	Mass. mil.....	Private....	77	Lincoln.	
'35c	Jones, James.......	Mass. line.....	Private....	64	Kennebec ...	('20) d. Jan. 26, 1829.
'35c	Jones, John........	Mass. line.....	Corporal ..	84	Lincoln.....	('20) d. June, 1824
'35d	Jones, John........	Mass. mil.....	Private....	78	Cumberland.	
'35d	Jones, Joshua......	Mass. line.....	Private....	76	Cumberland.	('20).
'35c	Jones, Lazarus.....	Mass. line.....	Private....	80	Somerset....	('20).
'40	Jones, Mehitable....	....	....	75	Kennebec ...	(Res. Gardiner.
'35c	Jones, Samuel......	Mass. line.....	Private....	78	Kennebec ...	('20) d. Sept 1. 1832.
'35d	Jones, Silvester.....	Mass. state....	Private....	74	Kennebec ...	Same as Jones, Sylvester.
'35c	Jones, Solomon.....	Mass. line.....	Private....	65	Cumberland.	('20) d. June 4, 1824.
'40	Jones, Sylvester....	....	....	79	Kennebec ...	Res. Fayette.
'35c	Jones, Thomas, 2d .	N. H. line.....	Private....	96	Waldo.	
'35c	Jones, Thomas.....	Mass. line.....	Private....	70	York........	('20).
'40	Jones, Thomas.....	....	....	62	Washington .	Res. Pembroke.
'35c	Jordan, Abner.....	Mass. line.....	Private....	58	Lincoln.....	('20) d. Sept. 22. 1820. See also JOurdan.
'35c	Jordan, Abraham...	Mass. line.....	Private....	73	Cumberland.	('20.)
'35c	Jordan, David.....	Mass. line.....	Private....	73	Oxford......	Same as Jordon, David.
'35c	Jordan, David.....	Mass. line.....	Private....	67	Oxford......	('20.)
'35c	Jordan, Elijah.....	Mass. line.....	Private....	80	Kennebec ...	('20) d. Dec. 26, 1827.
'35c	Jordan, Hezekiah ..	Mass. line.....	Private....	75	Cumberland.	('20) Jordon.
'35c	Jordan, Humphrey .	Mass. line.....	Private....	80	Cumberland.	('20 '31 b.) d. Oct. 13, 1833.
'20	Jordan, Ignatius ...	Mass..........	Private.			
'40	Jordan, Joanna.....	....	....	76	Cumberland.	Res. Danville.
'35d	Jordan, John.......	Mass. mil.....	Private....	86	Cumberland.	d. Nov. 25, 1833.
'35d	Jordan, Samuel....	Mass. mil.....	Private....	78	Cumberland.	
'35c	Jordan, Thomas....	Mass. line.....	Private....	68	Cumberland.	('20, '31 b.)
'40	Jordan, Timothy...	....	....	74	Oxford......	Res. Norway. See also Jourdan.
'40	Jordon, David.....	....	....	79	Oxford......	Res. Albany. Same as Jordan, David.
'35d	Josselyn, Nathaniel.	Mass. state....	Private....	80	Cumberland.	
'35c	Jotham, Calvin....	Mass. line.....	Private....	74	Kennebec ...	('20).
'35c	Jotham, Luther....	Mass. line.....	Private....	83	Kennebec ...	('20) d. June 22, 1832.
'40	Jourdan, Hannah ..	....	....	83	Waldo......	Res. Monroe.
'35d	Judkins, Benj., wid- ow.	Mass. line.....	Private....	85	Kennebec ...	d. Dec. 20, 1833.
'35c	Judkins, Jacob.....	N. H. line.....	Private....	62	Kennebec ...	('20) d. Sept. 2, 1822.
'35c	Judkins, Jonathan..	N. H. line.....	Private....	74	Kennebec.	
'35c	Judkins, Philip.....	N. H. line.....	Private....	82	Somerset....	('20).
'40	Judkins, Philip.....	....	....	82	Somerset....	Res. Cambridge.
'20	Judkins, Samuel....	N. H..........	Private.			
'35c	Judkins, Samuel....	Mass. line.....	Private....	74	Kennebec.	
'35c	Jumper, Daniel....	Mass. line.....	Private....	70	Cumberland.	('20).
'40	———	....	....	76	Cumberland.	Res. Harrison.
'20	Junkins, John......	....	Mariner			Ship "Ranger" Same as Jenkins, J.?
'35c	Kavan, James......	Mass. line.....	Private....	68	Cumberland.	d. Feb. 22, 1823.
'35c	Keath, Cornelius...	Mass. line.....	Private....	77	Lincoln.....	d. Jan. 9, 1830. Same as Keith?

List.	Name.	Service.	Rank.	Age.	County.	Remarks.
'40	Keen, Isaac........	....	....	86	Kennebec...	Res. Clinton.
'35c	Keen, James.......	Mass. line.....	Private....	70	Oxford......	('20).
'35d	Keen, John........	Mass. state....	Private....	74	Oxford.	
'40	———	....	....	79	Oxford......	Res. Turner.
'35d	Keen, Meshack....	Mass. line.....	Private....	75	Oxford......	('20, Mehach)
'40	———	....	....	83	Oxford......	Res. Sumner.
'35c	Keene, Isaac......	Mass. line.....	Private....	59	Kennebec...	('20). Same as Keen, Isaac?
'35c	Keene, William....	Mass. line.....	Private....	80	Lincoln.....	('20, '31 b).
'20	Keith, Cornelius....	Mass.........	Private....	—	....	See also Keath.
'35c	Keith, James......	Mass. line.....	Major.....	77	Washington.	('20, '28) d. May 14, 1829.
'40	Keler, Henry......	....	....	48	Hancock....	Res. Castine.
'40	Keller, David......	....	....	82	Lincoln.....	Res. St. George
'35c	Kelley, Joseph.....	Mass. line.....	Private....	62	Kennebec...	('20 Kelly).
'35c	Kelley, Joshua.....	Mass. line.....	Private....	93	Oxford......	('20 Kelly) d. in 1822.
'40	Kelley, Sarah	....	....	78	Kennebec...	Res. Monmouth.
'35c	Kelley, William....	N. H. line.....	Private....	71	Kennebec...	('20 Kelly)
'35c	Kellock, David.....	Mass. line.....	Private....	76	Lincoln.....	('20) See also Kollock.
'35c	Kellock, Matthew..	Mass. line.....	Mariner...	92	Lincoln.....	('20 Frigate Boston) d. March, 1825.
'35d	Kellogg, Elijah.....	Mass. line.....	Musician & D'm maj.	72	Cumberland.	('20, '31b).
'40	———	....	....	79	Cumberland.	Res. Portland.
'31b	Kellogg, Joseph....	....	Private.			
'35d	Kelly, Stephen.....	Mass. mil.....	Private....	92	Waldo......	See also Kelley.
'35c	Kemp, Ebenezer....	Mass. line.....	Private....	84	Cumberland.	('20).
'20	Kench, Thomas....	Mass.........	Private....	—	....	Same as Kinch?
'40	Kendall, Abigail....	....	....	74	Somerset....	Res. Fairfield.
'35d	Kendall, Chever....	Mass. state....	Pvt.& Serg.	79	Waldo.	
'40	Kendall, Mary.....	....	....	76	York........	Res. Limington.
'20	Kendall, William...	Mass.........	Private....	—	....	Same as Kindall, W.?
'40	Keniston, David...	....	....	82	Lincoln.....	Res Boothbay. Same as Kenniston?
'31a	Kennard, Timothy	....	Private....	—	....	Rejected as serving six months only.
'35d	Kennard, Timothy.	Mass. line.....	Private....	78	York.	
'35c	Kennedy, James....	N. H. line.....	Private....	70	Lincoln.....	('20) d. in 1825.
'35c	Kenney, Israel.....	Mass. line.....	Private....	—	Hancock....	('20) d. Mar. 5, 1820. See also Kinney.
'35c	Kenney, Thomas...	Mass. line.....	Private....	64	Kennebec...	d. April 11, 1825.
'35c	Kenniston, David ..	N. H. line.....	Private....	59	Lincoln.....	Same as Keniston? See also Kinerson.
'35d	Kent, John........	Mass. mil.....	Pvt.& Corp	79	Kennebec.	
'40	Keyes, Jemima.....	....	....	75	Franklin....	Res. Jay.
'35d	Keys, Ebenezer....	Mass. line.....	Private....	70	Oxfprd......	('20 Keyes).
'35c	Kezer, David......	Mass. line.....	Private....	74	Washington.	('20).
'35c	Kilborn, John......	Mass. line.....	Private....	80	York........	('20 & '31 b. Kilbourn).
'40	Kilborn, John......	....	....	85	Cumberland.	Res. Bridgton.
'35c	Kilburn, John......	Mass. line.....	Private....	64	Cumberland.	
'35e	Kilburn, John......	Mass. line..... 3d regt........	Sergeant ..	—	Cumberland.	('29 Killburn)
'20d	Kilegore, John.....	Mass.........	Corporal.			
'35c	Kilgore, James.....	Mass. line.....	Private....	76	Oxford......	('20).
'40	———	....	....	82	Oxford......	Res. Lovell.
'35c	Kilgore, John......	Mass. line.....	Private....	68	Oxford......	
'40	———	....	....	—	Oxford......	Res. Newry.
'35	Kilgore, Joseph....	Mass. line.....	Private....	71	Lincoln.....	('20 Killgore).
'35c	Kilgore, Trueworthy	Mass. line.....	Private....	71	Hancock....	('20 Kilgour) d. Mar. 4, 1830.
'40	Kimbal, Nathaniel .	....	....	83	Kennebec ...	Res. Winthrop. Same as Kimball, Nathaniel.
'35c	Kimball, Abraham .	Mass. line.....	Private....	73	York........	('20) d. Feb. 13, 1829.
'35d	Kimball, Benjamin.	Mass. line.....	Private....	83	York........	('20 '31b).
'35c	Kimball, David....	Mass. line.....	Private....	70	Somerset....	('20).
'35c	Kimball, Hezekiah .	Mass. line.....	Private....	79	York........	('20 Hezediah) d. Jan. 1828.
'35c	Kimball, Joseph....	Mass. line.....	Private....	76	Oxford......	('20).

List.	NAME.	Service.	Rank.	Age.	County.	Remarks.
'40	Kimball, Joseph....		....	81	Cumberland	Res. Bridgton.
'35c	Kimball, Moses....	N. H. line.....	Private....	85	Oxford......	('20).
'35c	Kimball, Nathan...	Mass. line.....	Corporal ..	84	York........	('20).
'35d	Kimball, Nathaniel .	Mass. line.....	Pvt.& Serg.	77	Kennebec ...	Same as Kimbal, Nathaniel.
'35d	Kimball, Simeon...	Mass. mil.....	Private....	74	Kennebec.	
'35c	Kincade, Reuben...	Mass. line......	Private....	75	Lincoln.	
'40	Kincaid, John......			78	Kennebec ...	Res. Augusta.
'35c	Kinch, Thomas....	Mass. line.....	Private....	87	Hancock....	('20) d. Jan. 17, 1831. Same as Kench.
'35c	Kindall, William...	Mass. line.....	Private....	59	Somerset....	Same as Kendall.
'35c	Kinerson, John.....	Mass. line.....	Private....	75	Oxford......	('20) d. Nov. 1, 1833. See also Kenniston.
'35c	King, Ichabod.....	Mass. line.....	Private....	75	Cumberland .	('20).
'40	King, Mary........			70	Cumberland .	Res. Minot.
'35c	Kingsbury, John...	Mass. line.....	Private....	67	York........	('20, '31b).
'35d	Kingsley, Azel.....	Mass. line.....	Private & Fifer.	72	Cumberland .	Same as Kinsley?
'35d	Kingsley, Daniel....	Mass. line.....	Pvt.& Serg.	76	Cumberland .	Same as Kinsley?
'35e	Kinnaston, Daniel.	N. H. line.....	Corporal ..	—	Lincoln.....	('29). Same as Keniston and Kenniston?
'35d	Kinney, Abijah..., .	Mass. mil.....	Private.....	73	Lincoln.....	See also Kenney.
'40	Kinney, Abijah.....			85	Lincoln.....	Res. Boothbay.
'35d	Kinney, Benjamin..	Mass. line.....	Private....	77	Lincoln.	
'35d	Kinney, Samuel....	Mass. mil.....	Private....	79	Lincoln.	
'40	Kinsley, Azael......			79	Cumberland .	Res. Minot. Same as Kingsley.
'40	Kinsley, Daniel....			82	Cumberland .	('20 Sergeant). Res. Minot.
'35c	Kitfield, William...	Mass. line.....	Private....	77	Hancock....	('20).
'35d	Knapp, Joseph.....	Mass. line.....	Private....	71	Kennebec.	
'35d	Kneeland, Adam...	Mass. mil.....	Private....	81	Cumberland .	
'35c	Knight, Abraham ..	N. H. line.....	Private....	73	Cumberland .	('20).
'40	———			74	Cumberland .	Res. Poland.
'35c	Knight, Daniel.....	Mass. line.....	Private....	74	Cumberland .	('20).
'40	———			81	Oxford......	Res. Norway.
'40	Knight, Elizabeth...			79	York........	Res. Elliot.
'35c	Knight, Jacob......	Mass. line.....	Private....	77	Cumberland	
'40	———			83	Cumberland .	Res. Falmouth.
'31a	Knight, John......		Private....	—	....	Rejected as serving 8 months only.
'35d	Knight, John......	Mass. line.....	Private & Drum.	87	Cumberland .	d. June 28, 1832.
'35c	Knight, John......	Mass. line.....	Private....	75	Cumberland .	
'40	———			83	Cumberland .	Res. Otisfield.
'35c	Knight, Jonathan,2d	Mass. line.....	Private....	76	Cumberland .	
'35d	Knight, Jonathan ..	Mass. line.....	Private....	72	Cumberland .	('20).
'35d	Knight, Jonathan ..	Mass. line.....	Private....	72	York........	('20 '31b).
'40	———			77	York........	Res. Waterborough.
'35c	Knight, Joseph, 1st.	Mass. line.....	Private....	79	York........	('20).
'35c	Knight, Joseph, 2d .	Mass. line.....	Private....	78	Oxford......	('20).
'35d	Knight, Mark......	Mass. mil.....	Private....	77	Cumberland .	
'35c	Knight, Zachariah..	Mass. line.....	Private....	78	Cumberland .	d. Dec. 1, 1828.
'35d	Knowles, Ezekiel...	N, H. line.....	Private....	83	Kennebec ...	d. Oct. 15, 1832.
'35c	Knowles, Isaac.....	Mass. line.....	Private....	80	Kennebec ..	('20) d. Mar. 3, 1822.
1794	Knowles, John.....	Stickney's regt.	Private....	—	....	Res. Sterling, Me. Wounded at Bennington, 1777.
'35d	Knowles, John.....	Mass. mil.....	Private....	82	Somerset.	
'40	Knowles, Lydia.....			84	Kennebec ...	Res. Litchfield.
'35e	Knowles, Simon....	Dearborn's regt	Private....	—	Waldo......	('29 from N. H. '31 b).
'35c	Knowles, Simon....	N. H. line.....	Private....	62	Hancock....	('20).
'35c	Knowlton, Abraham	Mass. line.....	Private....	75	York........	('20). d. Jan. 12, 1830.
'35c	Knowlton, Andrew .	Mass. line.....	Private....	82	Lincoln.....	('20).
'40	———			89	Lincoln.....	Res. Noblebo-rough.
'40	Knowlton, Dorcas...			69	York........	Res. Elliot.
'35d	Knowlton, Joseph..	Mass. line..... Mass. state....	Private.... Sergeant.	84	Kennebec ...	('20, '31b).
'40	Knowlton, Joseph..			90	Waldo......	Res. Liberty.
'35c	Knowlton, Thomas.	Mass. line.....	Private....	68	Kennebec.	
'35c	Knox, David......	Mass. line.....	Private....	72	York........	('20) d. Sept. 1, 1830.

58

List.	Name.	Service.	Rank.	Age.	County.	Remarks.
'35c	Knox, John	Mass. line	Private	77	York	('20) d. Sept,1821.
'35d	Kollock, Ebenezer	Mass. mil	Private	72	Cumberland	See also Kellock.
'35d	Lachanie, Antoine	Mass. state	Private & Mariner	83	Penobscot.	
'35c	Lake, John	Mass. line	Private	81	Lincoln	('20). d. in 1823.
'40	Lamb, James			79	Kennebec	Res. Leeds. Same as Lumb?
'40	Lamb, James			69	Kennebec	Res. Clinton.
'35c	Lammas, Dyre	Cont. navy	Mariner	81	Somerset	('20, ship "Warren").
'35c	Lamont, John	Mass. line	Captain	83	Lincoln	('20) d. Feb. 23, 1827.
'35c	Lampson, William	Mass. line	Private	73	Lincoln	('20) d. Oct. 8, 1823. See also Lanson.
'35d	Lancaster, Ezekiel	Mass. state	Pvt.& Corp	75	Kennebec.	
'35d	Lancaster, John	Mass. mil	Private	73	Lincoln.	
'40	Lancaster, John			78	Kennebec	Res. Augusta.
'35c	Lancaster, Joseph	Mass. line	Private	77	Lincoln	('20).
'40	Lancaster, Joseph			83	Cumberland	Res. Durham.
'40	Lancey, Elis abeth			74	Somerset	Res. Palmyra.
'35d	Lancy, Samuel	Mass. mil	Private	75	Somerset.	
'35c	Landerkin, Daniel	Cont. navy	Mariner	76	Lincoln	('20 ship "Boston").
'40	Landerkin, Daniel			90	Lincoln	Res. Boothbay.
'35c	Lane, Francis	Mass. line	Private	73	Oxford	('20) d. Dec.,1829.
'35d	Lane, Isaac	Mass. mil	Private & Fifer	71	York.	
'35c	Lane, Jabez	Mass. line	Captain	81	York	('20, '28) d. Oct. 25, 1825.
'35d	Lane, Samuel	Mass. mil	Private	72	Cumberland.	
'35d	Lang, John	N. H. mil	Private	81	Waldo	d. June 26, 1833.
'31b	Langley, Asa		Private.			
'35d	Langley, Eli	Mass. mil	Private	73	Cumberland.	
'40	Lanson, Martha			80	Waldo	Res. Liberty.
'35c	Lara, James	Mass. line	Private	77	Cumberland	('20).
'40	Larbree, Mary			78	Kennebec	Res. Wales.
'40	Laria, James			85	Oxford	Res. Turner.
'40	Larrabe, Jacob			76	Cumberland	Res. Danville.
'35c	Larrabee, Isaac	Mass. line	Private	79	Cumberland	('20).
'35d	Larrabee, Jacob	Mass. mil	Private	72	Cumberland	Same as Larabee J.
'35d	Larrabee, Jonathan	Mass. mil	Pvt.& Corp	86	Cumberland.	
'35d	Larrabee, Samuel	Mass. mil	Private	85	York.	
'35d	Larrabee, Stephen	Mass. state	Private	79	Kennebec.	
'35c	Larry, Michael	Penn. line	Private	80	Kennebec.	
'35c	Lasdell, Asa	Mass. line	Private	72	Waldo	('20).
'40	Lassell, Asa			78	Waldo	Res. Burnham. Same as Lasdell.
'35c	Lassell, Cabel	Mass. line	Private	73	York	('20).
'40				79	York	Res. Waterborough.
'35d	Lathrop, George	Mass. state	Pvt. of art.	69	Kennebec.	
'35d	Lathrop, Joseph	Mass. line	Private	79	Oxford.	
'35d	Laughton, James	Mass. mil	Sergeant	91	Lincoln	d. June 20, 1833.
'35d	Lawrence, Amos	Mass. line	Private	79	Lincoln.	
'40				86	Lincoln	Res. Warren.
'35c	Lawrence, Isaac	Mass. line	Private	75	Penobscot	('20 Lawrence).
'40				81	Penobscot	Res. Newport.
'35d	Lawrence, Isaac	Mass. state	Private	75	Penobscot	20 d. June 20, 1833.
'35d	Lawrence, John	Mass. line	Private	78	Cumberland	('20, '31b).
'35d	Lawrence, John	Mass. line	Private	—	Cumberland.	
'35d	Lawrence, Rogers	Mass. mil	Pvt.& Mar.	92	Hancock.	
'35c	Lawrence, William	Cont. navy	Mariner	87	Lincoln.	
'40	Lawyer, Luke			80	Somerset	Res. Starks.
'35d	Layton, Ephraim	Mass. mil	Private	69	Kennebec	Same as Leighton.
'35c	Leach, Benjamin	N. H. line	Private	80	York.	
'35c	Leach, George	Mass. line	Private	78	Cumberland	('20).
'40				83	Cumberland	Res. Danville.
'35d	Leach, John	Mass. line	Matross	77	Kennebec.	
'40	Leach, John			83	Piscataquis	Res. Sangerville.
'35c	Leach, Mark	Mass. line	Private	79	Cumberland	('20). d. Jan. 23, 1822.
'35c	Leadbetter, Increase	Cont. navy	Mariner	70	Kennebec	('20 ship "Boston").
'40	Leadbetter, Increase			90	Kennebec	Res. Leeds.
	Leaher, Peter	see Lehr				

List.	Name.	Service.	Rank.	Age.	County.	Remarks.
'35c	Leatherhead, Robert, alias Bell.	Cont. navy....	Musician..	78	Somerset....	('20 mariner ship "Alliance").
'35c	Leathers, Enoch....	Mass. line.....	Private....	71	Penobscot.	
'40	Leathers, Enoch....			79	Piscataquis.,	('20). Res. Sangerville.
'35c	Leathers, Levi.....	N. H. line.....	Private....	73	Lincoln.....	('20).
'40	Leathhead, Robert..			81	Somerset....	Res. Anson. Same as Leatherhead.
'35c	Leaver, William....	N. H. line.....	Private....	74	York........	('20).
'35c	Leavett, Edward ...	N. H. line.....	Private....	60	Somerset....	('20 '29 sergeant of inf.)
'35c	Leavett, Nathaniel.	N. H. line.....	Lieutenant	69	York........	('20) Leavitt) d. Feb. 1825.
'40	Leavitt, Betsey......			72	York........	Res. Sanford.
'35e	Leavitt, Edmund...	N. H. line, 2d. regiment.	Sergeant ..	So	merset......	d. July 27, 1831.
'35d	Leavitt, Joseph.....	R. I. line......	Pvt.&Corp.	85	Kennebec ...	('31b).
'40	Leavitt, Mary......			79	York........	Res. Limerick.
'35d	Leavitt, William...	N. H. line.....	Private....	83	York........	('20 '31b).
'35d	Lee, William.......	Mass. state....	Lieutenant	81	Lincoln.	
'35c	Leeman, Daniel....	Mass. line.....	Private....	74	Washington.'	
'35d	Leeman, Samuel....	Mass. mil......	Private....	70	Lincoln......	d. Apr. 30, 1833.
'35d	Legro, David......	Mass. mil......	Private....	74	York.	
'35c	Legrow, Joseph....	Mass. line.....	Private....	72	Hancock....	('20 Legro) d. Feb. 25, 1832.
'35c	Lehr, Peter........	Mass. line.....	Private....	64	Lincoln.....	d. in 1822.
'40	Leighton, Ephraim .			72	Kennebec ...	Res. Augusta. Same as Layton.
'35d	Leighton, Joseph...	Mass. mil......	Private....	80	Washington.	
'35d	Leighton, Robert...	Mass. mil......	Private....	77	Cumberland .	
'35c	Leighton, Tobias...	Mass. line.....	Private....	79	Somerset....	('20) d. in 1822.
'35c	Leissner, George ...	Mass. line.....	Sergeant ..	75	Lincoln.....	('20).
'35d	Leland, Henry.....	Mass. line.....	Private....	74	Penobscot.	
'35c	Leland, Joseph.....	Mass. line.....	Lieutenant	62	York........	('20, '29) (35e, 8th regiment.)
'40	Lement, Thomas...			81	Lincoln.....	Res. Bath.
'35d	Lemoat, David.....	Mass. mil......	Private....	75	Lincoln.	
'35d	Lemoat, Thomas...	Mass. line.....	Private....	75	Lincoln.	Same as Lement?
'35d	Lennell, Samuel....	Mass. mil......	Private.....	72	Cumberland .	
'35d	Leonard, Caleb.....	Mass. mil......	Private....	75	Kennebec.	
'40				80	Kennebec ...	Res. Windsor.
'40	Lerry, David......			86	Somerset....	Res Starks.
'20	Lervey, Jacob......	Mass. line.....	Private....	—		Same as Lurvey.
'40	Levering, Nathaniel.			77	Kennebec ...	Res. Winthrop. Same as Lovering.
'35c	Lewis, Abijah......	Mass. line.....	Private.	74	Oxford......	('20, d. June 1831.
'35d	Lewis, Archelaus...	Mass. mil......	Lieutenant	81	Cumberland .	
'35d	Lewis, Joseph.....	Mass. line.....	Private....	70	York........	('20).
'35c	Lewis, Nathan.....	Mass. line.....	Private....	63	Cumberland .	('20). d. Dec. 5, 1822.
'35d	Lewis, William.....	Mass. mil......	Sergeant ..	78	Lincoln.	
'35d	Libbee, Robert.. ..	Mass. line.....	Private...,.	77	Cumberland .	('20).
'35c	Libbey, Benjamin,2d	Cont. navy....	Mariner...	76	Kennebec ...	('20 Benjamin 2d; ship "Ranger").
'35d	Libbey, David.....	Mass. state....	Pvt. of art.	79	Washington.	
'35c	Libbey, Ezirah.....	Mass. line.....	Private....	58	York........	('20 Ezriah).
'35d	Libbey, James.....	Mass. line.....	Private....	72	York........	d. June 22, 1832.
'35c	Libbey, James.....	Mass. line.....	Private....	71	Cumberland .	('20 Libby) d. May, 1828.
'35d	Libbey, Joseph.....	Mass. line.....	Private....	86	Washington.	
'35d	Libbey, Josiah.....	Mass. state....	Pvt. of art.	79	Washington.	
'35c	Libbey, Nathan....	Mass. line.....	Private....	89	Cumberland .	d. Apr. 14, 1823.
'35c	Libbey, Reuben....	Mass. line.....	Private....	83	Cumberland .	('20 Libby) d. in 1822.
'35c	Libbey, Richard M .	Mass. line.....	Private....	61	Cumberland .	('20 Richard H. Libby) d. Mar. 27, 1820.
'35c	Libbey, Samuel....	Cont. navy....	Mariner...	69	York........	('20 ship "Ranger") d. Jan. 14, 1829.
'35c	Libbey, Simeon....	Mass. line.....	Corporal ..	63	Cumberland .	('20 & '31b, Libby).
'35c	Libbey, Solomon...	Mass. line.....	Private....	76	York........	('20) d. Mar. 1, 1831.
'40	Libby, Abigail......			78	Cumberland .	Res Scarborough.
'40	Libby, Abigail......			77	Cumberland .	Res. Scarborough.
'40	Libby, Abigail......			76	Cumberland .	Res. Scarborough.
'35c	Libby,Benjamin, 1st	Mass. line.....	Private....	70	Lincoln.....	d. Aug. 10, 1833.
'40	Libby, Dorothy.....			78	Cumberland .	Res. Scarborough.'
'35d	Libby, Edward ...	Mass. line.....	Private....	73	Cumberland .	('20).
'40	Libby, Edward.....			70to 80,	Cumberland .	Res. Gorham.

List.	Name.	Service.	Rank.	Age.	County.	Remarks.
'35d	Libby, Eliakim	Mass. line	Private	89	Cumberland	
'35d	Libby, Francis	Mass. line	Private	83	York	('20).
'35d	Libby, George	Mass. state	Private	74	York.	
'35d	Libby, Harvey	Mass. line	Private	80	York	('20, '31 b).
'35d	Libby, Isaac	Mass. mil	Private	70	York.	
'40	Libby, Joseph			92	Washington	Res. Harrington.
'20	Libby, Jotham	Mass. line	Private.			
'35d	Libby, Mark	Mass. line	Private	84	Cumberland	
'40	————			90	Cumberland	Res. Scarborough.
'35d	Libby, Nathaniel	Mass. line	Private	71	York	('20 '31b).
'40	————			77	York	Res. Limerick.
'35d	Libby, Robert	Mass. mil	Private	73	York.	
'40	Libby, Robert			79	Cumberland	Res. Sebago. Same as Libbee?
'35d	Libby, Seth	Mass. mil	Private	79	Cumberland	
'40	Libby, Theophilus			47	Cumberland	Res. Danville.
'35c	Libby, Thomas	Mass. line	Private	65	Cumberland	('20 Libbey).
'35d	Libby, William	Mass. line	Private	80 or 84	York	('20, '31b).
'35d	Libby, Zebulon	Mass. line	Private	77	Cumberland	('20).
'35c	Lilley, Benjamin	Mass. line	Private.	75	Lincoln	('20) d. Jan. 31, 1828.
'31b	Lincken, Joseph		P ivate.			
'35c	Lincoln, David	N. Y. line	Private	75	Lincoln.	
'35c	Lincoln, Elisha	Mass. line	Private	64	Somerset	('20)d. May3,1824
'35c	Lincoln, John	Mass. line	Private	75	Cumberland	('20).
'40	Lincoln, Loved			82	Lincoln	Res. Lewiston.
'35d	Lincoln, Royall	Mass. mil	Bomb'd'r & Sea'n.	79	York.	
'35d	Lincoln, Sherman	Mass. mil	Private	72	Kennebec.	
'40	————			83	Kennebec	Res. China.
'35c	Lindsay, James	Mass. line	Private	79	Kennebec	('20 Lindsey).
'40	————			84	Kennebec	Res. Leeds.
'35c	Linn, John	Mass. line	Private	70	Kennebec	('20) d. Apr. 28, 1834.
'40	Linn, Joseph			55	Kennebec	Res. Windsor.
'35c	Linnekin, Joseph	Mass. line		67	Lincoln	('20 Linekin).
'40	Linnen, Thomas			79	Lincoln	Res. Georgetown.
'35c	Linscott, Theodore	Mass. line	Private	71	York	('20).
'35c	Litchfield, Noah	Mass. line	Private	74	Hancock	('20 Linchfield) d. Nov. 17, 1827.
'40	Little, John			84	Lincoln	Res. Bristol. See also Lyttle.
'35c	Littlefield, Abraham	Mass. line	Private	71	York	('20) d. July 20, 1831.
'35d	Littlefield, Benjamin 1st.	Mass. state	Private	90	York.	
'35d	Littlefield, Benja- min, 2d.	Mass. state	Private	76	York.	
'35d	Littlefield, Daniel	Mass. line	Private	76	York	('20).
'35d	Littlefield, David	Mass. line	Private	73	York.	
'40	*Littlefield, Dorothy*			92	York	Res. Kennebunk.
'35d	Littlefield, Elijah	Mass. mil	Private	77	Cumberland	
'35d	Littlefield, Ephraim	Mass. mil	Private	82	York.	
'40	*Littlefield, Joanna*			72	York	Res. Lyman.
'35c	Littlefield, Joel	Mass. line	Private:	72	York	Transf. from Mass. 1820.
'35c	Littlefield, Johnson	Mass. line	Private	60	York	('20, '31 b).
'35c	Littlefield, Jotham	Mass. line	Private	87	York	('20) d. Mar. 7, 1834.
'40	*Littlefield, Miriam*			85	York	Res. Wells.
'35c	Littlefield, Moses	Mass. line	Private	80	Waldo.	
'40	Littlefield, Moses			85	Penobscot	Res. Dixmont.
'35c	Littlefield, Noah M.	Mass. line	Lieut. Col.	84	York	('20) d. Oct. 25, 1821.
'40	*Littlefield, Susannah*			81	York.	
'35c	Littlefield, Timothy	Mass. line	Private	72	Kennebec.	
'40	Littlefield, Timothy			81	Kennebec	Res. Waterville.
'35c	Lombard, Butler	Mass. line	Private	70	Somerset	('20) d. March, 1826.
'40	Lombard, Jedediah			81	Cumberland	Res. Standish.
'35d	Lombard, John	Mass. mil		77	Cumberland	
'40	————			80 to 90	Cumberland	Res. Gorham.
'35d	Lombard, John	Mass. line	Private	70	Oxford.	
'40	Lombard, John			76	Cumberland	Res. Otisfield.
'35d	Lombard, Nathaniel	N. H. line	Sergeant & Corp.	76	Somerset	('31 b) Same as Lumbard.
'35d	Lombard, Thomas	Mass. mil	Private	73	Lincoln	
'35d	Lombard, Thomas	Mass. mil	Private	72	Oxford.	
'40	*Longfellow, Mary*			81	Waldo	Res. Palermo.
'35c	Longfellow, Samuel	N. H. line	Private	78	Waldo	('20). d. Feb. 3, 1834.

61

List.	Name.	Service.	Rank.	Age.	County.	Remarks.
'35d	Longley, Asa	Mass. line	Private	72	Somerset	('20).
'40				78	Somerset	Res. Palmyra.
'35c	Longley, Jonathan	Mass. line	Private	72	Oxford	('20) d. March, 1833.
'35c	Longley, Zachariah	Mass. line	Private	78	Penobscot	('20) d. June 28, 1825.
'29	Loomis, Joseph	Conn	Dragoon			
'35c	Loomis, Roger	R. I. line	Private	64	Kennebec	('20) d. Sept. 1822
'40	Lord, Abigail			79	Oxford	Res. Paris.
'35c	Lord, Benjamin	Mass. line	Private	80	Oxford	d. Nov. 15, 1829.
'40	Lord, Daminicus			79	York	Res. Kennebunk.
'35c	Lord, Daniel	Mass. line	Private	76	Hancock	('20).
'35c	Lord, Daniel, 2d	Mass. line	Private	75	York	('20) d. Dec. 15, 1833.
'35c	Lord, Daniel, 3d	N. H. line	Private	70	York	('20).
'35d	Lord, Dominicus	Mass. mil	Private	72	York	Same as Lord, Daminicus.
'35c	Lord, Elias	Mass. line	Private	75	Kennebec	('20).
'35c	Lord, Elisha	Mass. line	Private	56	York	('20).
'40	Lord, Elizabeth			78	York	Res. Lyman.
'40	Lord, Hannah			77	York	Res. Limerick.
'35d	Lord, Ichabod	Mass. line	Private	79	York	('20, '31 b).
'35c	Lord, James	Mass. line	Private	93	Lincoln	d. Feb. 13, 1830.
'35d	Lord, James	Mass. mil	Private	71	Kennebec	
'28	Lord, James	Mass	Lieutenant	—		('20).
'35c	Lord, Joseph	N. H. line	Private	57	York	('20, '31b).
'35d	Lord, Nathan	Mass. line	Private	77	York	('20, '31b) d. Nov. 26, 1833.
'35d	Lord, Richard	Mass. line	Private	77	York	('20, '31b) d. Aug. 25, 1833.
'35d	Lord, Samuel	N. H. state	Private	74	York.	
'40				80	York	Res. Berwick.
'40	Lord, Wentworth			84	York	Res. Parsonsfield. ('20).
'35c	Lord, Wintworth	Mass. line	Private	78	York	Same as preceding.
'35d	Lothrop, Daniel	Mass. mil	Serg. & Lt.	88	Kennebec.	
'35d	Lothrop, Jacob	Mass. mil	Private	72	Oxford	d. Aug. 2, 1833.
'20	Loud, Benjamin	Mass. line	Private			
'35c	Loveland, James	Conn. line	Private	68	Somerset	('20) d. March, 1827.
'35c	Lovell, Josiah	Mass. line	Private	62	Cumberland	('20).
'35d	Lovering, Nathaniel	Mass. mil	Private	72	Kennebec	Same as Levering.
'35c	Low, Bezaleel	Mass. line	Private	70	Somerset	('20).
'35c	Low, John	Mass. line	Captain	75	York	('20).
'40	Low, Mary			80	Lincoln	Res. Bath.
'35c	Low, Phineas	Mass. line	Private	64	York	('20) d. March, 1824.
'35d	Low, Robert	Mass. mil	Private	74	Kennebec.	
'40	Low, Robert			80	Oxford	Res. Livermore.
'35d	Lowe, Jonathan	Mass. line	Private	76	Kennebec	('20 & '31b Low).
'35c	Lowell, Benjamin	Mass. line	Private	—	Hancock	('20).
'35e	Lowell, Benjamin	Crane's art	Matross	—	Hancock.	
'35d	Lowell, John	Mass. line	Private	76	Lincoln.	
'40	Lowell, John			83	Kennebec	Res. Gardiner.
'35c	Lowell, Paul	Mass. line	Private	75	Oxford	('20).
'35c	Lowell, Thomas	Mass. line	Private	74	Penobscot	('20).
'40				78	Penobscot	Res. Dixmont.
'35d	Luce, Seth	Mass. line	Private	82	Lincoln.	
'35c	Luce, Shubael	Mass. line	Private	77	Kennebec	('20, '31b).
'40	Lufkin, Benjamin			78	Oxford	Res. Roxbury. Same as Lupkin, B.
'35d	Lumb, James	Mass. mil	Private	74	Kennebec	Same as Lamb.
'35c	Lumbard, Caleb	Mass. line	Private	69	Oxford	('20) d. Apr. 19, 1833. See also Lombard.
'40	Lumbard, Hannah			68	Oxford	Res. Turner.
'20	Lumbard, Nathaniel	Mass	Sergeant			
'35d	Lunt, Amos	Mass. line	Sergeant & Ens.	81	Cumberland	('20).
'35c	Lunt, Daniel	N. H. line	Private	84	York	('20).
'35d	Lunt, Daniel	Mass. mil	Pvt.&Serg.	72	Cumberland	
'40				78	Cumberland	Res. Falmouth.
'35c	Lunt, Daniel	Mass. line	Captain	68	Cumberland	('20).
'40	Lunt, John			—	Cumberland	Res. New Gloucester.
'35d	Lupkin, Benjamin	Mass. mil	Private	72	Oxford	Same as Lufkin B.
'35c	Lurvey, Jacob	Mass. line	Private	58	Hancock.	
'35d	Lydstow, William	Mass. mil	Private	79	Kennebec.	
'35d	Lyttle, John	Mass. mil	Private	78	Kennebec	Same as Little, J?

List.	Name.	Service.	Rank.	Age.	County.	Remarks.
'35d	McAlester, Richard...	N. H. line.....	Private....	75	Lincoln......	
'40	McAlester, Richard...			or74 78	Waldo......	Res. Montville.
'35c	McCastin, Alexander..	Mass. line.....	Private....	72	Hancock....	
'35c	M'Causland, Henry...	Mass. line.....	Private....	75	Kennebec....	d. Aug. 21, 1829
'35c	McCausland, James...	Mass. line.....	Private....	60	Kennebec....	d. Mar. 4, 1826
'40	McCausland, Mary...			75	Kennebec....	Res. Gardiner
	McCausland, Robert..					s e e Causland, Robert M.
'35c	M'Clellan, John......	N. H. line.....	Private....	74	Penobscot...	Same as Mc-Lellan, J.?
'35c	McClellan, Prince....	Cont. navy....	Seaman...	90	Cumberland.	d. July 19, 1829.
'35c	McCormick, James...	Mass. line.....	Private....	88	Cumberland..	d. Sept. 2, 1829.
'35c	McDaniel, James.....	Mass. line.....	Private....	62	York........	d. Aug. 1821.
'35d	McDaniel, John......	Mass. mil......	Private....	70	Lincoln......	
'40	McDaniel, Susannah..			74	York........	Res. York.
'35c	McDonald, John.....	Mass. line.....	Sergeant...	77	Cumberland.	d.Feb. 8, 1825.
'35c	McDonald, Pelatiah..	Mass. line.....	Private....	80	Cumberland.	
'40				86	Cumberland.	Res. Standish.
'40	McDuffin, David.....			66	Kennebec....	Res. Winthrop
'35d	Mace, Andrew.......	Mass. mil......	Pvt. & Ser.	76	Kennebec....	
'40				83	Kennebec....	Res.Readfield.
'35d	M'Farland, Benjamin.	Mass. line.....	Private....	83	Lincoln......	
'35c	McFarland, Elijah....	Mass. line.....	Private....	77	Somerset....	d. Mar. 1828.
'36c	M'Farland, James....	Mass. line.....	Private....	75	Kennebec....	d.Mar. 3, 1834.
'35c	McFarland, James....	Mass. line.....	Private....	67	Somerset....	d. Mar. 1, 1824.
'35c	McFarland, William..	Mass. line.....	Private....	55	Lincoln......	d. Apr. 2,1823.
'35c	McFarlin, Solomon...	Mass. line.....	Private....	55	Somerset....	
'35c	McGaughlin, William.	Mass. line.....	Private....	66	Cumberland.	d. Feb. 20,1820. See also Mc-Laughlin.
'35c	M'Gee, Neil.........	Mass. line.....	Private....	63	Hancock....	d. Sept. 2, 1825.
'40	McGill, Martha......			85	Cumberland.	Res. Brunswick See also Magill.
'35d	McIntire, Phineas....	Mass. line.....	Private....	82	York........	
'35c	McIntosh, John......	Mass. line.....	Private....	73	Cumberland.	
'35d		Mass. line.....	Private....	78 & 73	Cumberland.	
'40	McKenney, Jonathan.	Mass. line.....	Private....	80	Cumberland.	Res. Scarbor'gh Same as McKinney.
'35d	McKenney, Joseph...	Mass. line.....	Sergeant...	78	Kennebec....	
'40	McKenney, Margaret..			70	Lincoln......	Res. Georgetown.
'40	McKenney, Sarah....			74	York........	Res. Waterborough.
'35c	Mckinney, Isaac......	Mass. line.....	Private....	91	Cumberland.	

List.	Name.	Service.	Rank.	Age.	County.	Remarks.
'35d	McKinney, Jonathan.	Mass. mil.	Private.	72	Cumberland.	Same as McKenney.
'35d	M'Kinney, Robert.	Mass. mil.	Private.	76	Lincoln.	
'35c	McKinney, William.	Mass. line.	Lieutenant	84	Cumberland.	d. Jan. 27, 1823
'35c	McLain, Samuel.	Mass. line.	Private.	80	Lincoln.	
'35c	McLane, Ichabod.	Mass. line.	Private.	89	Kennebec.	
'40	*McLaughlin, Hannah.*			78	Cumberland.	R c s. Scarborough. See also McGaughlin.
'40	McLellan, John.			79	Penobscot.	Res. Glenburn Same as McClellan?
'40	McLellan, John.			74	Cumb.	Res. Portland. 3 d. Ward.
'40	McLellan, William.			80	Cumberland.	Res. Gorham.
'35d	McLelland, William.	Mass. line.	Private.	to90 77	Cumberland.	See also McLellan.
'35d	M'Lure, James.	N. H. line.	Serg. & Pvt	81	Waldo.	
'35c	McMahan, Joseph.	Mass. line.	Private.	73	Lincoln.	d. Aug. 22, 1825.
'35c	McMahon, Daniel.	Mass. line.	Private.	83	Lincoln.	
'35d	M'Manners, Daniel.	Mass. mil.	Private.	68	Lincoln.	
'40	McManus, Daniel.			74	Cumberland.	Res. Brunswick.
'35c	McManus, John.	Mass. line.	Corporal.	75	Cumberland.	
'40	—			80	Cumberland.	Res. Brunswick.
'35d	McMichael, James.	Mass. line.	Private.	73	Lincoln.	
'35c	McMullen, Archibald.	Mass. line.	Private.	61	Hancock.	
'40	McNally, Michael.			88	Kennebec.	Res. Clinton.
'35c	Macomber, South'th.	Mass. line.	Private.	70	Cumberland.	
'35c	Madden, John.	Mass. line.	Private.	77	Hancock.	
'40	Maddin, John.			83	Waldo.	Res. Waldo. Plantation.
'35c	Maddock, Henry.	R. I. line.	Private.	65	York.	d. Aug. 25, 1821.
'35c	Maddocks, Samuel.	Mass. line.	Private.	72	Hancock.	
'40	—			78	Hancock.	Res. Ellsworth.
'35c	Magill, William.	Mass. line.	Private.	81	Cumberland.	d. Sept. 25,1828. See also Mc Gill.
'35d	Main, Amos.	Mass. line.	Sergeant.	84	York.	
'40	Maine, William.			82	Lincoln.	Res. Phipsburg
'35c	Mallet, William.	Mass. line.	Private.	77	Kennebec.	
'40	Mallett, William.			83	Lincoln.	Res. Topsham.
	Maloon, see Baloon.					
'35d	Mann, Amos.	Mass. line.	Private.	72	Penobscot.	
'35d	Mann, David.	Mass. line.	Private.	75	Penobscot.	
'35d	Mann, Joseph.	Mass. mil.	Private.	73	Cumberland.	
'35d	Mann, Oliver.	Mass. line.	Surgeon's mate.	76	Hancock.	
'40	Mann, Robert.			52	Penobscot.	Res. Bangor.
'35d	Mansell, Joseph.	Mass. line.	Serg. & Lt.	84	Penobscot.	
'40				89	Penobscot.	
'35c	Mansfield, JamesM.	Penn. line.	Private.	73	Kennebec.	d. Feb. 22, 1825
'35d	Manson, Thomas.	Mass. mil.	Private.	86	York.	
'40	Manton, Joseph P.			78	Kennebec.	Res. Fayette.
'35c	Marble, John.	N. H. line.	Private.	70	Kennebec.	
'35c	Marble, Samuel.	N. H. line.	Private.	74	Somerset.	
'35d	March, James.	Mass. mil.	Private.	73	York.	
'40	March, Matthias.			80	Cumberland.	Res. Gorham.
'35d	March, William.	Mass. line.	Private.	to90 71	Penobscot.	
'35c	Margary, Jonathan.	Mass. line.	Private.	68	Cumberland.	d. Mar. 5, 1821.
'35c	Marr, James.	Mass. line.	Corporal.	81	York.	
'40	*Marr, Lydia.*			72	York.	Res. So. Berwick.
35'c	Marsdon, Theodore.	N. H. line.	Private.	64	Kennebec.	
'35c	Marsh, Noah.	N. H. line.	Private.	75	Somerset.	d.Oct. 25, 1830.
'35d	Marsh, Stephen.	N. H. State.	Private.	74	York.	
'40				79	York.	Res.Acton.
'40	Marshall, George D.			—	Penobscot.	Res. Bradford.
'35c	Marshall, Benjamin.	Mass. line.	Private.	63	Hancock.	d. March, 1822.
'40	Marshall, Benjamain.			49	Lincoln.	Res. St. George.
'35d	Marston, David.	N. H. line.	Private.	78 & 76	York.	

List.	Name.	Service.	Rank.	Age.	County.	Remarks.
'40				82	Kennebec	Res. Monmouth
'35d	Marston, Joseph	Mass. State	Private	72	Kennebec	
'35c	Marston, Nathaniel	N. H. line	Private	67	Kennebec	d. June 4, 1824.
'35c	Marston, Samuel	N. H. line	Private	74	Washington	
'35c	Martin, David	Mass. line	Private	73	Cumberland	
'40	Martin, Elizabeth			66	Cumberland	Res. Portland. 7th. ward.
'35c	Martin, John	Mass. line	Drummer	72	Cumberland	d. May 23, 1820
'40	Martin, Joseph			79	Waldo	Res. Prospect.
'35c	Martin, Joseph	Cont. line	Prinate	74	Waldo	
'35d	Martin, Nathaniel	Mass. line	Private	88	Penobscot	
'35c	Martin, Robert	Mass. line	Private	81	Cumberland	
'35c	Mason, Broadstreet	N. H. line	Private	64	Waldo	d. June, 1824.
'35d	Mason, Ebenezer	Mass. mil	Private	71	Kennebec	
'40				77	Kennebec	Res. Vienna.
'40	Mason, Eunice			80	Cumberland	Res. Bethel.
'35c	Mason, John	Mass. line	Private	65	Cumberland	Oct. 22, 1824. d.
'35d	Mason, Moses	N. H. mil	Private	77	Oxford	
'35d	Mason, Tilley	Mass. mil	Private	74	Somerset	
'40	Massman, Aaron			82	Lincoln	Res. Thomaston. Same as Moosman.
'35d	Masterson, James	Mass. mil	Pvt. & Sea	75	Oxford	
'35c	Mathews, Daniel 2'd	Mass. line	Private	64	Cumberland	d. Feb. 10, 1823
'40	Mathews, Desire			78	Kennebec	Res. Vassallborough.
'35c	Mathews, John 1st	Mass. line	Private	89	Oxford	d. Jan., 1826.
'35c	Mathews, Daniel	N. H. line	Private	61	Somerset	d. in 1826.
'35c	Mathews, John 2'd	Mass. line	Private	79	York	
'40	Maxfield, Daniel			55	Penobscot	Res. Bradford.
'35c	Maxfield, Robert	Mass. line	Private	74	Cumberland	
'40				78	Cumberland	Res. No. Yarmouth.
'35d	Maxfield, William	Mass. mil	Private	74	Cumberland	
'40	Maxwell, Robert			74	Cumb.	Res. Danville.
'35c	Maxwell, William	Mass. line	Private	8	Kennebec	
'40	Maxwell, William			80	Cumberland	Res. Danville.
'35d	Mayberry, John	Mass. line	Private	70	Cumberland	
'35d	Mayberry, Thomas	Mass. line	Private	74	Cumberland	
'35c	Mayberry, William	Mass. line	Private	75	Cumberland	
'40				82	Cumberland	Res. Raymond.
'40	Mayhew, James			81	Penobscot	Res. Bangor.
'40	Mayhew, James			81	Penobscot	Res. Carmel.
'35c	Mayhue, James	Mass. line	Private	75	Penobscot	Same as Mayheu?
'35c	Mayhue, Joshua	Mass. line	Private	83	Hancock	d. Jan. 11, 1820.
'35d	Maynard, Joseph	Mass. line	Sergeant	76	Somerset	
'40				81	Somerset	Res. Madison.
'35d	Mayo, Isaac	Mass. line	Private	76	Waldo	
'35c	Meader, Francis	Mass. line	Private	87	Somerset	
'40	Means, James			86	Waldo	Res. Brooks.
'35c	Means, James	Mass. line	Captain	65	Cumberland	
'35e		2'd. Regt.	Captain	—	Cumberland	d. Oct. 15, 1832.
'35c	Means, Thomas	1st. Mass. line	Private	72	Kennebec	d. Jan. 5, 1828.
'35d	Meharin, Isaac	Mass. line	Private	72	Oxford	
'35c	Meldrum, John	Mass. line	Private	70	York	d. Dec. 7, 1822.
'35c	Melvin, David	Mass. line	Private	77	Hancock	d. Jan. 20, 1830.
'35c	Melvin, John	Mass. line	Private	85	Kennebec	
'40	Mendum, Anna			81	York	Res. York.
'35c	Mendum, William	Cont. Navy	Mariner	77	York	d. Feb. 18, 1831.
'40	Menow, Margaret			86	Cumberland	Res. Standish. See also Merro.
'40	Merb, Josiah			85	Lincoln	Res. Warren. Same as Mero.
'35c	Merchant, John	Mass. line	Sergeant	67	Kennebec	d. Feb. 5, 1819.
'35d	Mero, Amariah	Mass. line	Sergeant	77	Lincoln	Same as Meso?
'35d	Mero, Josiah	Mass. mil	Private	79	Lincoln	Same as Merb.
'35d	Merrick, John	Mass. line	Pvt. & C'p.	73	Somerset	
'35d	Merrill, Abel	Mass. State	Pvt. & Mus.	78	York	
'40	Merrill, Abner			49	Piscataquis	Res. Parkman.
'35d	Merrill, Amos	Mass. line	Private	82	Cumberland	
'35d	Merrill, Jacob	Mass. line	Private	79	Cumberland	
'35d	Merrill, Jacob	Mass. line	Private	75	York	
'40				84	York	Res. Kennebunkport.
'35d	Merrill, James	Mass. line & mil	Private	73	Cumberland	

List.	Name.	Service.	Rank.	Age.	County.	Remarks.
'40	Merrill, John			81	Cumberland.	Res. Gray.
'40	Merrill, John			80	Lincoln	Res. Lewiston.
'35d	Merrill, Moses	Mass. line	Serg. & Lieut.	90	Cumberland.	
'35d	Merrill, Nathan	Mass. line	Private	82	Cumberland..	
'35d	Merrill, Roger	Mass. State	Private	72	Kennebec	
'40				78	Kennebec	Res. Litchfield.
'35d	Merrill, Samuel	Mass. line	Private	80	York	
'40	Merit, Mary			78	Lincoln	Res. Bremen.
'40	Merit, William			81	Washington..	Residence. Addison.
'35d	Merritt, Jonathan	Mass. State	Private	80	Lincoln	
'35c	Merritt, William	Mass. line	Private	64	Washington..	
'35c	Merrow, William	Mass. line	Private	75	Cumberland.	d. Aug. 2, 1823. See also Merrow
'35c	Meseroe, Solomon	Mass. line	Ensign	77	Cumberland.	
'35c	Meserve, Nathaniel	Mass. line	Private	87	York	d. Jan. 1825.
'40	Meso, Amreah			83	Somerset	Res. Starks. Same as Mero?
'35d	Metcalf, Titus	Mass. State	Private	80	Waldo	
'40				85	Waldo	Res. Appleton.
'35d	Michals, William	Mass. mil	Private	71	Waldo	
'35c	Miller, Asa	Mass. line	Private	85	Somerset	
'35d	Miller, Frank	Mass. State	Private	69	Lincoln	
'40				75	Lincoln	Res. Waldoborough.
'35c	Miller, John	Mass. line	Private	72	York	d. Nov. 28, 1825
'35d	Miller, Lemuel	Mass. line	Lieutenant.	84	York	
'40				89	York	R e s. Kennebunkport.
'40	Miller, Noah			66	Waldo	Res. Lincolnville.
'35c	Millet, John	N. H. line	Private	93	York	
'35c	Millet, Thomas	Cont. Navy	Mariner	87	Kennebec	d. Sept. 6, 1824.
'40	Millett, John			77	York	Res. Kennebunkport.
'35c	Milligin, Joel	Mass. line	Private	72	Cumberland.	
'40	Milliken, John			78	Waldo	Res. Montville. Same as Mulliken.
'35d	Milliken, Joshua	Mass. line	Private	79	Cumberland.	d. Nov. 27, 1832
'35d	Milliken, Lemuel	Mass. line	Serg. & Lt.	86	Cumberland.	
'40	Milliken, Lydia			79	Cumberland.	R e . Scarborough.
'40	Milliken, Margaret			83	Cumberland.	Res. Scarborough.
'35c	Millikin, Abner	Mass. line	Private	78	Hancock	
'35c	Millikin, Josiah	Mass. line	Private	76	Cumberland.	d. Jan. 7, 1832.
'35d	Mills, Phillip	Mass. mil	Private	80	Oxford	
'35d	Mink, John	Mass. mil	Private	71	Lincoln	
'40				77	Lincoln	Res. Waldoborough.
'35d	Mink, Paul	Mass. mil	Private	81	Lincoln	
'35c	Mink, Valentine	Mass. line	Private	80	Kennebec	d. June 19, 1832
'40	Mitchell, Ammi			47	Oxford	Res. Mexico.
35c	Mitchell, James M	Mass. line	Private	74	Lincoln	
'40				80	Lincoln	Res. Bath.
'35c	Mitchell, John	Mass. line	Private	64	Washington..	
'35c	..itchell, Joshua	Mass. line	Private	67	Lincoln	d. Nov. 6, 1826.
'35c	Mitchell, Josiah	Mass. line	Private	70	Kennebec	d. Nov. 12, 1819
'40	Mitchell, Pammey			80	Lincoln	Res. Bath.
'35d	Mitchell, Richard	Mass. mil	Private	76	Cumberland.	
'35c	Mitchell, Samuel	Mass. line	Private	82	Kennebec	
'35c	Mitchell, William	N. H. line	Private	74	York	d. March, 1827.
'35d	Monk, Elias	Mass. mil	Private	73	Oxford	
'40	Monk, Elias			86 or 87	Oxford	Res. Hebron.
'35c	Monroe, Abijah	Mass. line	Private	75	Oxford	
'35c	Monroe, Hugh	Mass. line	Private	66	Lincoln	d. June 22, 1832
'35d	Moody, Edward	N. H. line	Private	76	Somerset	
'35c	Moody, George	Mass. line	Private	73	York	
'35d	Moody, John	Mass. line	Pvt. & Co'p	82	Lincoln	
'40	Moody, John			59	Kennebec	Res. Monmouth
'35c	Moody, Joshua	Mass. line	Private	82	Cumberland.	d. Dec. 28, 1828
'40	Moody, Lucy			76	Cumberland.	Res. Minot.
'40	Moody, Rebecca			83	Cumberland.	Res. Sebago.
'35d	Moody, Samuel	Mass. State	Fifer&Serg.	76	Kennebec	

List.	Name.	Service.	Rank.	Age.	County.	Remarks.
'35c	Moore, Benjamin...	N. H. line.....	Private....	69	York........	d. May 14, 1826.
'35c	Moore, Edward....	Mass. line......	Private....	68	York........	d. Sept. 1826.
'40	Moore, Elizabeth....			77	York........	Res. Biddeford.
'35d	Moore, Goff.......	N. H. line.....	Private....	73	Kennebec.	
'35d	Moore, Isaac.......	N. H. line.....	Private....	80	Lincoln.	
'40	———			88	Lincoln......	Res. Edgecomb.
'35c	Moore, James......	N. H. line.....	Private....	73	Kennebec.	
'35c	Moore, John.......	Mass. line......	Private....		York.	
'35c	Moore, Joshua.....	Mass. line.....	Private....	77	Kennebec.	
'40	Moore, Josiah......			80	Washington..	Res. Addison.
'35d	Moore, Nathaniel...	Mass. line.....	Private....	74	Penobscot.	
'40	Moore, Nathaniel...			84	Lincoln......	Edgecomb.
'35c	Moore, Pelatiah....	Mass. line.....	Private....	82	York.	
'35c	Moores, David.....	Cont. Navy...	Mariner...	73	Kennebec.	
'40	Moores, David.....			84	Kennebec....	Res. Pittston.
'35c	Moores, Jonathan..	Mass. line.....	Private....	64	Cumberland.	
'35d	Moores, Peter......	Mass. mil......	Private....	82	Kennebec.	
'35d	Moores, Samuel....	Mass. mil......	Private....	86	Kennebec.	
'35d	Moosman, Aaron...	Mass. line.....	Private....	78or 76	Lincoln.....	Same as Massman
'35c	Morgan, Jonathan..	N. H. line.....	Private....	83	Kennebec....	d. Dec. 2, 1831.
'40	Morr. Mary......			97	Cumberland.	Res. Freeport.
'35c	Morrill, Jacob......	N. H. line.....	Private....	78	Hancock....	d. Dec. 15, 1830.
'35c	Morrill, Moses.....	Mass. line.....	Private....	77	Cumberland.	d. Oct. 27, 1823.
'40	Morrill, Stephen....			65	Kennebec....	Res. Rome
35c	Morris, William....	Cont. Navy....	Lieutenant.	66	York........	d. Dec. 20, 1822.
'35d	Morrison, James....	N. H. line.....	Private....	81	York.	
'35c	Morrison, Moses...	Mass. line.....	Private....	78	Lincoln.	
'40	———			84	Lincoln......	Res. Phipsburg.
'35d	Morrison, William..	Mass. mil......	Private....	75	Kennebec.	
'35c	Mors, Mark.......	Mass. line.....	Private....	70	York.	
'40	Morse, Daniel......			94	Lincoln......	Res. Phipsburg.
'35d	Morse, Daniel......	Mass. State....	Private....	86	Lincoln.	
'40	Morse, David......			79	Somerset....	Res. Lexington.
'35d	Morse, Eliphalet...	Mass. line.....	Private....	79	Oxford.	
'35d	Morse, Enoch......	Mass. line.....	Pvt. of art	71	Cumberland.	
'35c	Morse, Isaac.......	N. H. line.....	Private....	84	Kennebec.	
'35c	Morse, Jacob......	N. H. line.....	Fifer......	69	Kennebec.	
'40	———			75	Kennebec....	Res. Sidney.
'35d	Morse, Jonathan...	Mass. mil......	Private....	79	Lincoln.	
'35c	Morse, Josiah......	Mass. line	Private....	60	Penobscot...	d. June 2, 1824.
'35d	Morse, Levi, 2d....	Mass. mil......	Private....	73	Lincoln.	
'40	———			78	Lincoln......	Res. Union.
'35d	Morse, Levi........	Mass. line.....	Private....	72	Cumberland.	

List.	Name.	Service.	Rank.	Age.	County.	Remarks.
'35d	Morse, Philip	Mass. line & State	Private	79	Kennebec.	
'40				85	Kennebec	Res. Fayette.
'35d	Morse, Seth	Mass. mil	Pvt. & Corp	70	Oxford.	
'40				76	Oxford	Res. Paris.
'35d	Morse, William	Mass. line	Private	73	Kennebec.	
'40	Morton, Benjamin			55	Cumberland.	Res. Standish.
'35c	Morton, David	Mass. line	Private	60	Cumberland.	
'35d	Morton, James	Mass. line	Private	83	Cumberland.	
'35d	Morton, Thomas	Mass. line	Private	70	Cumberland.	
'40				70 to 80	Cumberland.	Res. Gorham.
'35c	Moses, Daniel	Mass. line	Sergeant	72	Cumberland.	d. Feb. 8, 1824
'35d	Moses, Josiah	Mass. line	Private	78	Cumberland.	
'35d	Moulton, Daniel	Mass. line	Private	82	York.	
'35d	Moulton, David	N. H. line	Pvt. & Serg	80	York.	
'35d	Moulton, David	N. H. mil	Private	74	Oxford.	
'35d	Moulton, Joseph	Mass. State	Private	75	Cumberland.	
'40	Moulton, Joseph			83	Cumberland.	Res. Scarborough.
'35d	Moulton, Simeon	N. H. line	Private	73	York.	
'40	Mountfort, Elizabeth			72	Cumberland.	Res. Portland. 1st. Ward.
'35d	Mowen, Samuel	Mass. mil	Private	73	Kennebec	Same as Mower.
'35d	Mower, John	Mass. mil	Private	75	Kennebec.	
'40				81	Kennebec	Res. Greene.
'40	Mower, Samuel			79	Kennebec	Res. Greene. Same as Mower.
'35c	Mudget, John	N. H. line	Sergeant	84	Somerset.	
'35c	Mugford, John	Mass. line	Private	67	Cumberland.	
'40	Mugford, John			79	Cumberland.	Res. Windham.
'40	Mulikin, Edward			71	Kennebec	Res. Sidney.
'40	Mulligan, Patrick			52	Washington.	Res. Eastport.
'35d	Mulliken, Edward	Mass. mil	Private	68	Kennebec.	
'35d	Mulliken, John	Mass. mil	Private	72	Waldo	Same as Milliken.
'40	Mun, Joseph			79	Cumberland.	Res. Freeport.
'35c	Murch, Matthias	Mass. line	Private	75	Cumberland.	
'35d	Murdock, James	Mass. line	Private	80	Cumberland.	
'40	Murdock, James			83	Cumberland.	Res. Minot.
'35c	Murphy, Pierce	Cont. Navy	Marine	82	York.	
'35c	Murphy, Thomas	1st Conn. line	Private	88	Washington.	d. June 1, 1825.
'35d	Murphy, Thomas	Cont. Navy	Mariner	78	York.	
'40	Murray, Cotton				Cumberland	Res. Cumberland.
'35d	Murray, William	Mass. line	Private	75	York	d. Sept. 14, 1833.
'40	Nasan, Betsey			81	York	Res. S. Berwick.
'35d	Nash, Jonathan	Mass. mil	Pvt. & Serg.	81	Cumberland.	
'40				87	Cumberland.	Res. Minot.
'35d	Nason, Edward	Mass. line	Private	78	York	See also Nasar.
'40	Nason, Edward			85	York.	Res. Kennebunk- port.
'35d	Nason, John	Mass. mil	Private	74	Waldo	See also Nayson.
'35c	Nason, Jonathan	Mass. line	Private	93	York	d. Mar. 8, 1831.
'35c	Nason, Nathaniel	Mass. line	Captain	73	York	d. July 27, 1818.
'40	Nayson, John			84	Waldo	Res. Hope.
'40	Neal Isaac			58	Waldo	Res. Belmont.
'35c	Neal, John	N. H. line	Ord. serg	91	Lincoln.	
'35d	Neal, Walter	Mass. mil	Private	76	York	d. Aug. 12, 1833.
'35d	Neale, Thomas	Mass. line	Private	80	Kennebec.	
'40	Nealey, Benjamin			51	York	Res. S. Berwick.
'35d	Needham, John	Mass. line	Private	75	Oxford.	
'40	Needham, Mary			75	Oxford	Res. Norway.
'35c	Nelson, Daniel	Cont. Navy	Mariner	73	Somerset.	
'40	Nelson, Nason			80	Oxford	Res. Oxford.
'35d	Nelson, Nathan	Mass. mil	Private	74	Oxford.	
'35d	Nowbegin, George	Mass. line	Private	71	York.	
'40				76	York	Res. Parsonsfield.
'35c	Newell, Jonathan	Mass. line	Captain	74	York	d. Jan. 5, 1821.
'35d	Newell, Zachariah	Mass. line and mil.	Sergeant	65 or 83	Cumberland.	
'35c	Newman, Ebenezer	Mass. line	Private	78	Oxford.	
'35d	Newman, Josiah	Mass. mil	Pvt. Serg. & Corp.	76	Oxford.	
'35d	Nicholls, John	Mass. mil	Private	75	Kennebec	d. May 12, 1833.
'35c	Nichols, Bela	Mass. line	Lieutenant	77	Hancock	See also Nickels.
'40	Nichols, Estor			78	Lincoln	Res. Georgetown.
'40	Nichols, John			81	Lincoln	Res. Bristol.
'35c	Nichols, John	N. H. line	Private	66	Lincoln	d. in Jan. 1825.
'35c	Nichols, Nathaniel	R. I. line	Private	80	Waldo.	

List.	Name.	Service.	Rank.	Age.	County.	Remarks.
'35c	Nichols, Samuel....	Cont. Navy....	Musician..	70	Hancock....	d. in 1826.
'35c	Nicholson, Luke....	Mass. line.....	Private....	83	Cumberland.	d. May 4, 1829.
35d	Nickells, William...	Mass. mil......	Sergeant...	83	Lincoln......	d. Aug. 19, 1832.
'40	Nickerson, ———			82	Waldo......	Res. Frankfort.
'35c	Nickerson, Moses...	Mass. line.....	Private....	70	Hancock....	
'40	Nickerson, Moses...			81	Kennebec....	Res. Readfield.
'35c	Nickerson, Paul....	Mass. line.....	Private....		Penobscot.	
'35c	Nickerson, Reuben.	Mass. line.....	Private....	74	Penobscot...	d. Aug. 17, 1821.
'35c	Noble, Anthony....	Mass. line.....	Private....	64	Cumberland.	d. Mar. 2, 1826.
'35c	Noble, John.......	Del. line.......	Private....	76	Washington..	
'40	Noble, John.......			78	Washington..	Res. Calais.
'35d	Noble, Stephen.....	Mass. mil......	Private & Mariner.	77	York.	
'35d	Nook, Jonathan.....	N. H. line.....	Private....	76	York.	
'35	Nocke, Sylvanus...	N. H. line.....	Private....	76	York.	
'35c	Norman, John.....	Mass. line.....	Private....	81	York........	d. May 19, 1820.
'40	Norris, James F....			67	Kennebec....	Res. Monmouth.
'40	Norris, Ruth......			74	Kennebec....	Res. Monmouth.
'40	Norton, Elihu......			53	Franklin.....	Res. Farmington.
'35d	Norton, Elijah.....	Mass. line.....	Pvt. of art.	75	Lincoln.	
'35c	Norton, Joseph.....	Mass. line.....	Private....	82	Kennebec....	d. Oct. 7, 1822.
'35c	Norton, Josiah.....	Mass. line.....	Private....	86	Waldo.	
'40	Norton, Mary......			73	Lincoln......	Res. Cushing.
'35c	Norton, Nathaniel..	Mass. line.....	Private....	64	York.	
'35d	Norton, Nathaniel..	Mass. mil......	Mariner...	72	Lincoln.	
'40				79	Lincoln......	Res. Wiscasset.
'35d	Norton, Noah.....	Mass. State...	Private & Coporal	86	Hancock.	
'40	Norton, Noah.....			92	Waldo......	Res. Montville.
'35d	Norton, Samuel....	Mass. State...	Artificer...	77	York.	
'35d	Norton, Stephen....	Mass. line.....	Private....	77	Lincoln.	
'35c	Norwood, Moses...	Mass. line.....	Private....	75	Washington..	d. Dec. 9, 1833.
'35d	Nowell, Mark......	Mass. line.....	Private & Musician	72	York.	
'35c	Nowell, Paul.......	Mass. line.....	Private....	82	Lincoln.	
'35c	Noyes, Bela.......	Mass. line.....	Private....	63	Oxford......	d. Aug. 21, 1833.
'35d	Noyes, John.......	Mass.line.....	Private....	79	Cumberland.	
'35d	Noyes, Timothy....	N. H. mil ...	Pvt.&Corp		Cumberland.	Residence N. H. Paid in Portland.
'35c	Nutting, Abel......	Mass. line.....	Private....	67	Lincoln......	d. Sept. 4, 1827.
'35c	Nutting, Thomas...	Mass. line.....	Private....	69	Kennebec.	
'35d	Nye, Elisha........	Mass. line.....	Lieutenant & Captian.	or68 74	Kennebec.	
'35d	Nye, Jonathan.....	Mass. line.....	Private & Sergeant...	80 or76	Somerset.	
'35c	Oaks, John........	Mass. line.....	Private....	80	Penobscot.	
'35c	Oaks, Joshua.......	N. H. line.....	Musician .	74	Hancock.	
'40	Oaks, Joshua......			81	Washington..	Res. Lubec.
'35d	O'Brien, John......	Mass. line.....	Private....	73	York.	
'40	O'Brion, John......			78	York........	Res. Cornish. Same as preceding
'35c	Odiorne, Samuel....	Cont. Navy....	Seaman...	76	Lincoln.	
'35d	Oliver, David......	Mass. state....	Private of . Art.	75	Lincoln.	
'35d	Oliver, Henry......	Mass. state.....	Private of Art........	79	Lincoln.	
'35d	Oliver, John........	Mass. state.....	Private....	78	Lincoln......	d. May 7, 1834.
'35d	Oliver, Jonathan...	Mass. line.....	Private....	84	Lincoln.	
'40	Oliver, Mary.......			70	Lincoln......	Res. Georgetown.
'35c	Oliver, Thomas.....	Mass. line.....	Sergeant...	83	Lincoln.	
'35d	Oliver, William.....	Mass. state.....	Private....	79	Lincoln.	
'35c	O'Rian, John......	Mass. line.....	Private....	98	York........	d. Dec. 28, 1822.
'35d	Osborn, James.....	Mass. line.....	Private....	75	York.	
'35c	Osborn, Michael....	Mass. line.....	Private....	73	Lincoln.	
'35c	Osbourne, Hugh....	Cont. navy.....	Mariner...	72	Kennebec.	
'35d	Osgood, Asa.......	Mass. line.....	Sergt. Maj.	79	Oxford.	
'35c	Osgood, Chri'o'nr..	Mass. line.....	Private....	72	Penobscot...	d. July 31, 1823.
'35d	Oshee, Joseph......	Mass. state.....	Lieutenant	88	Lincoln.	
'40	Ott, Beulah........			82	Lincoln......	Res. Thomaston.
'40	Ott, Beulah........			82	Waldo......	Res. Camden.
'35d	Overlock, Charles...	Mass. state.....	Private....	74	Lincoln.	
'35d	Owen, Hugh.......	Mass. state.....	Private....	66	Lincoln.	
'40	Owen, Hugh.......			71	Kennebec....	Res. Wales.
35d	Owen, Philip.......	Mass. line.....	Private....	78	Cumberland.	
'40				84	Cumberland.	Res. Brunswick.
'35c	Paccard, Daniel....	Mass. line.....	Private....	84	York.	

List.	Name.	Service.	Rank.	Age.	County.	Remarks.
'35c	Packard, David	Mass. line	Private	79	Lincoln,	D. Feb. 9, 1833.
'35c	Packard, James	Conn. line	Private	76	Oxford	
'40	Packard, James			82	Waldo	Res. Unity.
'35d	Packard, Job	Mass. mil	Private	72	Oxford.	
'40				77	Oxford	Res. Buckfield.
'35c	Packard, Jonathan	Mass. line	Private	71	Oxford	d. Aug 30, 1825.
'40	Packard, Nehemiah			74	Cumberland.	Res. Minot.
'35c	Page, Abraham	N. H. line	Sergeant	64	Kennebec	d. Mar. 6, 1822.
'35c	Page, Caleb	Mass. line	Private	70	Kennebec.	
'35c	Page, Chase	N. H. line	Private	65	Penobscot	d. May 1825.
'35c	Page, Edward	N. H. line	Private	77	York.	
'35d	Page, Enoch	N. H. line	Private & Sergeant	90	Somerset	d. Nov. 22, 1832.
'35d	Page, Nathan	Mass. mil	Private	71	Waldo.	
'35c	Page, Philip	Mass. line	Private	72	Oxford.	
'35c	Page, William	Mass. line	Private	84	Lincoln	d. Jan. 9, 1821.
'35d	Paine, Thomas	Mass. line	Sergeant	78	Cumberland	
'40				84	Cumberland.	Res. Pownal.
'40	Pallman, Peleg			77	Lincoln	Res. Bath.
'35c	Palmer, Bezaleel	Mass. line	Private	64	Lincoln	
'35c	Palmer, Jenkins	Mass. line	Private	78	Washington.	
'35c	Palmer, John	Mass. line	Private	80	Kennebec.	
'35c	Palmer, Nathaniel	Mass. line	Private	76	Lincoln.	
'35d	Palmer, Nathaniel	Mass. line	Private	76	Lincoln.	
'40	Palmer, Sarah			80	Lincoln	Res. Bremen.
'35c	Palmer, Simeon	N. H. line	Private	83	Kennebec.	
'40	Palmer, Simeon			79	Kennebec	Res. Windsor.
'35c	Parcher, George	Mass. line	Private	81	Kennebec	d. Apr. 16, 1831.
'35	Parker, Aaron	Mass. mil	Private	75	Cumberland.	
'40d				81	Cumberland.	Res. Standish.
'35c	Parker, Barnabas	Mass. line	Private	77	Kennebec.	
'35d	Parker, Benjamin	Mass. mil	Private & Sergeant	85	Kennebec.	
'35c	Parker, Daniel	Mass. line	Private	68	Lincoln	d. in 1822.
'35c	Parker, Ebenezer	Mass. line	Private	94	Somerset.	
'35d	Parker, Edmund	Mass. line	Private	73	Somerset.	
'40	Parker, Fred G			85	Hancock	Res. Bucksport.
'35d	Parker, Freegrove	Mass. mil	Private	79	Hancock.	
'35d	Parker, Josiah	Mass. line	Private	79	Somerset.	
'40	Parker, Josiah			75	Waldo.	
'35d	Parker, Josiah			76	Somerset	Res. N. Portland.
'35d	Parker, William	Mass. mil	Private	81	Somerset.	
'35c	Parkhurst, George	Mass. line	Private	79	Lincoln	d. Nov. 21, 1830.
'35c	Parkman, Daniel	Mass. line	Private	81	Somerset	d. Oct. 1824.
'35c	Parlin, Ebenezer	Mass. line	Private	76	Somerset.	
'40	Parlin, Eleazer			83	Franklin	Res. Freeman.
'35d	Parris, Josiah	Mass. line	Private & Sergeant	73	Oxford.	
'40	Parris, Josiah			75	Oxford	Res. Buckfield.
'35d	Parris, Samuel	Mass. state	Lieutenant & Serge a n	78	Oxford.	
'35d	Parsons, Eleazer	Mass. mil	Private	72	Oxford.	
'40				79	Oxford	Res. Buckfield.
'35c	Parsons, Josiah	Mass. line	Private	70	Lincoln	d. Aug. 31, 1826.
'35c	Parsons, Nathan	Mass. line	Ensign	73	Penobscot	d. in 1824.
'35c	Parsons, Nathaniel	N. H. line	Private	78	Penobscot.	
'40	Parsons Thom s B.			51	Cumberland	Res. Portland 6th Ward.
'35c	Partridge, David	Mass. line	Private	87	Cumberland.	
'40	Partridge, Mary			90	Cumberland.	Res. Poland.
'35c	Patch, John	Mass. line	Private	85	York	d. July 29, 1828.
'40	Patten, Benjamin			80	Somerset	Res. Solon.
'35e	Patten, James, alias Underwood Edward	Mass. line	Private		Lincoln..	
'35c	Patten, Nathaniel	Mass. line	Sergeant	73	Penobscot.	
'40				79	Hancock	Res. Penobscot.
'35c	Patterson, Adam	N. H. line	Private	85	Hancock	d. Feb. 8, 1827.
'35d	Patterson, Alexander	Mass. mil	Private	81	Washington.	
'40	Patterson, Mary			90	Waldo	Res. Belfast.
'35d	Patterson, William	Mass. mil	Private & Seaman	83	Lincoon.	
'35c	Pattin, John	Mass. line	Private	68	Penobscot	d. Dec. 22, 1820.
'35c	Paul, David	Mass. line	Private	70	Lincoln.	
'40	Paul, David			79	Lincoln	Res. Lewiston.
'35d	Paulson, Nathan	Mass. mil	Private	84	Somerset	d. Dec. 18, 1833.
'35d	Payne, John	Mass. mil	Private	79	York.	

List.	Name.	Service.	Rank.	Age.	County.	Remarks.
'35c	Payne, William	Mass. line	Private	76	Somerset.	
'35c	Payson, Ephraim	Mass. line	Private	80	Waldo.	
'35c	Payson, Samuel	Mass. line	Captain	85	Lincoln	d. June 19, 1819.
'35c	Payson, Samuel	Mass. line	Private	72	Lincoln.	
'40	Paysons, Samuel			79	Lincoln	Res. Cushing. Same as Payson
'40	Peabody, Charles			44	Penobscot	Res. Dixmont.
'35c	Peabody, Seth	Mass. line	Sergeant	70	Kennebec	d. Jan. 24, 1828.
'35c	Pearce, James	Mass. line	Private	59	Lincoln.	
'35d	Pearcy, Stephen	Mass. line	Private	84	Oxford.	
'40	Pearl, John			41	Oxford	Res. Porter.
'35c	Pearson, Mark	Mass. line	Private	63	Kennebec	d. Jan. 21, 1821.
'35c	Pease, Samuel	N. H. line	Drum. maj.	80	York.	
'35d	Pease, Zebulon	Mass. mill.	Private	73	York.	
'40	Peavy, John S			44	Penobscot	Res. Exeter.
'35c	Peavy, Winthrop	N. H. line	Private	68	Kennebec.	
'35d	Peck, George	R. I. state	Captain & Lieut. Col.	96	Washington.	
'35c	Peck, Joshua	Mass. line	Private	74	Kennebec	
'35d	Peebles, William W.	Mass. mil.	Private	69	Cumberland.	
'35c	Pelton, Joel	Mass. line	Private	78	Oxford.	
'40	Pelton, Joel			83	Franklin	Res. Madrid.
'40	Pendexter, Thomas			68	York	Res. Parsonsfield. See also Pindexter.
'35d	Pengree, Stephen	Mass. mil.	Private	81	Oxford.	
'35d	Penley, Joseph	Mass. mil.	Pvt. & Serg	78	Cumberland.	
'40				83	Cumberland.	Res. Danville.
'35d	Pennell, Joseph	Mass. mil.	Pt. & Crop.	87	Cumberland.	
'35c	Penney, John	Mass. line	Private	74	Kennebec	
'35c	Penney, Salathiel	Mass. line	Private	81	Kennebec.	
'50	Penney, Salathiel			83	Kennebec	Res. Waterville.
'35d	Penny, Benjamin	Mass. line	Private	79	York.	
'40	Penny, Benjamin			79	York	Res. Wells.
'35d	Perkins, Abner	Mass. mill.	Private	72	Lincoln.	
'35d	Perkins, Daniel	Mass. state	Private	76	York.	d. July 31, 1832.
'40	Perkins, Ebenezer			83	Oxford	Res. Hebron.
'35d	Perkins, Enoch	Mass. mil.	Musician	72	Cumberland.	
'35c	Perkins, James	Mass. line	Private	63	Lincoln.	
'35d	Perkins, Joseph	Mass. line	Private	..	Oxford.	
'40	Perkins, Mehitable			70	Oxford	Res. Paris.
'40	Perkins, Oliver			42	York	Res. Kennebunk.
'35d	Perkins, Pelatiah	Mass. mil.	Private	80	York.	
'40				86	York	Res. York.
'40	Perkins, Sarah			77	Oxford	Res. Oxford.
'35c	Perkins, William	Mass. line	Private	61	York.	
'35d	Perley, Daniel	Mass. mil.	Pvt. of art.	83	Cumberland.	
'35d	Perry, David	Mass. mil.	Pvt. of art.	73	Lincoln.	
'40				77	Lincoln	Res. Richmond.
'35d	Perry, James	Mass. state	Pvt., Corp & Serg	76	Oxford.	
'35c	Perry, Jesse	Mass. line	Private	75	Washington	d. Dec. 18, 1832.
'35d	Perry, Job	Mass. mil.	Private	68	Lincoln.	
'40				75	Lincoln	Res. Thomaston.
'35d	Perry, Joseph	Mass. line	Private	74	Lincoln.	
'40				79	Lincoln	Res. Thomaston.
'35c	Perry, Reuben	Mass. line	Private	69	Oxford.	
'35c	Peterson, Andrew	Mass. line	Private	72	Oxford.	
'40	Peterson, Joseph			57	Oxford	Res. Dixfield & Peru.
'35d	Pettingall, Obadiah	Mass. line	Pvt. & Serg	72	Kennebec	Same as Pettingill, O.
'35d	Pettingell, Matthew	Cont. navy	Mariner	79	Kennebec.	
'35d	Pettingell, William	Mass. state	Private	74	Kennebec	Same as Pettingill, W.
'40	Pettingill, Obadiah			78	Kennebec	Res. Leeds. Same as Pettingall.
'40	Pettingill, William			80	Kennebec	Res. Leeds. Same as Pettingell.
'35c	Phelps, Samuel	N. H. line	Private	62	Oxford	
'40	Philbric, Nathaniel			47	Oxford	Res. Roxbury.
'35c	Philbrook, David	Mass. line	Private	99	Kennebec	d. Feb. 17, 1831.
'35d	Philbrook, William	Mass. state	Private	75	Waldo.	
'40				80	Waldo.	Res. Thorndike.
'35c	Philbrook, William	Cont. navy	Marine	77	Hancock	d. Nov. 2, 1829.
'40	Phillips, Abigail			84	Oxford	Res. Turner.
'35c	Phillips, Ichabod	Mass. line	Private	55	Kennebec.	

List.	Name.	Service.	Rank.	Age.	County.	Remarks.
'35c	Phillips, Jarius	Mass. line	Private	64	Kennebec.	
'35d	Ph llips, John	Mass. line	Private	87	Penobscot.	
'35d	Philips, Norton	Mass. line	Private	84	York.	
'40	*Phillips, Silence*			74	Oxford	Res. Turner
'35d	Phinney, Ithamar	Mass. line	Private	69	Oxford	
'35c	Phinney, John	Mass. line	Private	72	York.	
'40	Phinney, John			70to 80	Cumberl'd	Res. Gorham
'35d	Pickett, William	Mass. line	Private	69	York.	
'40	Pickett, William			76	Cumberland.	New Gloucester.
'40	*Pierce, Abigail*			60	Hancock	Res. Sullivan.
'35d	Pierce, Benjamin	Mass. state	Private	74	York.	
'35c	Pierce, David	Mass. line	Private	83	Somerset.	
'40	*Pierce, Hannah*			81	York	Res. So.'Berwick
'35c	Pierce, James	Mass. line 8th. Regiment.			Lincoln.	
'35c	Pierce, John	Mass. line	Corporal	72	York.	
'35c	Pierce, Lemuel	Mass. line	Private	64	Lincoln	d. Sept. 22, 1818.
'35d	Pierce, Nathaniel	Mass. state	Private	83	Penobscot.	
'40	Pierce, Nathaniel			92	Penobscot	Res. Orrington.
'40	Pierce, Peace			69	York	Res. Sou. Berwick
'35d	Pike, Dudley	N. H. mil.	Private	71	Oxford.	
'35d	Pillsbury, Joseph	Mass. mil.	Private	81	Cumberland.	
'40				84	Cumberland.	Res. Scarborough
'35c	Pindexter, Paul	Mass. line	Private	71	York	See also Poudexter
'35d	Pinkham, Calvin	R. I. line	Private	79	Lincoln	
'35d	Pinkham, Nathaniel	Mass. line	Private	82	Lincoln.	
'35d	Piper, John	Mass. line	Private	73	Somerset.	
'40				79	Somerset	Res. Madison.
'35d	Pitts, Seth	Mass. mil.	Pvt. & Serg	76	Kennebec.	
'40				82	Kennebec	Res. Augusta.
'35d	Pitts, Shubael	Mass. state	Private	69	Kennebec.	
'40				74	Kennebec	Res. Augusta.
'35c	Pittsbury, Nathan	Mass. line	Private	68	Lincoln.	
'35c	Place, Amos	Mass. line	Private	78	York.	
'35d	Plaisted, John	Mass. line	Private	78	Cumberland.	
'35d	Plaisted, John	Mass. line	Private	75	Cumberland.	
'40	*Plaisted, Lydia*			72	Cumberland.	Res. Standish.
'40	Plaisted, Roger			86	York	Res. Buxton.
'35c	Plummer, Daniel	Mass. line	Private	75	Cumberland.	
'40	Plummer, Daniel			85	Waldo	Res. Palermo.
'35c	Plummer, Edward	Mass. line	Musician	76	Kennebec.	
'40	Plummer, Edward			86	Kennebec	Res. Albion.
'35c	Plummer, Isaac	Mass. line	Private	74	Cumberland.	
'40	Plummer, Isaac			56	Piscataquis	Res. Guilford.
'35c	Plummer, John	Mass. line	Private	80	Oxford.	
'35c	Plummer, John	Mass. line	Private	76	Waldo.	
'40	Plummer, John			69	Waldo	Res. Freedom.
'35c	Plummer, Joseph	Mass. line	Private	63	Cumberland.	
'35c	Plummer, William	N. H. line	Private	78	Cumbérland.	
'35c	Poland, Moses	Mass. line	Sergeant	81	Oxford	d. Jan. 28, 1821.
'35c	Poland, Seward	Mass. line	Private	76	Lincoln	d. June 19, 1831.
'35c	Poleresky, John	deLouzen's	Corps Maj.	71	L ncoln	d. June 8, 1830.
'35c	Pollard, Barton	N. H. line	Sergeant	75	Kennebec.	
'35c	Pollard, Jonathan	Mass. line	Private	65	Cumberland.	d. May 6, 1824.
'35c	Pollard, Timothy	N. H. line	Private	82	Somerset	d. in 1822.
'35c	Pompilley, Bennet	Mass. line	Private	70	Oxford.	
'35d	Pompilley, Bennet	Mass. line	Pvt. &Serg.	74	Oxford	See also Pumpilly
'40	Pomroy, Joseph			67	Penobscot	Res. Levant.
'35c	Pool, Job	Mass. line	Private	71	Cumberland.	
'40				76	Cumberland.	Res. Falmouth.
'35d	Pool, Joshua	Mass. mil.	Private	73	Oxford.	
'40				78	Oxford	Res. Greenwood.
'35d	Pool, Samuel	Mass. line	Pvt. &Serg.	72	Kennebec.	
'35c	Pool, Thomas	Mass. line	Sergeant	79	Cumberland.	d. Mar. 4, 1824.
'35c	Poole, Abijah	Mass. line	Lieutenant	78	Kennebec	d. May 9, 1820
'35c	Pope, Isaac	Mass. line	Captain	74	York	d. June 1820.
'35c	Porter, Benjamin J.	Mass. line	Surgeon's Mate	56	Lincoln	(35c Benj. Jones.
'40	Porter, Benjamin J.			77	Waldo	Res. Camden.
'35c	Porter, Frederick	R. I. line	Private	73	Kennebec	d. Sept. 1824.
'35c	Porter, Moses	Mass. line	Ensign	82	Kennebec.	
'35d	Porter, Nehemiah	N. H. line	Private	76	Cumberland	
'40				83	Cumberland.	Res. North Yarmouth.
'35d	Porter, Tyler	Mass. mil.	Private	76	Cumberland.	
'40				83	Cumberland.	Res. Sebago.

List.	Name.	Service.	Rank.	Age.	County.	Remarks.
'40	Porterfield, Cath'ine			84	Cumberland.	Res. Westbrook.
'35d	Porterfield, John...	Mass. line.....	Private....	76	Cumberland.	
'35c	Potter, Hugh......	Mass. line.....	Private....	70	Kennebec.	
'40	Potter, Hugh......			78	Kennebec....	Res. Gardiner.
'35c	Potter, James......	Mass. line.....	Private....	78	Lincoln.	
'40	Potter, James......			88	Lincoln......	Res. Bowdoin.
'35c	Potter, Oliver......	Mass. line.....	Private....	75	Washington..	d. Aug. 23, 1831.
'35c	Potter, William....	Mass. line.....	Private....	77	Lincoln......	d. Aug. 11, 1829.
'35d	Prastoe, Jonathan..	Mass. line.....	Pvt.& Serg.	79	Lincoln.	
'35c	Pratt, Benjamin....	Mass. line.....	Private....	68	Kennebec. ..	d. Sept. 8, 1825.
'35d	Pratt, Cushing.....	Mass. line.....	Private....	74	Cumberland.	d. May 14, 1833.
'35d	Pratt, Dan........	R. I. state.....	Private....	72	Oxford.	
'40				79	Oxford......	Res. Turner.
'35d	Pratt, Elam........	Mass. mil......	Pvt.& Serg.	82	Kennebec.	
'35c	Pratt, George......	Mass. line.....	Private....	70	Somerset.	
'40	Pratt, George......			76	Franklin.....	Res. Salem.
'35d	Pratt, Joseph......	Mass. mil......	Pvt. &Serg.	75	Kennebec.	
'40	Pratt, Joseph......			82	Somerset....	Res. Palmyra.
'40	Pratt, Lydia......			78	Somerset....	Res. Bloomfield.
'35c	Pratt, Seth 2nd.....	Mass. line.....	Private....	75	Hancock.	
'35c	Pratt, Seth........	Mass. line.....	Private....	71	Kennebec.	
'35d	Pratt, Solomon.....	Mass. mil......	Pvt. & Mat ross......	80	Somerset....	d. Feb. 6, 1832.
'35c	Pratt, Thaddeus....	Mass. line.....	Private....	79	Oxford.	
'40				85	Oxford......	Res. Buckfield.
'35c	Pray, Abraham.....	Mass. line.....	Private....	81	Kennebec.	
'40	Pray, Abraham.....			79	Kennebec...'.	Res. Hallowell.
'35d	Pray, Peter........	Mass. line.....	Pvt. &Serg.	87	York.	
35d	Pray, Samuel.......	Mass. line.....	Private....	79	York.	
'40	Pray, Sarah.......			74	Somerset....	Res. Chandlerville
'40	Preble, Mary.......			65	Cumberland.	Res. Portland 5th. Ward.
'35c	Prentiss, Valentine..	Mass. line.....	Sergeant...	84	Kennebec....	d. Sept. 4, 1822.
'35d	Prescott, Nathan...	N. H. line.....	Pvt. &Serg.	75	Kennebec.	
'35c	Prescott, Samuel...	Mass. line.....	Private....	81	Kennebec.	
'40	Prescott, Samuel...			83	Kennebec...	Res. Hallowell.
'40	Pribou, Amasa.....			81	Cumberland.	Res. Minot.
'35d	Pride, John........	Mass. line.....	Pvt. &Serg.	82	Cumberland.	
'35d	Pride, Thomas.....	Mass. mil......	Private....	70	Cumberland.	
'35d	Prince, Amory.....	Mass. mil......	Private....	81	Cumberland.	
'35c	Prince, Benjamin...	Mass. line.....	Private....	77	Cumberland.	
'40				83	Cumberland.	Res. Falmouth.
'40	Prince, Dinah......			105	York........	Res. York.
'35d	Pritchard, James...	Mass. mil......	Private....	75	Waldo.	
'40	Procter, Josiah.....			79	Oxford	Res. Waterford.
'35d	Proctor, Josiah.....	Mass. mil......	Mariner & Seaman...	71	Oxford......	'35c.
'35c	Pulcifer, Joseph....	Mass. line.....	Private....	80	Kennebec....	d. Nov. 27, 1820.
'40	Pulcifer, Joseph....			75	Lincoln......	Res. Bath.
'35c	Pullen, Oliver	Mass. line.....	Private....	86	Waldo.	
'40	Pullen, Oliver......			78	Waldo.......	Res. Palermo.
'35c	Pullen, William....	R. I. line......	Private....	67	Kennebec.	
'40	Pumpilly, Elizabeth.			67	Oxford......	Res. Turner See also Pompilly.
'35d	Purham, Peter.....	Mass. line.....	Private....	84	Penobscot..	
'40	Putnam, Tamar....			74	Penobscot...	Res. Eddington.s
'35d	Putney, James.....	N. H. line.....	Pvt. &Serg.	77	Kennebec.	
'35c	Quimby, Benjamin.	N. H. line.....	Private....	75	Kennebec.	
'40	Quint, John........			79	York........	Res. Sanford.
'35c	Rackliff, Joseph....	Mass. line.....	Private....	69	Cumberland.	d. Dec. 15, 1828.
'35c	Radford, Benjamin.	Mass. line.....	Private....	72	Cumberland.	d. May 20, 1820.
'40	Ralf., Jeremiah.....			82	Piscataquis..	Res. Abbot.
'40	Ramsdell, Ebenezer.			78	Washington.	Res. Lubec.
'35c	Ramsdell, James...	Mass. line.....	Private....	63	Washington..	d. June 3, '29.
'40	Ramsey, Robert....			76	Washington.	Res. Charlotte.
'35c	Rand, James.......	Mass. line.....	Private....	77	Cumberland.	d. Oct. 18, 1827.
'35d	Rand, John........	N. H. line.....	Private....	75	Lincoln......	d. Nov. 11, 1826.
'35c	Rand, Michael.....	Mass. line.....	Private....	64	York........	d. Sept. 1824.
'35c	Rand, Reuben.....	N. H. line.....	Private....	67	Kennebec....	d. June 1, 1831.
'35d	Rand, Thomas.....	N. H. line.....	Private....	74	Lincoln.	
'40	Randal, Caleb......			87	Kennebec....	Res. Vassalborough.
'35d	Randall, Job.......	Mass. line.....	Private....	91	Oxford.	
'40	Randall, Oliver.....			79	Penobscot...	Res. Bangor.
'35d	Randall, Samuel....	N. H. line.....	Corporal ..	76	Kennebec.	
'35d	Randall, Stephen...	Mass. mil......	Private....	75	York.	
'35d	Randler, Noah.....	Mass. mil......	Private....	72	York.	

List.	Name.	Service.	Rank.	Age.	County.	Remarks.
'35c	Rankin, Robert	Mass. line	Private	71	Lincoln.	
'40	Rankins, Abigail			68	Waldo	Res. Lincolnville.
'35c	Rankins, Andrew	Mass. line	Private	81	York	d. June 11. 1829.
'35c	Rankins, John	Mass. line	Sergeant	80	Kennebec	d. May 1, 1828.
'35c	Rawlings, Joseph	Mass. line	Sergeant	78	Kennebec.	
'40	Ray, Eunice			94	Cumberland.	Res. Otisfield.
'35d	Raymond, Nathan.	Mass. state	Pvt. &Serg.	80	York.	
'40				86	York.	Res. Lyman
'35c	Raymond, William.	Mass. line	Private	77	Kennebec	
'40	Raymond, William.			92	Kennebec	Res. Fayette.
'35d	Rea, Benjamin	Mass mil	Private & Corporal	83	Hancock.	
'35d	Read, George	Mass. state	Private & Corporal	75	Kennebec.	
'40				80	Kennebec	Res. Augusta.
'40	Read, John P			46	Lincoln	Res. Lewiston
'40	Record, Abigail			82	Oxford	Res. Buckfield.
'40	Record, Jane			82	Oxford	Res. Buckfield.
'35d	Record, Jonathan	Mass. line	Private	84	Oxford.	
'40				90	Oxford	Res. Buckfield.
'35d	Record, Simon	Mass. line	Private	81	Oxford.	
'40				87	Oxford	Res. Buckfield.
'35d	Redington Asa	Mass. state	Private & Corporal	72	Kennebec.	
'40				78	Kennebec	Res. Waterville.
'35c	Redlon, Ebenezer	Mass. line	Private	76	Cumberland.	
'35c	Redlon, Ephraim	Mass. line	Private	74	York.	
'35d	Redlow, Matthias	Mass. mil	Corporal	84	Kennebec.	
'35c	Reed, Abraham	N. H. line	Private	94	Cumberland.	d. July 15, 1832.
'40	Reed, David			74	Lincoln	Res. Boothbay.
'35d	Reed, David, 2nd	Mass. mil	Private	67	Lincoln.	
'35c	Reed, Jonathan	N. H. line	Private	81	Cumberland.	
'35d	Reed, Josiah	Mass. line	Private	73	Cumberland.	
'35d	Reed, Ward	Mass. line	Private & Sergeant	75	Penobscot.	
'40	Reed, William W			85	Penobscot	Res. Dixmont.
'40	Reed, Josiah			79	Cumberland.	Res. Freeport.
'40	Remick, Phebe			73	Hancock	Res. Eden.
'35c	Remick, Samuel	N. H. line	Private	58	York.	
'35c	Rendall, James	Mass. line	Private	60	York.	
'35c	Reynolds, Daniel	Mass. line	Private	78	Kennebec	d. May 13, 1832.
'35d	Reynolds, David	Mass. line	Private	75	Kennebec.	
'40				82	Kennebec	Res. Sidney.
'35c	Reynolds, David	Conn. line	Private	72	Washington.	
'35c	Reynolds, Eliphalet	Conn. line	Private	74	Washington.	
'40				80	Washington.	Res. Addison.
'35c	Rhodes, Jacob	Mass. line	Private	80	York.	
'40	Rhodes, Jacob			76	York	Res. Lyman.
'35c	Rhodes, Moses	Mass. line	Private	78	York.	
'40	Rhodes, Moses			74	York	Res. Waterborough.
'40	Riant, Thomas			80	Franklin.	Res. Farmington.
'35d	Rice, Ashbell	Mass. line	Private	79	Washington.	
'35c	Rice, David	Cont. navy	Mids'pm'n	61	Cumb.	d. Aug. 11, 1821.
'35d	Rice, Gideon	Mass. line	Private	74	Cumberland.	
35d	Rice, John	Mass. mil	Private	74	Kennebec.	
'35c	Rice, Joseph	Mass. line	Private	67	Kennebec	d. Sept. 11, '26.
'35c	Rice, Lemuel	Mass. line	Private	72	Cumb.	d. Jan. 16, 1827.
'35c	Rice, Luther	Mass. line	Private	73	Oxford	d. Mar. 8, 1831.
'35c	Rich, Joel	Mass. line	Private	81	Waldo.	
'35c	Richards, Bradley	N. H. line	Ensign	73	Kennebec	d. June 12, '21.
'35c	Richards, John	N. H. line	Private	80	York.	
'35d	Richards, Jonathan	Mass. line	Private	73	Waldo.	
'35c	Richards, Joseph 2d	N. H. line	Private	78	Somerset.	
'35d	Richards, Joseph	Mass. line	Private	75	York.	
'35d	Richards, Mitchell	Mass. line	Private	74	Kennebec.	
'40	Richards, Mitchell			81	Franklin	Res. Temple.
'40	Richardson, Eben'er			38	Hancock	Res. Castine.
'35d	Richardson, Edward	Mass. state	Lieutenant & Captain.	86	Oxford.	
'35d	Richardson, James	Mass. mil	Private & Seaman	81	Hancock.	
'35c	Richardson, Joel	Mass. line	Private	65	Lincoln	d. Feb. 23, 1827.
'35d	Richardson, Joseph	Mass. line	Private	71	Cumberland.	
'40	Richardson, Lydia			82	Penobscot	Res. Newport.
'40	Richardson, Molly			87	Cumb.	Res. Baldwin.
'35d	Richmond, Nathan	Mass. state	Private	79	Kennebec	
'35c	Ricker, George	Mass. line	Private	81	York	d. Dec. 25, 1833.

List.	Name.	Service.	Rank.	Age.	County.	Remarks.
'35d	Ricker Maturian...	N. H. line.....	Private & Seaman...	74	York.	
'35d	Ricker, Noah......	Cont. Navy....	Marine....	72	York.	
'40				78	York........	Res. Waterborough.
	Ricker, Reuben....	....	....	83	York........	Res. Lyman.
'40	Ricker, Reuben....	Cont. Navy....	Seaman....	65	Waldo.	
'35c	Ricker, Simeon.....	Mass. line.....	Private....	80	York.	
'35d	Ricker, Stephen....	Mass. line.....	Private....	78	York.	
'35c	Ricker, Timothy...	Mass. mil......	Private....		York.	
'35d	Ricker, Tobias.....	N. H. line.....	Private....	74	Oxford.	
'35d				80	Oxford.......	Res. Buckfield.
'40	Ricker, Wentworth.	N. H. line.....	Private....	81	Cumberland.	
'35d	Rideout, Benjamin.	Mass. mil......	Private....	79	Lincoln......	d. Aug. 3, 1833.
'35d	Rideout, Stephen...	....	....	80	Lincoln......	Res. Bowdoin.
'40	Rider, John........	Mass. line.....	Private....	70	Kennebec.	
'35c	Rider, Stephen.....	....	....	79	Kennebec....	Res. Albion.
'40	Ridley, Daniel.....	Mass. line......	Private....	75	Lincoln..	
'35c	Ridley, David......	Mass. line.....	Private....	72	Kennebec.	
'35c	Ridley, George.....	Mass. line.....	Private....	57	Lincoln......	d. Dec. 31, 1818.
'35c	*Ridlow, Mary*......	....	....	74	Kennebec....	Res. Winsdor.
'40	Ridout, Abraham...	Mass. line.....	Private....	76	York.	
'35c	Ridout, Stephen....	Mas. line......	Private....	74	Lincoln.	
'35c	Rines, Samuel......	Mass. line.....	Private....	76	York.	
'35c	*Ripley, Lucy*.......	....	....	75	Waldo......	Res. Montville.
'40	Ripley, William....	Mass. line.....	Private....	67	Lincoln......	d. June 27, 1823.
'35c	*Roach, Abigail*.....	....	....	73	Franklin.....	Res. Wilton.
'40	Roach, John.......	Mass. line.....	Private....	85	Kennebec....	d. Aug. 22, 1828.
'35c	Robbins, Asa......	Mass. line.....	Corporal..	75	Kennebec.	
'35d				81	Kennebec....	Res. Winthrop.
'40	Robbins, Daniel 2nd	Mass. line.....	Private...	77	Kennebec.	
'35c	Robbins, Daniel....	Mass. line.....	Private....	73	Kennebec.	
'35c	Robbins, Eli. halet..	Mass. line.....	Private....	73	Kennebec.	
'35c	Robbins, Jonathan.	Mass. line.....	Corporal ..	73	Oxford.	
'35c	Robbins, Joseph....	N. H. line.....	Private....	76	Kennebec....	d. Aug. 7, 1825.
'35c	Robbins, Luther....	Mass. mil......	Private & Quarter Master....	76	Kennebec.	
'35d	Robbins, Otis......	Mass. line	Private....	77	Lincoln.	
'35c	Robbins, Samuel...	N. H. line.....	Private....	75	Lincoln......	d. Oct. 28, 1832.
'35c	Robbins, William...	Mass. line.....	Private....	59	Lincoln.	
'35c	Roberts, George....	Mass. line.....	Private....	72	Somerset.	
'35d	Roberts, Jeremiah..	Mass. State....	Private....	81	York.	
'40				86	York........	Res. Lyman.
'35d	Roberts, Joseph....	Mass. line.....	Private....	75	Waldo.	
1794	Roberts, Joseph....	....	Carpenter.		....	Res. Berwick. Lost left arm on ship of war "Hampden" at Siege of Penobscot Aug. 15, 1779.
'40	Roberts, Joseph....	....	....	87	Waldo......	Res. Brooks.
'35c	Roberts, Love......	N. H. line.....	Private....	84	York.	
'40				88	York........	Res. Lebanon.
'35d	Roberts, Paul......	Mass. line.....	Private....	74	York.	
'40				78	York........	Res. Newfield.
'35c	Roberts, Samuel....	N. H. line.....	Private....	62	York.	
'35d	Roberts, Simon.....	N. H. line.....	Seaman...	73	York........	d. Oct. 5, 1832.
'40	Robinson, Andrew I.	....	....	84	Waldo......	Res. Searsmont.
'35d	Robinson, Andrew..	Mass. line.....	Private....	75	Lincoln.	
'40	Robinson, Daniel...	....	....	86	Cumb.......	Res. Durham.
'40	*Robinson, Deborah*..	....	....	77	York........	Res. Limington.
'35c	Robinson, George...	Mass. line.....	Private....	62	York........	d. Mar. 13, 1819.
'35c	Robinson, James...	Mass. line.....	Private....	66	Lincoln......	d. Jan. 18, 1833.
'35d	Robinson, Jedediah.	Mass. mil......	Private....	08	Kennebec.	
'40	Robinson, Jedediah.	....	....	87	Kennebec....	Res. Gardiner.
'35d	Robinson, John....	Mass. line.....	Private....	81	Cumberland.	
'35c	Robinson, John....	Mass. line.....	Private....	66	Cumberland.	d. Feb. 13, 1827.
'35c	Robinson, John....	Mass. line.....	Private....	58	York.	
'35d	Robinson, Joshua...	Mass. mil......	Private & Sergeant...	81	Kennebec.	
'35d	Robinson, Meshuck	Mass. state....	Private....	70	Penobscot.	
'35d	Robinson, Moses...	Mass. mil......	Sergeant...	78	Waldo.	
'40	*Robinson, Phebe*....	....	....	72	Cumb.......	Res. Sebago.
'35c	Robinson, Thomas..	Mass. line.....	Ensign....	79	Somerset.	

75

List.	Name.	Service.	Rank.	Age.	County.	Remarks.
'35c	Rockwood, Ebenezer	Mass. line	Private	64	Lincoln	d. June 1831.
'35d	Rogers, Alexander	Mass. mil	Private	73	Lincoln	
'35c	Rogers, David	Mass. line	Private	74	York	d. Apr. 1, 1828.
'35d	Rogers, James	Mass. mil	Sergeant	77	Lincoln	
'35c	Rogers, John	N. H. line	Private	78	Kennebec	
'35d	Rogers, John 2nd	Mass. line	Private	69	Lincoln	d. Apr. 18, 1824.
'35d	Rogers, William	Mass. line	Private	78	Lincoln	
	Rogues	(See Bogues)				
'35c	Rolf, Jeremiah	Mass. line	Private	74	Somerset	See Ralf.
'35d	Rolfe, Joseph	Mass. line	Private	80	Kennebec	
'35d	Rolings, Nathaniel	Mass. mil	Private	73	Kennebec	
'40	Rollins, David			65	Kennebec	Res. Pittston.
'35c	Rollins, Eliphalet	Mass. line	Private		Somerset	
'35c	Rollins, Jabez	N. H. line	Private	74	Kennebec	
'40	Rollins, Jabez			73	Kennebec	Res. Sidney.
'35d	Rollins, James	Mass. mil	Private	71	Lincoln	
'35c	Rollins, John	R. I. line	Private	77	Kennebec	
'40	Rollins, John			74	Kennebec	Res. Augusta.
'40	Rollins, Joseph			85	Kennebec	Res. Gardiner.
'40	Rollins, Susannah			87	Penobscot	Res. Cornith.
'40	Rose, Joseph			78	York	Res. Limington.
'35d	Ross, Isaac	Mass. line	Private	77	Cumberland	
'40	———			84	Cumb	Res. No. Yarmouth
'35d	Ross, Jonathan	Mass. mil	Private	86	York	
'40	———			91	York	Res. Shapleigh.
'35c	Ross, Joseph	Mass. line	Private	73	Cumb	d. Feb. 2, 1827.
'40	Ross, Sarah			82	Cumb	Res. Brunswick.
'40	Roundy, Benjamin			48	Kennebec	Res. Clinton.
'35d	Rounds, Joseph	Mass. mil	Private	81	York	
'35c	Rounds, Theodore	Mass. line	Private	80	York	
'35c	Row, John	Mass. line	Private	77	Oxford	
'35c	Row, John	N. H. line	Private	72	Kennebec	
'35c	Row, Webber	N. H. line	Private	71	York	
'35c	Rowe, Caleb	Mass. line	Private	66	Kennebec	d. July 1, 1821.
'35c	Rowe, John	Mass. line	Ensign	60	Oxford	
'40	Rowe, John			82	Oxford	Res. Paris.
'35c	Rowe, Lazarus	M. H. line	Private	108	Kennebec	
'35c	Rowe, William	N. H. line	Private	82	Kennebec	
'35d	Rowe, Zebulon	Mass. line	Corporal	85	Cumberland	
'40	Rowe, Zebulon			91	Cumb	Res. New Gloucester.
'35d	Rummery, Dom'c's	Mass. line	Private of Artillery	70	Washington	
'35d	Rumsdell, Ebenezer	Mass. line	Private	74	Washington	
'35c	Rundle, Nathaniel	R. I. Corps	Private	80	Lincoln	d. Jan. 7, 1825.
'35d	Runnells, Samuel	Mass. State	Sergeant	83	Washington	
'40	Runnells, Thomas			79	Cumb	Res. Portland 7th Ward.
'40	Russell, Hannah			82	Lincoln	Res. Waldoboro'.
'40	Russel, Andrew			81	Somerset	Res. Madison.
'35c	Russel, Levi	Mass. line	Private	82	Lincoln	
'40	Russel, Solomon			82	Somerset	Res. Solon.
'35c	Russell, Andrew	Mass. line	Private	76	Somerset	
'35d	Russell, Benjamin	Mass. state	Private	71	Oxford	
'40	———			76	Oxford	Res. Newry.
'35c	Russell, Calvin	Mass. line	Private	72	Somerset	
'40	———			78	Somerset	Res. Bingham.
'40	Russell, Jonathan			87	Kennebec	Res. Winthrop.
'35c	Russell, Solomon	Mass. line	Private	76	Cumberland	
'35d	Russell, Solomon	Mass. line & Mass. mil	Private & Sergeant	76	Cumberland	
'35d	Russell, William	Mass. state	Private	74	Oxford	
'35d	Ryant, Joseph	N. H. line	Private & do	78	Kennebec	
'35c	Sadler, John	Mass. line	Private	72	Cumberland	
'35c	Sadler, John	Mass. line	Private	72	Lincoln	
'40	Sadler, John			70	Lincoln	Res. Georgetown.
'35d	Sampson, James	Mass. line	Private	70	Cumberland	
'40	Sampson ———			76	Cumb	Res. Otisfield.
'35d	Sampson, Luther	Mass. mil	Private	74	Kennebec	
'40	———			80	Kennebec	Res. Readfield.
'35d	Sanborn, Abner	N. H. line	Private	88	York	
'35d	Sanborn, Benjamin	N. H. line	Private	72	Washington	
'40	———			78	Washington	Res. Cherryfield.
'35c	Sanborn, Benjamin 2nd	Mass. line	Private	70	Cumberland	
'40	Sanborn, Hannah			77	Cumb	Res. Minot.

List.	Name.	Service.	Rank.	Age.	County.	Remarks.
'35c	Sanborn, John 2nd..	Mass. line.....	Private....	92	Cumb.......	d. Jan. 4, 1832.
'35c	Sanborn, John......	Mass. line.....	Private....	76	Cumberland.	
'35d	Sanborn, Matthew..	N. H. line.....	Private & Sergeant...	72 to 77	Somerset.	
'40	Sanborn, Matthew P	....	....	81	Somerset....	Res. Solon.
'35c	Sanborn, Paul......	Mass. line.....	Private....	72	Cumberland.	
'35c	Sanborn, Peter.....	Mass. line.....	Private....	75	Cumb.......	d. Aug. 6, 1827.
'35c	Sanborn, Simon....	Mass. line.....	Private....	73	Oxford......	d. Nov. 25, 1833.
'40	Sanburn, John.....	....	....	50	Waldo.......	Res. Monroe.
'35d	Sanderson, Rufus...	Mass. line.....	Private....	76	Somerset.	
'40				82	Somerset....	Res. Mercer.
'40	Sanford, John......	....	....	80	Lincoln.....	Res. Bath.
'40	Santell, John.......	....	....	81	Waldo......	Res. Camden.
'35c	Sargeant, Charles...	Mass. line.....	Private....	73	York.	
'35c	Sargeant, Daniel...	Mass. line.....	Private....	67	York........	d. in 1827.
'35c	Sargeant, P. Dudley	Mass. line.....	Colonel...		Hancock.	
'35d	Sargent, Benjamin..	Mass. line......	Private....	70	Penobscot.	
'40	*Sargent, Charity*...	....	....	76	York........	Res. Kittery.
'40	Sargent, Charles....	....	....	86	York........	Res. So. Berwick.
'35d	Sargent, Chase.....	Mass. state....	Private....	79	York.	
'40				83	York........	Res. Cornish.
'35c	Sargent, Daniel 2nd	N. H. line.....	Private....	61	Cumb.......	d. Aug. 16, 1821.
'35d	Sartell, John.......	Mass. mil......	Private....	75	Waldo.	
'35c	Sautell, Jonas......	Mass. line.....	Private....	62	Somerset.	
'40	Savage, Elijah D....	....	....	52	Kennebec....	Res. Augusta.
'35c	Savage, Jacob......	Cont. navy....	Mariner...	68	Somerset....	d. Nov. 7, 1826.
'40	*Savage, Sarah*......	....	....	77	Hancock....	Res. Mt. Desert.
'40	*Sawtelle, Eunice*...	....	....	82	Penobscot...	Res. Corinna.
'35d	Sawyer, Barnabas..	Mass. mil......	Private & Fifer....	74	York.	
'35d	Sawyer, Ebenezer...	Mass. line.....	Private....	76	York.	
'40	Sawyer, George....			82	Somerset....	Res. Smithfield.
35d		Mass. line......	Private & Sergeant...	76	....	do.
'35d	Sawyer, Isaac......	Mass. mil......	Private....	75	Cumberland.	
'40d	Sawyer, Jabez......	....	....	72	York........	Res. Buxton.
'40	Sawyer, Jacob......	....	....	92	Penobscot...	Res. Dixmont.
'35	Sawyer, Jacob......	Mass. mil......	Private....	86	Kennebec.	
'35c	Sawyer, John......	Mass. line......	Corporal..	74	Cumberland.	
'35d	Sawyer, John......	Mass. mil......	Private....	75	Cumberland.	
'40	Sawyer, John......	....	....	75	Cumb.......	Res. Westbrook.
'35c	Sawyer, Josiah.....	Mass. line.....	Private....	71	Washington.	
'35d	Sawyer, Luke......	Mass. mil......	Private....	74	Somerset.	
'35d	Sawyer, Solomon...	Mass. mil......	Private....	77	Cumberland.	
'35d	Sawyer, Thomas....	Mass. line.....	Private....	75	Cumb.......	d. April 11, 1833.
'40	Sawyer, William....	....	....	77	Kennebec....	Res. Greene.
'35d	Sawyer, William....	Mass. mil...... Mass. line.....	Private & Surgeon's. Mate.....	71	Kennebec.	
'35d	Sayer Nathaniel....	Mass.line......	Private....	75	York.	
'35d	Sayward, George...	Mass. mil......	Lietuenant. of Artillery	81	Lincoln.	
'40	*Sayward, Susan*....	....	....	87	Waldo.......	Residence Waldo Plantation.
'35d	Scales, Samuel.....	Mass. mil......	Private....	70	Cumberland.	
'35d	Schwartze, Peter...	Mass. line.....	Private....	77	Lincoln.	
'35d	Scribner, Stephen...	Mass. mil......	Private....	75	Kennebec.	
'40	Scriggins, Thomas..	....	....	76	York........	Res. Elliot.
'40	Seales, Samnet.....	....	....	81	Cumb.......	Res. Freeport.
'35c	Sears, Barnabas....	Mass. line.....	Private....	86	Somerset....	d, June 29, '21.
'35c	Sears, Willard......	N. H. line.....	Private....	82	Kennebec....	d. Dec. 13, 1831.
'35c	Seates, John.......	Mass. line.....	Private....	82	York.	
'40	Seavy, Ebenezer....	....	....	53	Oxford......	Res. Bloomfield.
'35d	Seavy, Thomas.....	N. H. state....	Private & Teamster..	69	Hancock.	
'35d	Seawell, Thomas...	Mass. mil......	Private....	83	Kennebec....	d. May 4, 1833.
'35d	Sedgeley, John.....	Mass. mil......	Private....	75	Lincoln.	
'40	Sedgeley, John.....	....	....	80	Lincoln......	Res. Bowdoinham
'35d	Seger, Nathaniel....	Mass. line.....	Private....	79	Oxford.	
'40				85	Oxford......	Res. Bethel.
'35c	Selsby, Samuel.....	Mass. line.....	Private....	68	Hancock....	d. Feb. 10, 1826.
'35d	Senter, Abel.......	Mass. line.....	Private....	76	Cumberland.	
'40	*Senter. Sally*......	....	....	76	Cumb.......	Res. Naples.
'40	Servall, Henry.....	....	....	87	Kennebec....	Res. Augusta.

77

List.	Name.	Service.	Rank.	Age.	County.	Remarks.
'35c	Sessions, David	N. H. line	Sergeant	69	Cumberland.	d. Sept. 22, 1824.
'35c	Severance, Caleb	Mass. line	Private	79	Penobscot.	
'40	Severance, Elizabeth.			69	Penobscot	Res. Orrington.
'35d	Sev'.ance, Joshua	Mass. line	Private	78	Penobscot.	
'35c	Sevey, Eliakim	Mass. line	Private	71	York.	
'40				77	York	Res. York.
'35c	Sewall, Dummer	Mass. line	Private	74	Kennebec.	
'35c	Sewall, Henry	Mass. line	Captain	67	Kennebec.	
'35e		N. H. line 2nd. Regiment.			Kennebec.	
'40	Shackford, Samuel			79	York	Res. Sanford.
'35d	Shackley, Joseph	Mass. line	Private	70	York.	
'40	Shattuck, James			83	Lincoln	Res. Westport.
'35d	Shaw, Abraham	Mass. line	Private	71	York.	
'40				71	York	Res. York.
'35c	Shaw, Benjamin	Mass. line	Ensign	80	Washington.	
'35d	Shaw, Eliab	Mass. line	Private	76	Kennebec	d. Apr. 24, 1833.
'35d	Shaw, Elisha	Mass. state	Sergeant & Ensign	76	Kennebec.	
'35c	Shaw, Ephraim	Mass. line	Private	83	Kennebec.	
'35c	Shaw, George	Cont. navy	Mariner	80	Penobscot.	
'40				86	Penobscot	Res. Exeter.
'35c	Shaw, Jacob	Mass. line	Private	60	Kennebec	d. Aug. 29, 1820.
'35d	Shaw, Jairus	Mass. mil	Private	79	Oxford.	
'35c	Shaw, James	Mass. line	Ensign	76	Kennebec	d. April 1822.
'35c	Shaw, John	Mass. line	Private	74	Lincoln.	
'40	Shaw, John			88	Lincoln	Res. Woolwich.
'35d	Shaw, Joseph	Mass. mil	Private & Seaman	72	Cumberland.	
'40	Shaw———			78	Cumb	Res. Cumberland.
'35d	Shaw, Levi	N. H. mil	Private & Corporal	75	Cumberland.	
'35d	Shaw, Nathaniel	Mass. state	Private & Sergeant	89	Oxford.	
'35d	Shaw, Nathaniel	Mass. mil	Private	71	Oxford.	
40				76	Oxford	Res. Turner.
'35c	Shaw, Nathaniel	Mass. line	Private	59	Cumberland.	
'40	Shaw, Polly			77	Cumb	Residence Portland 5th. Ward.
'35d	Shaw, Samuel	Mass. state	Private	77	York.	
'40				83	York	Res. Sanford.
'35d	Shaw, Thomas	Mass. line	Private	80	Cumberland.	
'35c	Shaw, William	Mass. line	Private	90	York	d. in 1822.
'35c	Shean, Richard	Mass. line	Private	77	Cumb	d. Mar. 31, 1820.
'35c	Shed, Daniel	Cont. navy	Seaman	73	Penobscot.	
'40				77	Penobscot	Res. Brewer.
'35d	Shed, John	Mass. line	Private	71	Kennebec.	
'35d	Shed, Jonathan	Mass. line	Private	73	Oxford.	
'35d	Sheldon, Ephraim	Mass. mil	Private	70	Waldo.	
'40				75	Waldo	Res. Camden.
'35c	Sheldon, William	Mass. line	Private	73	Lincoln	d. Sept. 26, 1831.
'35c	Shepherd, James	Mass. line	Private	57	Lincoln.	
'40	Shepherd, Levi			76	Kennebec	Res. Pittston.
'35c	Shepherd, Lewis	Mass. line	Private	90	Cumb	d. Nov. 28, 1822.
'40	Shepherd, Mary			79	Lincoln	Res. Jefferson.
'35c	Shepherd, William	Mass. line	Private	60	Lincoln	d. in 1824.
'35c	Sheppard, Levi	Mass. line	Private	81	Kennebec.	
'40	Sherburn, Job			82	Kennebec	Res Readfield.
'35c	Sherburne, Job	N. H. line	Private	76	Kennebec.	
'35d	Sherman, Isasac	Mass. mil	Private	78	York.	
'35d	Sherman, Joseph	Mass. mil	Private	77	Waldo.	
'35d	Sherman, Nathan	Mass. mil	Private	72	Lincoln.	
'40				78	Lincoln	Res. Thomaston.
'40	Shorey, Samuel			47	Kennebec	Res. Sidney.
'35d	Shuckford, Samuel	Mass. mil	Private	73	York.	
'35c	Shurtliff, William	Mass. line	Private	68	Cumb	d. July 3, 1825.
'35d	Sias, John	N. H. line	Private	77	Oxford.	
'35d	Sidgeley, Joseph	R. I. State	Private	78	Lincoln	
'40	Silley, Benjamin			73	Waldo	Res. Brooks.
'35c	Silly, Benjamin	Mass. line	Private	73	Waldo.	
'35d	Silvester, Thomas	Mass. line	Private	75	Cumberland.	
35d	Simons Ichabod	Mass. line	Private	72	Somerset	d. Jan. 12, 1833.
'35d	Simmons, Isaac	Mass. line	Private of Inf. & Cav.	72	Lincoln.	
'35d	Simmons, Lebbeus	Mass. line	Private	85	Waldo.	
'35c	Simmons, Samuel	Conn. line	Corporal	79	Oxford.	

List.	Name.	Service.	Rank.	Age	County.	Remarks.
'35c	Simonton, Walter...	Mass. line.....	Private....	66	Cumb.......	d. in 1826.
'35d	Simpson, Benjamin.	Mass. line.....	Private....	74	York........	d. Feb. 9, 1833.
'40	Simpson, Lucy.....			82	York........	Res. Elliot.
'35c	Simpson, Simon....	Mass. line.....	Private....	68	Kennebec.	
'35d	Simpson, Zedekiah..	Mass. state....	Private....	78	York........	d. Jan. 8, 1833.
'40	Simson, Simon.....			76	Kennebec....	Res. Winslow.
'35c	Sinclair, Joshua....	N. H. line.....	Private....	74	Waldo.	
'40	Sinclair, Joshua....			..	Penobscot...	Res. Old Town.
'35c	Skinner, Elisha.....	Mass. line.....	Surgeon...	73	Penobscot...	d. Nov. 1827.
'35d	Skinner, John......	Mass. line.....	Sergeant...	84	Lincoln.	
'40				87	Lincoln......	Res. Lewiston.
'35c	Small, Daniel 3rd...	Mass. line.....	Private....	91	Cumb.......	d. Feb. 21, 1821.
'35d	Small, Daniel......	Mass. line & Mass. mil......	Private....	78	Washingtom.	
'35d	Small Daniel.......	Mass. line.....	Private....	80	Cumberland.	
'35d	Small, Daniel 2nd...	Mass. line.....	Private....	75	York.	
'40..				80	York........	Res. Limington.
'40	Small, Daniel......			76	Cumb.......	Res. Raymond..
'35c	Small, Elisha......	Mass. line.....	Private....	78	Cumberland.	
'40	Small, Elisha.......			82	Washington..	Res. Cherryfield.
'40	Small, Elizabeth....			81	York........	Res. Limington.
'40	Small, Ephraim.....			81	Lincoln......	Res. Baldwin.
'35d	Small, Ephraim.....	Mass. state....	Private....	74	Kennebec....	
'35c	Small, Henry......	Mass. line.....	Private....	63	York.	
'35d	Small, James.......	Mass. line.....	Sergeant...	77	Cumberland.	
'40				83	Cumb.......	Res. Scarborough.
'35c	Small, Jeremiah....	Mass. line.....	Private....	84	Cumberland.	
'35d	Small, Samuel......	Mass. state....	Private....	77	Lincoln.	
'40				83	Lincoln......	Res. Phipsburg.
'35d	Small, William.....	Mass. mil......	Private & Sergeant...	75	York	
'35c	Small, Zachariah...	Mass. l ne.....	Private....	56	Cumberland.	
'35c	Smart, Richard.....	N. H. line.....	Private....	71	Hancock....	d. May 1827.
'35d	Smith, Abraham....	Mass. mil......	Private....	72	Kennebec.	
'40	Smith, Abraham....			78	Franklin.....	Res. Farmington.
'35d	Smith Benjamin,...	Mass. line.....	Private & Sergeant...	78	Waldo.	
'40				83	Waldo.......	Res. Hope.
'35c	Smith, Charles 2nd..	Mass. line.....	Private....	79	Waldo..	
'40				85	Waldo.......	Res. Belfast.
'35c	Smith, Charles.....	Mass. line.....	Private....	66	Lincoln......	d. Dec. 17, 1831.
'35d	Smith, Daniel......	Mass. state....	Private....	72	Washington..	
'35c	Smith, Daniel......	N. H. line.....	Private....	67	Kennebec....	d. Aug. 24, 1824.
'35c	Smith, David......	N. H. line.....	Private....	74	Hancock.	
'40	Smith, David......			42	Kennebec....	Res. Readfield.
'35c	Smith, Dominicus..	Mass. line.....	Private....	79	York.	
'35c	Smith, Ebenezer....	Mass. line.....	Private....	75	Kennebec....	d. Sept. 1822.
'35c	Smith, Ebenezer....	Mass. line.....	Captain...	75	Lincoln.	
'40	Smith, Elizabeth....			85	York........	Res. Waterborough.
'35d	Smith, Ephraim . .	Mass. line.....	Private....	82	Cumberland.	
'40	Smith, Hannah.....			73	Waldo......	Res. Belfast.
'35c	Smith, Heman......	Mass. line.....	Sergeant...	73	Lincoln......	d. Jan. 7, 1820.
'35d	Smith, Isaac.......	Mass. line.....	Private....	69	Lincoln.	
'35c	Smith, Jacob.......	Mass. line.....	Private....	73	York.	
'35c	Smith, James......	Mass. line.....	Private....	76	York.	
'35d	Smith, Jaziel.......	R. I. line......	Private....	72	Kennebec.	
'35c	Smith, Jeremiah....	N. H. line.....	Private....	80	Cumb.......	d. Aug. 12, 1832.
'35c	Smith, Jesse.......	Mass. line.....	Private....	69	Penobscot...	d. Nov. 22, '29.
'35c	Smith, John 4th....	Mass. line.....	Private....	81	Hancock....	d. Jan. 7, 1828.
'35d	Smith, John........	Mass. line.....	Private & Fife Major.	77	Kennebec.	
'40				83	Kennebec....	Res. Wayne.
'35c	Smith John 1st.....	Mass. line.....	Private....	74	Cumberland.	
'35d	Smith, John.......	Mass. line.....	Private....	74	Cumberland.	
'35d	Smith, John 2nd...	Mass. line.....	Private....	74	Cumberland.	
'35c	Smith, John 3rd....	Mass. line.....	Private....	72	Hancock....	d. May 11, 1824.
'35c	Smith, John K......	Mass. line.....	Captain...	68	Cumberland.	
'40	Smith, John K......			86	Cumb.......	Res. Portl'd 5th. Ward.
'35e	Smith, Kilby.......	Mass. line.....	6th. Regiment Captain.......	..	Cumberland.	
'35d	Smith, Jonathan....	Mass. mil......	Sergeant...	76	Somerset....	d. June 14, '33.

List.	Name.	Service.	Rank.	Age.	County.	Remarks.
'40	Smith, Josiah			77	Oxford	Res. Buckfield.
'40	Smith, Judith			79	Kennebec	Res. Winthrop.
'35d	Smith, Laban	Mass. line	Private	74	Oxford	
'40	Smith, Laban			79	Kennebec	Res. Mt. Vernon.
'35c	Smith, Moses	Mass. line	Private	74	Waldo	
'40				81	Waldo	Res. Prospect.
'35c	Smith, Nathan	N. H. line	Private	69	Kennebec	d. Aug. 25, 18_2.
'35c	Smith, Nathaniel	N. H. line	Private	76	Kennebec	d. May 2 1833.
'35c	Smith, Noah	Mass. line	Private	73	York	d. Dec. 3, 1829.
'35c	Smith, Peleg	Mass. line	Private	83	Lincoln	d. June 12, 1832.
'35c	Smith, Peter 2nd	Mass. line	Private	74	Cumberland	
'35c	Smith, Rowland	Mass. line	Private	71	Kennebec	
'35d	Smith, Samuel	Mass. line	Sergeant	85	York	
'40				91	York	Res. Kennebunkport.
'35c	Smith, Samuel	Mass. line	Private	76	Waldo	
'40				82	Waldo	Res. Monroe.
'35d	Smith, Samuel	Mass. mil	Private	75	York	
'40	Smith, Sarah			73	Waldo	Res. Knox.
'35c	Smith, Stephen	Mass. line	Private	83	Waldo	
'35d	Smith, Thomas	Mass. line	Private & Sergeant	81	Lincoln	
'35c	Smith, William	Mass. line	Private	74	York	d. April 1828.
'35c	Smith, William	Mass. line	Private	64	York	
'35e	Smith, William	Mass. line	Sergeant		York	
'35d	Snell, Thaddeus	Mass. line	Private	77	Kennebec	
'35c	Snow, Aaron	R. I. line	Private	80	York	
'35d	Snow, Harding	Mass. line	Private	79	Penobscot	
40'				84	Penobscot	Res. Hampden.
'35c	Snow, James	Mass. line	Private	80	Cumberland	
'40	Snow, James			87	Cumb	Res. Scarborough.
'35c	Snow, James	Mass. line	Sergeant	75	Cumberland	
'35c	Snow, Joshua	Mass. line	Sergeant	59	Cumberland	
'35e	Snow Joshua	N. H. line	Sergeant		Cumberland	
'40	Snowdeul. Elizabeth			75	Lincoln	Res. Thomaston.
35c	Sommers, Jonathan	Mass. line	Corporal	67	Cumberland	
'35c	Soul, James	Mass. line	Private	81	Cumberland	
'35c	Soule, Asa	Mass. line	Private	70	Penobscot	
'40	Soule, James			85	Cumb	Res. Freeport.
'35d	Soule, Jesse	Mass. state	Private & Mariner	75	York	
'35d	Soule, Jonathan	Mass. mil	Private	78	Cumberland	
'40				84	Cumberland	Res. Freeport.
'35c	Sourcee, Francis	N. H. line	Private	67	Kennebec	
'35c	Southard, Abraham	Mass. line	Private	78	Kennebec	
'35c	Southart, Constant	Mass. line	Private	63	Somerset	d. March 1826.
'35c	Soward, Richard	N. H. line	Private	92	York	d. Oct. 6, 1832.
'35d	Spalding, William	Mass. line	Private	75	Somerset	
'35c	Sparks, David	Mass. line	Private	75	Lincoln	d. Mar. 6, 1820.
'35c	Sparrock or Sparhawk, Jacob	Mass. line	Private	69	Kennebec	
'35c	Spaulding, Eleazer	Mass. line	Private	77	Penobscot	
1794	Spaulding, Ezekiel	7th. Mass. regt	Sergeant			Res. Georgetown, Injured 1777, loading a wagon
'40	Spaulding, Joseph			79	Penobscot	Res. Dixmont
'35d	Spaulding, Josiah	Mass. line	Private	84	Somerset	
'40	Spaulding, Josiah			79	Somerset	Res. Norridgewock.
'35c	Spaulding, Samuel	N. H. line	Private	71	Waldo	
'40				76	Waldo	Res. Frankfort.
'40	Spaulding, William			82	Somerset	Res. Norridgewock.
'35c	Spearing, John	N. H. line	Private	67	Waldo	d. Nov. 9, 1831.
'40	Spencer, Eleanor			75	Cumb	Res. Baldwin.
'35c	Spencer, Solomon	Mass. line	Private	72	Somerset	
'35c	Spencer, Thomas	Mass. line	Private	69	York	
'35c	Spencer, William	Mass. line	Private	73	York	
'35c	Spinney, Caleb	N. H. line	Sergeant	95	York	
'35d	Spinney, Caleb	Mass. state	Corporal & Sergeant	84	York	
'40	Spinney, Hannah			86	York	Res. Elliot.
'35d	Spinney, Jeremiah	Mass. line	Private of Artillery	74	Lincoln	

List.	Name.	Service.	Rank.	Age.	County.	Remarks.
'40				77	Lincoln	Res. Georgetown.
'35d	Sprague, James	Mass. line	Private	95	Oxford.	
'35c	Sprague, John	Mass. line	Private	67	Kennebec	d. Jan. 4, 1821.
35d	Sprague, Samuel	Mass. line	Private	81	Somerset.	
'35d	Sprague, William	Mass. line	Private	68	Lincoln.	
'40				73	Lincoln	Res. Phipsburg.
'35c	Sprague, William	Mass. line	Private	61	Kennebec.	
'35c	Spring, Josiah	Mass. line	Private	75	Oxford.	
'35d	Spring, Seth	N. H. line	Private	80	York.	
'35d	Spring, Thomas	Mass. mil	Private		Oxford.	
'35d	Springer, John	Mass. mil	Private	75	Lincoln.	
'35d	Springer, John	Mass. mil	Private	72	Hancock.	
'40	Sproul, Jean			78	Lincoln	Res. Bristol.
'35d	Sproul, Robert	Mass. mil	Private	79	Lincoln.	
'35d	Sproul, William	Mass. line	Private	74	Lincoln.	
'35d	Spurr, Enoch	Mass. line	Pvt. & Ser.	73	Cumberland.	
'40				79	Cumb	Res. Otisfield.
'40	Stacey, Eunice			80	Yor'.	Res. Elliot.
'35d	Stackpole Absalom	Mass. state	Private	82	York.	
'40	Stacpole, Absalom			88	York	Res. No. Berwick.
'35c	Stacy, John	N. H. line	Private	80	York.	
'35c	Stacy, William	Cont. navy	Seaman	76	York.	
'35c	Stanford, John 2nd.	Mass. line	Private	77	Lincoln.	
'35c	Stanford, John	Mass. line	Private	73	Cumberland.	
'40				77	Cumb	Res. Cape E'zab'h
'35d	Stanley, Adin	Mass. line	Private &	80		
		Mass. state	Matross	73	Kennebec.	
'40				78	Kennebec	Res. Winthrop.
'35c	Stanley, James	Mass. line	Private	71	York.	
'35d	Stanley, Nathaniel	Mass. mil	Corporal	79	Washington.	
'35d	Stanley, Real	Mass. mil	Drummer&			
			& Fifer	76	Kennebec.	
'40	Stanley, Rial			80	Kennebec	Res. Winthrop.
'35d	Stanton, Paul	Mass. mil	Private	76	Cumberland.	
'40				82	Cumb	Res. Poland.
'35c	Stanwood, Daniel	Mass. line	Lieutenant	82	Lincoln.	
'35c	Staples, Edward	N. H. line	Private	78	York.	
'35c	Staples, John	R. I. line	Private	70	Hancock.	
'35c	Staples, Joseph	Mass. line	Private	72	York	d. Jan. 21, 1832.
'40	Staples, Louisa			77	York	Res. Biddeford.
'35d	Staples, William	Mass. state	Private	76	York.	
'35c	Staples, William	Mass. line	Private	72	Oxford	d. Feb. 5, 1832.
1792	Starbard, Anthony	Col Rose's regt	Private			(1794). Res. Pepperreiboro u g h. Lost sight of one eye and received other injures about Apr. 1777.
'35c	Starbird, Anthony	Mass. line	Private	93	York	d. Aug. 15, 1823.
'35c	Starbird, John	Mass. line	Ensign	68	Cumb	d. Nov. 4, 1824.
'35d	Starling, Josiah	Mass. mil	Private	70	Lincoln	d. Dec. 28, 1832.
'35c	Stenson, William	Mass. line	Musician	61	Lincoln.	
'35c	Stephens, Bartholomew	N. H. line	Private	75	Somerset	d. in 1823.
'35d	Stephens, James	Mass. mil	Private	73	Kennebec.	
'35d	Stephens, Jonas	Mass. line	Sergeant	84	Oxford	d. Feb. 9, 1823.
'40	Stephens, Jowel			94	York	Res. Kennebunk.
'35c	Stephens, Pelatiah	Mass. line	Private	77	York.	
'35c	Stephens, Samuel	Mass. line	Private	74	Kennebec	d. Sept. 14, '33.
'35d	Stephens, Sylvanus	Mass. line	Private & Musician	76	Oxford.	
'35c	Stephens, Thomas	Mass. line	Corporal	76	Lincoln.	
'35c	Stephens, Thomas	Mass. line	Private	70	Lincoln.	
'35c	Stephens, Thomas 3d	Mass. line	Private	69	Hancock.	
'35d	Stephens, William	N. H. line	Private	80	Kennebec.	
'35c	Sterry, David	Mass. line	Private	77	Kennebec.	
'35c	Stetson, Batchelor	Mass. line	Private	66	Kennebec.	
'35d	Stetson, Elijah	Mass. mil	Private	94	Cumberland.	
'35c	Stetson, Elijah	Mass. line	Private	70	Cumberland.	
'35d	Stetson, Elisha	Mass. state	Private	74	Cumberland.	
'40				81	Cumb	Res. Durham.
'35d	Stetson, Hezekiah	Mass. line	Private	81	Oxford.	
'35c	Stetson, Joseph	Mass. line	Private	71	Hancock	d. July 17, 1825.
'40	Stevens, James			44	Lincoln	Res. Warren.
'35d	Stevens, Jeremiah	Mass. mil	Private	79	Oxford.	

List.	Name.	Service.	Rank.	Age.	County.	Remarks.
'35d	Stevens, Joel	Mass. mil	Private	85	York.	
'40	Stevens, Joel			88	Oxford	Res. Norway.
'35d	Stevens, Joel	Mass. mil	Private	79	Oxford	
'35d	Stevens, John	Mass. state	Private	76	York.	
'40	——			82	York	Res. Kittery.
'40	Stevens, Mary			92	Oxford	Res. Waterford.
'35d	Stevens, Moses	Mass. mil	Private	89	York	d. Dec. 5, 1832.
'40	Stevens, Peliliah			83	York	Res. So. Berwick.
'40	Stevens, Thomas			82	Kennebec	Res. Sidney.
'40	Stevens, Thomas			74	Hancock	Res. Brooksville.
'35d	Stevens, William	Cont. navy	Seaman	78	Cumberland.	
'40	Steward, Amasa			78	Somerset	Res. St. Albans.
'35d	Steward, Daniel	Mass. line	Private	76	Somerset.	
'40	Steward, Sally			77	Penobscot	Res. Newport.
'35d	Stewart, Amasa	Mass. line	Private	69	Somerset.	
'35c	Stewart, Benjamin	Mass. line	Private	67	Somerset	d. Feb. 7, 1820.
'35c	Stewart, Daniel	Mass. line	Private	76	York.	
'35c	Stewart, Henry	N. H. line	Private	71	Waldo.	
'35c	Stewart, Hugh	Mass. line	Private	83	Kennebec.	
'40	Stickney, Benjamin			84	Kennebec	Res. Hallowell.
'35d	Stickney, Benjamin	Mass. line	Musician also Private & FifeM'j'r		Kennebec.	
'40	Stickney, Polly			68	Piscataquis	Res. Brownville.
'35d	Stickney, Samuel	Mass. state	Musician	72	Penobscot.	
'35c	Stiles, Ezra	Mass. line	Private	78	Oxford	d. March 1826.
'35d	Stinchfield, Ephr'm	Mass. line	Private	73	Cumberland.	
'40	Stinson, Abiah			70	Kennebec	Res. Litchfield.
'35c	Stinson, Samuel	Mass. line	Private	75	Hancock.	
'40	——			81	Hancock	Res. Deer Isle.
'35c	Stinson, Thomas	Mass. line	Private	79	Lincoln.	
'35c	Stirbird, Samuel	Mass. line	Sergeant	77	Lincoln.	
'35e	Stober, Ebenezer	Mass. line 2nd. Regt	Lieutenant		Cumberland.	
'35c	Stockbridge, John	Mass. line	Private	61	Oxford	d. Aug. 23, 1820.
'35c	Stockbridge, Joseph	Mass. line	Private	74	Lincoln.	
'35d	Stockbridge, Micah	Mass. line	Private	77	Cumberland.	
'40	Stockbridge, Sarah			79	Lincoln	Res. Bath.
'35c	Stoddard, Nathaniel	Mass. line	Private	80	Washington.	
'35d	Stone, David	Mass. mil	Private	72	Oxford.	
'40	——			78	Oxford	Res. Sweden.
'35d	Stone, George	Mass. line	Private	79	York.	
'35d	Stone, John	Mass. line	Private	77	York.	
'35c	Stone, John	Cont. navy	Mariner	76	York.	
'40	Stone, John			82	York	Res. Parsonsfield.
'35d	Stone, Jonathan	Mass. mil	Private	88	York.	
'35d	Stone, Jonathan	Mass. line	Private & Corporal	80	Cumberland.	
'40	Stone, Jonathan			77	York	Res. Kennebunkport.
'35d	Stone, William	Mass. state	Private	88	York.	
'35d	Stone, William	Mass. mil	Private & Corporal	72	Kennebec.	
'40	Stone, William			75	Kennebec	Res. Augusta.
'40	Storer, Eben			80 to90	Cumberland	Res. Gorham.
'35c	Storer, Elias	Mass. line	Private	60	Lincoln	d. Sept. 1824.
'35d	Storer, Isaac	Mass. mil	Private	74	York.	
'35c	Storer, William	Mass. line	Private	63	Oxford	d. March 1826.
'35d	Storers, Joseph	Mass. state	Private & Musician	77	York	d. Sept. 30, 1833.
'35d	Story, William	Mass. mil	Private	68	Cumb	d. Nov. 5, 1832.
'35c	Stover, Christopher	Mass. line	Private	72	Lincoln	d. Sept. 8, 1823.
'40	Stowe, Anne			76	Kennebec	Res. Leeds.
'40	Stowers, Samuel				Franklin	Res. Farmington.
'35d	Stowers, Samuel	Mass. line & Mass. mil	Private	76	Kennebec.	
'35d	Stratton, Elijah	Mass. mil	Private & Treamster	71	Hancock.	
'35c	Stratton, Nehemiah	N. H. line	Private	76	Kennebec.	
'40	——			81	Kennebec	Res. Albion.
'35d	Straw, Daniel	N. H. state	Private	85	York	d. Nov. 7, 1833.
'35c	Strout, Prince	Mass. line	Private	80	Cumberland.	
'40	Stuart, Daniel			87	York	Res. Wells.
'40	Stuart, Hannah				Penobscot	Res. Newport.
'40	Stuart, Henry			78	Waldo	Res. Unity.

List.	Name.	Service.	Rank.	Age.	County.	Remarks.
'35d	Stuart, Peter	Mass. line	Private	90	Cumberland.	
'35c	Stuart, Samuel	N. H. line	Private	73	Penobscot	d. July 12, '32.
'40	Stubbs, Joseph			47	Waldo	Res. Frankfort.
'35c	Stubbs, Richard	Mass. line	Sergeant	73	Cumb	d. Jan. 21, 1820.
'35c	Stubbs, Samuel	Mass. line	Ensign	73	Kennebec	d. Mar. 3, 1823.
'40	Sturdevant, Andrew			79	Kennebec	Res. Fayette.
'35d	Sturges, Jonathan	Mass. line	Private	92	Cumberland.	
'35c	Sturtevant, Andrew	Mass. line	Private	94	Kennebec.	
'35c	Sturtevant, Asa	Mass. line	Private	74	Penobscot.	
'35d	Sturtevant, Francis	Mass. line	Sergeant & Pvt. of Art.	79	Oxford.	
'35c	Sturtevant, Jesse	Mass. line	Lieutenant	67	Hancock	d. Sept. 1, 1818.
'35c	Sturtevant, Joseph	Mass. line	Private	74	Oxford.	
'35c	Sturtevant, Lot	Mass. line	Private	75	Kennebec.	
'40	—			81	Kennebec	Res. Waterville.
'35c	Sturtevant, Seth	Mass. line	Private	74	Oxford.	
'40				80	Oxford	Res. Sumner.
'40	*Sufferance, Ruth*			76	Waldo	Res. Knox.
'35c	Sullivan, Barnabas	N. Carolina line	Private	70	Lincoln	d. May 7, 1830.
'35c	Sully, Daniel	R. I. line	Private	83	York.	
'35d	Summers, Thomas	Mass. mil	Private & Teamster	76	Hancock.	
'35d	Sunborn, Jonathan	Mass. mil	Private	73	Cumberland.	
'35c	Sutton, John	Mass. line	Private	82	York	d. Nov. 18, 1810.
'35c	Sutton, John	Mass. line	Private	75	York	d. Nov. 18, 1819.
'40	*Sutton, Lois*			76	York	Res. Limington.
'35d	Swain, Joseph	Mass. line	Sergeant	72	Oxford.	
'35d	Swain Samuel	Mass. mil	Private & Corporal	72	Oxford.	
'35d	Swan James	Mass. mil	Private	73	Oxford.	
'40				77	Oxford	Res. Bethel.
'35	Swan, Nathan	Mass. line	Private	80	Oxford	d. July 22, 1833.
'40	*Sweetland, Rebecca*			82	Kennebec	Res. Gardiner.
'40	Sweatland, Stephen			79	Waldo	Res. Hope.
'35d	Sweet, Ebenezer	Mass. mil	Private	94	Kennebec.	
'35c	Sweet, Israel	Mass. line	Private	76	Cumberland.	
'35d	Sweet, Joshua	Mass. line & Mass. state	Private	71	Cumberland.	
'35d	Sweet, Samuel	Mass. mil	Private	74	Cumberland.	
'35d	Sweetland, Stephen	Mass. mil	Private	73	Lincoln.	
'40	Sweetser, Richard			90	Kennebec	Res. Waterville.
'35c	Sweetsere Richard	Mass. line	Private	84	Kennebec.	
'35d	Swett, John	Mass. line & Mass. state	Private	77	Cumberland.	
'40				82	Cumb	Res. Windham.
'40	Swett, Joshua			70to 80	Cumb	Res. Gorham.
'40	Swett, Samuel			76	Cumb	Res. Gray.
'35d	Swift, Enoch	Mass. mil	Private	74	Kennebec.	
'35d	Swift, Joseph	Mass. line	Private	74	Oxford.	
'35d	Sylvester, Elisha	Mass. line	Priv of Art.	81	Kennebec.	
'35c	Sylvester, Job	Mass. line	Private	94	Cumberland.	
'35c	Symonds, Ebenezer	Mass. line	Private	65	York.	
'35d	Symonds, Thomas	Mass. line	Private	73	Oxford.	
1794	Symms, William	Kimball's Co. of militia	Private			Res. Washington, Wounded at battle of Bennington, Aug. 1777.
'35c	Taggart, John	N. H. line	Sergeant	93	Kennebec	d. in 1822.
'35c	Taggart, Robert	N. H. line	Private	72	Kennebec	d. July 29, '23.
'35c	Talbert, Abraham	Mass. line	Private	77	Kennebec.	
'35d	Talbot, Joseph	Mass. mil	Private	70	Cumberland.	
'40	—			76	Cumb	Res. Freeport.
'35c	Tarbell, Joseph	Mass. line	Private	76	Somerset.	
'40	Tarbox, Carll			70to 80	York	Res. Hollis.
'35d	Tarbox, Samuel	Mass. mil	Private	76	Cumberland.	
'40				82	Cumb	Res. Danville.
'35d	Tarr, Abraham	Mass. mil	Private	73	Lincoln.	
'40	Tarr, Abram			78	Lincoln	Res. Whitefield.
'35c	Tarr, Joseph	Mass. line	Private		Lincoln.	
'35d	Tarr, Joseph	Mass. mil	Private	76	Lincoln.	
'40				82	Lincoln	Res. Bowdoin.
'35d	Taylor, Elias	Mass. mil	Private	72	Kennebec.	
'35c	Taylor, Ephraim	Mass. line	Private	76	Lincoln.	
'40				81	Lincoln	Res. New Castle.
'35c	Taylor, John	N. H. line	Private	72	Oxford.	
'35d	Taylor, Samuel	Mass. line	Private	74	Lincoln.	

83

List.	Name.	Service.	Rank.	Age.	County.	Remarks.
'35c	Taylor, Simeon.....	Mass. line.....	Private....	78	Kennebec....	d. Feb. 3, 1823.
'35c	Teague, Benj........	Mass. line.....	Private....	70	Oxford......	d. Jan. 15, 1820.
'40	Tebbets, Ephraim...			78	York........	Res. Berwick.
'40	Temple, John.......			84	Lincoln......	Res. Bowdoin.
'35d	Temple, John.......	Mass. line.....	Lieutenant	77	Kennebec.	
'35c	Terry, David.......	Mass. line.....	Private....	99	Lincoln......	d. June 8 1828.
'35c	Terry, John........	Cont. navy....	Mariner...	70	Lincoln.	
'40	Terry, Susannah....			71	Waldo......	Res. Montville.
'35c	Thayer, Jeremiah...	Mass. line.....	Private....	76	Kennebec.	
'35c	Thayer, Philip.....	Mass. line.....	Private....	80	Kennebec.	
'35d	Thing, Levi........	Mass. mil......	Private & Corporal...	71	Kennebec.	
'35d	Thing, Nathaniel...	Mass. line......	Private & Sergeant...	87	York.	
'35d	Thomas, Charles...	Mass. mil......	Private....	84	Cumberland.	
'40	Thomas, Charles...			82	Cumb.......	Res. Brunswick.
'35d	Thomas, Charles...	Mass. line & Mass. state....	Private....	74	Cumberland..	
'35d	Thomas, Holmes...	Mass. state....	Private....	79	Oxford.	
'35d	Thomas, Ichabod...	Mass. mil......	Private....	77	Penobscot.	
'40	Thomas, Ichabod...			82	Piscataquis..	Res. Brownville.
'35d	Thomas, Joseph. ..	Mass. line & Mass. state....	Corporal...	94 or 87	Cumberland..	
'35d	Thomas, Joseph....	Mass. state....	Private of Artillery...	74	Cumberland.	
'35c	Thomas, Jonathan..	N. H. line.....	Sergeant...	84	Kennebec.....	d. June 1824.
'35c	Thomas, Joshua....	Mass. line.....	Private....	60	Hancock.	
'40	Thomas, Mary....			80	Lincoln......	Res. Thomaston.
'35d	Thomas, Nathan...	Mass. state....	Private & Bombardier	76	Hancock.	
'35d	Thomas Samuel.... Widow of........	Mass. line.....	Private & Corporal...	79	Hancock.....	d. Aug. 14, 1832.
'40	Thomas, Spencer...			76	York........	Res. Limington.
'40	Thomas, Spencer...			53	Oxford......	Res. Dixfield & Peru.
'35c	Thompson, Alex....	Mass. line.....	Private....	74	Lincoln.	
'35c	Thompson, Alex. 2d	Mass. line.....	Private....	64	Kennebec....	d. Feb. 23, 1830.
'35d	Thompson, Benj....	Mass. state....	Private....	80	York.	
1792	Thompson, Benj..	Col. Brewer's regt.........	Lieutenant			(1794) Res. Topsham. Commissioned Nov. 6, 1776. Contracted disease on retreat from Ticonderoga in 1777.
'35d	Thompson, Cornelius............	Mass. line.....	Private....	78	Hancock.	
'35c	Thompson, David..	Mass. line.....	Corporal..	77	York.	
'35c	Thompson, Ephr'm.	Mass. line.....	Private....	72	York.	
'35d	Thompson, James..	Mass. state....	Lieutenant	86	Lincoln.....	
'35d	Thompson, James..	Mass. line.....	Private....	73	York.	
'40				79	York........	Res. Kenneb'kp't
'40	Thompson, Joel....			86	Lincoln.....	Res. Lewiston.
'35d	Thompson, Joel....	Mass. mil......	Sergeant...	72	Lincoln.	
'35c	Thompson, John...	Mass. line.....	Private....	80	York.	
'40	Thompson, John...			71	Oxford......	Res. Porter.
'35c	Thompson, Jonath'n	Mass. line.....	Private....	94	York.	
'35d	Thompson, Joseph..	Mass. state....	Private & Musician..	82	York.	
'40				88	York........	Res. Cornish.
'35c	Thompson, Joseph..	Mass. line.....	Private....	72	Lincoln......	d. June 1827.
'35d	Thompson, Joseph..	Mass. line.....	Private....	69	York.	
'35d	Thompson, Nathan.	Mass. mil......	Private....	80	York.	
'40				85	York........	Res. Kennebunkport.
'35c	Thompson, Richard.	Mass. line.....	Private....	64	Lincoln.	
'35c	Thompson, Robert..	Mass. line.....	Private....	67	Oxford.	
'35d	Thompson, Samuel. Widow of........	Mass. mil......	Private....	79	Lincoln......	d. Dec. 13, 1833.
'35d	Thompson, William.	Mass. mil......	Private....	75	Cumberland.	
'35c	Thompson, William	Mass. line.....	Private....	74	Kennebec.	
'35c	Thoms, Samuel.....	Mass. line.....	Captain...	76	Penobscot...	d. Feb. 13, '23.
'35c	Thorndike, Joshua..	Mass. line.....	Private....	69	Lincoln......	d. Dec. 2, 1824.
'35d	Thorndyke, Robert.	Mass. mil......	Private & Seaman...	74	Lincoln.	

84

List.	Name.	Service.	Rank.	Age.	County.	Remarks.
'40	————			79	Lincoln......	Res. Thomaston.
'35c	Thornton, Michael..	Mass. line.....	Private...	72	Washington..	d. Dec. 2, '25.
'35c	Thorp, Thomas.....	Mass. line.....	Sergeant...	80	Washington.	
'35c	Thurlo, John.......	Mass. line.....	Private....	68	Cumb........	d. March 1, 1834.
'35d	Thurlow, Asa......	Mass. mil......	Private ...	74	Oxford.	
'35c	Thurston, Jacob....	Mass. line.....	Private....	57	Cumberland.	
'40	Tibbets, Ichabod....	....	....	90	Waldo........	Res. Liberty.
'35d	Tibbets, Nathaniel..	Mass. mil......	Private....	82	Kennebec.	
'40	Tibbets, Simeon....	....	....	88	York........	Res. Newfield.
'40	Tibbets, Stephen...	....	....	88	Lincoln......	Res. Bristol.
'35c	Tibbetts, Giles.....	Mass. line.....	Private....	77	Lincoln......	d. July 12, 1832.
'35d	Tibbetts, Ichabod..	Mass. state....	Private & Sergeant...	84	Lincoln.	
'35c	Tibbetts, John.....	R. I. line	Private....	71	Penobscot...	d. June 1826.
'40	Tibbetts, Nathaniel	....	....	85	Franklin.....	Res. New Sharon.
'35c	Tibbetts, Stephen.	Mass. line.....	Private..	80	Lincoln.	
'35d	Tibbitts, Ephraim..	Mass. line.....	Private...	72	York.	
'35d	Tillson, William....	N. H. line.....	Corporal & Sergeant...	80	Lincoln.	
'40	————			87	Lincoln......	Res Thomaston.
'35c	Tinan, Joseph......	Mass. line.....	Private....	72	York.........	d. Oct. 15, 1825.
'35c	Tinkham, John.....	Mass. line.....	Private....	71	Kennebec....	d. Dec. 21, 1827.
'35d	Titcomb, John.....	Mass. mil......	Private....	80	Cumb........	d. Feb. 3, 1833.
'35d	Titus, Samuel......	Mass. mil......	Private....	80	Kennebec.	
'35d	Tobey, Barnabas..	Mass. mil......	Private....	74	Lincoln.	
'35c	Tobey, John........	Mass. line.....	Private....	77	Cumberland.	
'40	Tobey, Mary.......	....	....	78	Lincoln......	Res. Jefferson.
'35d	Tobey, William.....	Mass. line.....	Private....	75	Lincoln.	
'35c	Tobin, Samuel.....	Mass. line.....	Private....	72	Cumberland.	
'40	Tolbot, Abram.....	....	....	87	Kennebec....	Res. China.
'35d	Tolman, Samuel....	Mass. mil......	Private....	84	Kennebec.	
'40	Toothaker, Seth....	....	....	82	Cumb........	Res. Brunswick.
'35c	Toothaker, Seth....	Mass. line.....	Private....	71	Cumberland.	
'35c	Toppon, Michael, ..	Mass. line.....	Private....	68	Lincoln......	d. Aug. 5, 1832.
'35c	Tory, Elisha.......	Mass. line.....	Private....	85	Cumb........	d. Nov. 20, 1828.
'35c	Tourtelott Abraham	R. I. line......	Lieutenant	74	Penobscot...	d. Dec. 6, 1820.
'40	Tourtelotte, Leah...	....	....	84	Penobscot...	Residence Mattamiscontis.
'35c	Tourtelott Orono...	R. I. line......	Private....	82	Penobscot.	
'35c	Tourtelott, Reuben.	R. I. line......	Private....	75	York........	d. Dec. 1825.
'35d	Towb, William.....	Mass. line.....	Private....	76	Somerset.	
'35c	Towle, Jeremiah....	N. H. line.....	Private....	75	Kennebec.	
'35c	Towle, Josiah......	N. H. line.....	Private....	80	Waldo.......	'40.
'40	Towle, Thomas.....	....	....	98	York........	Res. Parsonsfield.
'35d	Towle, Thomas.....	Mass. mil......	Private....	83	York.	
'35c	Town, Joseph......	Mass. line.....	Private....	72	York.	
'35c	Town, Noah.......	N. H. line.....	Private....	80	Lincoln.	
'40	Towne, Joseph.....	....	....	78	York........	Res. Kennebunk.
'40	Towns, Noah......	....	....	85	Kennebec....	Res. Litchfield.
'35c	Townsend, Isaac...	Mass. line.....	Private....	76	York........	d. Nov. 1, 1832.
'35c	Townsend, Joseph..	Mass. line.....	Private....	80	Cumberland.	
'35d	Townsend, Robert..	Mass. state....	Private....	74	Cumberland.	
'40	————			79	Cumb........	Res. Freeport.
'35c	Townsley, Gad.....	Mass. line.....	Private....	78	Washington.	
'35c	Townsley, Jacob....	Mass. line.....	Private....	85	Kennebec.	
'35c	Trafton, Benjamin..	Mass. line.....	Private....	63	York.	
'35c	Trafton, Eliphalet..	Mass. line.....	Private....	66	York.	
'35d	Trafton, Joshua....	R. I. line......	Captain...	89	York.	
'35c	Trafton, Josiah.....	Mass. line.....	Private....	66	York.	
'35d	Trask, Ebenezer....	R. I. mil.......	Private....	72	Kennebec.	
'40	————			77	Kennebec....	Res. Sidney.
'35d	Trask, Moses......	Mass. mil......	Private....	77	Lincoln.	
'35d	Trask, Obadiah....	Mass. mil......	Private....	69	Lincoln.	
'35c	Trask, Thomas Jr...	R. I. line......	Private....	76	Lincoln.	
'35d	Travis, Oliver......	Mass. mil......	Private....	72	Oxford.	
'35c	Treadwell, Marsters	Mass. line.....	Private....	..	Oxford.	
'35d	Treadwell, Samuel..	Mass. mil......	Private & Sergeant...	82	York.	
'40	Treadwell, Susan...	....	....	83	York........	Res. Kennebunk.
'35c	Trevett, John......	Mass. line.....	Sergeant...	82	Lincoln.	
'35c	Tripp, Robert......	Mass. line.....	Private....	70	York.	
'40	————			76	York........	Res. Sanford.
'35d	Trivett, Samuel....	Mass. mil......	Private....	77	Waldo.	
'35d	True, Aaron.......	Mass. mil......	Private....	76	Lincoln.	
'35d	True, Daniel.......	Mass. mil......	Private....	73	Lincoln.	
'35d	True, Edward......	Mass. mil......	Private....	80	Kennebec.	

List.	Name.	Service.	Rank.	Age.	County.	Remarks.
'35d	True, Jonathan	Mass. mil	Private	77	Somerset.	
'35c	True, Obadiah	Mass. line	Private	75	Oxford.	
'40	———			82	Oxford	Res. Denmark.
'40	True, Polly			80	Franklin	Res. Temple.
'40	True, William			80	Lincoln	Res. Lewiston.
'35d	True, William	Mass. line	Private	74	Cumberland.	
'35c	True, Zebulon	Mass. line	Private	65	Kennebec	d. Feb. 4, 1830.
'35c	Trumbull, William	Penn. line	Private	80	Somerset	d. Sept. 4, 1822.
'35c	Tubbs, Jacob	Mass. line	Private		Oxford.	
'40	Tucker, Aaron			56	Piscataquis	Res. Foxcroft.
'40	Tucker, Anna			84	Oxford	Res. Sumner.
'35d	Tucker, John	N. H. state	Matross	73	Penobscot.	
'40	———			80	Penobscot	Res. Dexter.
'35d	Tucker, Samuel	Cont. navy	Captain	86	Lincoln	d. Mar. 10, 1833.
'35d	Tukesbury, Thomas	N. H. state	Private	77	Penobscot.	
'35d	Tukey, William	Mass. mil	Private & Sergeant	70	Cumberland.	
'35c	Turner, Abial	Mass. line	Private	93	Oxford.	
'35c	Turner, David	Mass. line	Private	72	Somerset.	
'35c	Turner, Isaac	Mass. line	Private	78	Cumberland.	
'40	Turner, Isaac			87	Oxford	Res. Albany.
'40	Turner, Isaac			87	Oxford	Res. Norway.
'40	Turner, John			78	Kennebec	Res. Greene.
'40	Turner, Lydia			88	Kennebec	Res. Leeds.
'40	Turner, Oliver			79	Oxford	Res. Sumner.
'35d	Turner, Oliver	Mass. mil	Private	69	Oxford.	
'35d	Turner, Robert	Mass. mil	Musician & Sergeant	78	Lincoln.	
'35d	Turner, Samuel	Mass. mil	Private	79	Penobscot	
'35c	Turner, Starbird	Mass. line	Sergeant	81	Kennebec.	
'35d	Tuttle, Samuel	Mass. state	Sergeant & Private	80	Washington	
'40	Twitchell, Eli			81	Oxford	Res. Bethel.
'35d	Twitchell, Eli	Mass. mil	Private & Sergeant	73	Oxford.	
'35c	Twitchell, Moses	Mass. line	Private	75	Somerset.	
'35d	Twitchell, Peter	Mass. mil	Private	73	Oxford.	
'40	———			80	Oxford	Res. Bethel.
'35c	Twitchett, Ezra	Mass. line	Private	75	Oxford	d. May 16, 1821.
'35c	Tyler, Abraham	Mass. line	Private	71	York.	
'40				77	York	Res. Saco.
'40	Tyler, Andrew			80	Waldo	Res. Frankfort.
'35c	Tyler, Daniel	Mass. line	Private	75	Oxford.	
'35c	Tyler, Joseph	Mass. line	Private	74	York.	
'40	Tyler, Simon			87	Waldo	Res. Camden.
'35d	Tyler, Simeon	Mass. mil	Private & Sergeant	79	Waldo.	
'35d	Tyler, Andrew	Mass. line	Private	84	Waldo.	
'35d	———	Mass. line	Sergeant & Corporal	84	Waldo.	
'35c	Ulmer, George	Mass. line	Private	74	Waldo.	
'40				80	Waldo	Res. Hope.
'35d	Upton, Amos	Mass. mil	Sergeant	92	Oxford.	
'35c	Upton, Jeduthan	Mass. line	Private		Washington.	
'35c	Uran, James	Mass. line	Private	66	York.	
'35d	Vance, William	Mass. line	Private & Fifer	74	Kennebec.	
					Lincoln	'35c.
'35c	Varner, John	Mass. line	Private	88	York.	
'35c	Varney, Francis	Mass. line	Private	75	Cumberland.	d. Apr. 23, 1822.
'35c	Varney, Moses	Mass. line	Private	73	Kennebec.	
'35d	Varnum, Joel	Mass. line	Private	78	Franklin	Res. Temple.
'40	Varnum, Joel			81	Kennebec	d. Jan. 1828.
'35c	Varnum, Samuel	R. I. line	Private	77	Cumberland.	
'35d	Varrel, Samuel	Mass. mil	Private & Fifer	80	Kennebec.	
'35d	Veasey, Samuel	Mass. state	Private	89	Kennebec	d. Nov. 4, 1823.
'35c	Vickery, David	Mass. line	Private	82	Lincoln.	
'35c	Videto, Joseph	Mass. line	Private			
'35d	Vining, John	Mass. line & state	Private	71	Cumberland.	
'35c	Vose, Jesse	Mass. line	Sergeant	82	Kennebec	d. Sept. 1824.

List.	Name.	Service.	Rank.	Age.	County.	Remarks.
'35c	Wade, Abner	Mass. line	Captain	80	Lincoln	d. Oct. 1827.
'35d	Wade, John	Mass. line	Private	79	Waldo.	
'40				85	Waldo	Res. Lincolnville.
'35c	Wadlid, Daniel	Mass. line	Private	63	York.	
'35d	Wadsworth, John	Mass. line	Private & Musician	71	Kennebec.	
'35c	Wagg, James	Mass. line	Private	82	Cumberland.	
'40				86	Cumberland.	Res. Durham.
'35c	Waid, Henry	Conn. line	Private	73	York	d. Oct. 21, 1826.
'35d	Wait, William	Mass. line	Private & Corporal	80	Oxford.	
'35d	Wakefield, Ezekiel	Mass. state	Private & Sergeant	81	York.	
'40	Wakefield, Hannah			77	York	Res. Kennebunk
'35d	Wakefield, Nathan	Mass. mil	Private	74	York.	
'35c	Walch, Charles	Mass. line	Private	80	Lincoln.	
'40	Walch, James			50	Lincoln	Res. Woolwich.
'35c	Waldron, Ebenezer	N. H. line	Sergeant	64	Kennebec	d. in 1830.
'35c	Walker, Abraham	R. I. line	Private	80	Lincoln.	
'35d	Walker, Charles	Mass. line	Private & Sergeant	75	Cumberland.	
'35c	Walker, Edward	Mass. line	Private	73	York.	
'35c	Walker, John	Mass. line	Private	61	Somerset.	
'35d	Walker, Josiah	Mass. state	Private	78	Cumberland.	
'40				84	Cumberland.	Res. Pownal.
'35d	Walker, Lemuel	Mass. mil	Private & Matross	75	Lincoln.	
'40	Walker, Samuel			80	Lincoln	Res. Bowdoin.
'40	Waalker, Samuel C.			50	Somerset	Res. Madison.
'40	Walker, Timothy			82	Waldo	Res. Freedom.
'35c	Walker, Timothy	Mass. line	Private	74	Kennebec.	
'35c	Walker, William	N. H. line	Private	81	Oxford	d. Feb. 1, 1831.
'35d	Walker, William	Mass. mil	Private	80	Oxford	d. Dec. 1, 1833.
'40	Walker, William			73	Somerset	Res. Madison.
'35c	Wallace, Josiah	Mass. line	Drummer	72	Washington	d. Jan. 22, 1830.
'40	Walton, Benjamin			78	Penobscot	Res. Chester.
'35c	Walton, Reuben	Mass. line	Private	59	Oxford	d. March 1825.
'35c	Wurd, Benjamin	N. H. line	Private	74	Penobscot.	
'40	Ward, Nehemiah			55	Kennebec	Res. Windsor.
'35c	Ward, Thomas	Mass. line	Private	72	Kennebec.	
'35c	Warden, Thomas	Mass. line	Drummer	66	York	d. Feb. 15, 1827.
'35c	Wardley, Moses	Mass. line	Private	86	York	d, Sept. 1830.
'35c	Wardwell, Joseph	Mass. line	Ensign	74	Oxford.	
'40				80	Oxford	Res. Rumford.
'35d	Ware, Jason	Mass. mil	Private	79	Lincoln.	
'40	Ware, Jerson			84	Lincoln	Res. Union.
'35d	Ware, Nathan	Mass. line	Private of Art	78	Lincoln.	
'35d	Warren, Aaron	Mass. state	Sergeant & Sur. Mate.	76	York.	
'40				83	York	Res. Wells.
'35c	Warren, Aaron	Mass. line	Private	60	York.	
'35c	Warren, Abijah	Mass. line	Private	73	Oxford.	
'40				78	Oxford	Res. Sumner.
'35c	Warren, Daniel	Mass. line	Private	84	York.	
'35d	Warren, Daniel	Mass. line	Private	69	York.	
'40				75	York	Res. Limerick.
'40	Warren, George			39	Waldo	Res. Lincolnville.
'35d	Warren, Joshua	Mass. line	Private	76	York.	
'40				83	York	Res. Hollis.
'40	Warren, Keziah			81	York	Res. Shapleigh.
'35d	Warren, Moses	Mass. line	Private	74	Oxford.	
'35d	Warren, Nathan	Mass. mil	Private	81	Cumberland.	
'40	Warren, Nathan			77	Cumberland.	Res. Minot.
'35c	Warren, Nathaniel	Mass. line	Private	62	Oxford	d. Dec. 21, 1819.
'35c	Warren, Pelatiah	Mass. line	Private	80	Kennebec.	
'40				86	Kennebec	Res. Monmouth.
'35c	Warren, Peter	Virginia. line	Private	75	Kennebec.	
'35c	Warren, Richard	Mass. line	Private	78	Kennebec.	
'40				85	Kennebec	Res. Vassalborough.
'40	Warson, John			86	Hancock	Res. Brooksville.

List.	Name.	Service.	Rank.	Age.	County.	Remarks.
'35c	Warthen, Isaac	Cont. navy	Mariner	72	Waldo.	
'35c	Wasgate, David	Mass. line	Sergeant	83	Hancock.	
'35d	Washburn, Ebene'r.	Mass. line	Private	72	Oxford.	
'40	—			78	Oxford	Res. Hartford.
'35d	Washburn, Ephraim	Mass. mil	Private	74	Penobscot.	
'40	Washburn, Jennet			79	Oxford	Res. Hebron.
'35d	Wasson, John	Mass. line	Musician	81	Hancock.	
'35d	Wasson, John	Mass. line	Drummer		Hancock.	
'35d	Wasson, Samuel	Mass. mil	Drummer	74	Hancock.	
'35d	Wasson, Thomas	Mass. line	Fifer	73	Hancock.	
'35d	Waterhouse, George	Mass. line	Private	84	Cumberland.	
'40	Waterhouse, Hannah			84	York	Res. Kennebunk.
'35c	Waterhouse, John	Mass. line	Private	65	Cumberland.	d. Nov. 1833.
'35d	Waterhouse, Joseph.	Mass. line	Private	81	Cumberland.	
'35c	Waterman, Joseph	Cont. navy	Mariner	84	Waldo.	
'35c	Waterman, Malachi	Mass. line	Private	73	Cumberland.	d. Jan. 12, 1824.
'35d	Waterman, Noah	Mass. state	Private	79	Cumberland.	
'35d	Waston, John	Mass. line	Private	93	Cumberland.	
'35c	Waston, John	Mass. line	Private	69	Lincoln	d. June, 1824
'35d	Waston, Stephen	Mass. state	Private	72	York.	
'40	Waston, Thomas			77	Hancock	Res. Brooksville.
'40	Watts, Samuel			85	Washington	Res. Jonesborough.
'40	Waugh, Bethesda,			89	Somerset	Res. Starks.
'35d	Weare, Jeremiah	Mass. line	Private	75	York.	
'40	Weare, Jeremiah			83	York	Res. York
'35c	Webb, Edward	Mass. line	Private	75	Cumberland.	
'40	—			80	Cumberland.	Res. Gorham.
'35c	Webb, James	Mass. line	Ensign	75	Cumberland.	d. Sept. 1, 1825.
'35d	Webb, John	Mass. line	Private	70	Cumberland.	
'35c	Webb, Nathaniel	Mass. line	Corporal	79	Lincoln	d. Dec. 5, 1832.
'40	Webber, Abigail			79	Lincoln	Res. Richmond.
'35d	Webber, Asa	Mass. line	Private & Musician	74	Kennebec.	
'35c	Webber, Benjamin	Mass. line	Private	69	York.	
'35c	Webber, Daniel	Mass. line	Lieutenant	74	Hancock	d. Feb. 1, 1827.
'35c	Webber, Ezekiel	Mass. line	Private	76	Lincoln.	
'40	—			80to 87	Lincoln	Res. Boothbay.
'35d	Webber, George	Mass. line	Sergeant	74	Lincoln.	
'35c	Webber, Jonathan	Mass. line	Private	77	York.	
'35c	Webber, Joseph	R. I. line	Private	67	Kennebec	d. Sept. 4, 1822.
'35d	Webber, Lewis	R. I. line	Private	80	Kennebec.	
'35d	Webber, Lewis	R. I. state	Private	77	Kennebec.	
'35c	Webber, Noah	Mass. line	Private	57	Lincoln	d. in 1828.
'35c	Webber, Paul	Mass. line	Private	60	York	d. Dec. 21, 1819
'35d	Webber, Stephen	Mass. line	Private	78	do	
'35d	Webber, William	Mass. line	Sergeant	76	Hancock.	
'40	Weber, Nancy			73	Lincoln	Res. Georgetown.
'35c	Webster, Israel	N. H. line	Sergeant	69	Kennebec.	
'35d	Wedgwood, Jesse	Cont. navy & Mass. line	Mariner	73	York.	
'40	Wedgwood, Noah			81	York	Res. Parsonsfield.
'40	Weeks, Bethiah			78	Kennebec	Res. Wayne.
'40	Weeks, James			81	Lincoln	Res. Webster.
'35d	Weeks, James	Mass. mil	Private	72	Kennebec.	
'35c	Weeks, Pelatiah	N. H. line	Private	81	York	d. May 26, 1827.
'40	Welch, James			76	Cumberland.	Res. Gray.
'35c	Welch, Lemuel	Mass. line	Private		Lincoln.	
'35c	Welch, Paul	Mass. line	Private	68	York	d. Dec. 22, 1829.
'35c	Welch, William	Mass. line	Private	80	Lincoln.	
'35c	Welch, William	N. H. line	Private	80	Lincoln.	
'40	Welch, William			85	Lincoln	Res. Richmond.
'35d	Welder, Ephraim	Mass. mil	Private & Corporal.	88	York	d. Apr. 11, 1833.
'35c	Wellman, Abraham	Mass. line	Private	72	Kennebec.	
'40	Wellman, Mary			78	Lincoln	Res. Bremen.
'35c	Wellman, Samuel	Mass. line	Private	70	Waldo.	

List.	Name.	Service.	Rank.	Age.	County.	Remarks.
'35d	Wells, Joshua	Mass. line	Private	79	Kennebec.	
'40	Wells, Mary			76	Kennebec.	Res. Vienna.
'35c	Wells, Phineas	Mass. line	Private	75	Lincoln.	
'35d	Welsh, Jonathan	Mass. mil	Private	84	York.	
'35d	Welson, Jonathan	Mass. line	Private	72	Waldo	d. Apr. 13, 1833.
'35c	Wentworth, Andrew	Mass. line	Private	60	York.	
'35c	Wentworth, Enoch	Mass. line	Private	81	Hancock	d. Dec. 26, 1821.
'35d	Wentworth, Foster	Mass. mil	Private	70	Lincoln.	
'40	Wentworth, Ichabod			52	York	Res. Berwick.
'35c	Wentworth, John	Mass. line	Private	63	Hancock	d. June 18, 1824.
'35c	Wentworth, John 2d	Mass. line	Private	57	Somerset.	
'35c	Wentworth, Lemuel	N. H. line	Private	84	Lincoln.	
'40	Wentworth, Lemuel			86	Waldo	Res. Hope.
'35c	Wentworth, Paul	Mass. line	Private	75	Waldo	d. Sept. 3, 1833.
'40	Wentworth, Paul.. Widow of			76	Waldo	Res. Knox.
'35d	Wentworth, Rich'd	Mass. line	Private & Sergeant	88	York.	
'35d	Wentworth, Tim'y	Mass. state	Lieutenant	87	York.	
'40				93	York.	Res. Berwick.
'35c	Wescott, Joshua	Mass. line	Private	86	Oxford	d. Feb. 6, 1826.
'35d	West, Isaac	Mass. line	Private	81	Kennebec.	
'35c	West, Peter	Mass. line	Private	83	Somerset	d. Feb. 5, 1828.
'35c	Weston, Daniel	N. H. line	Private	73	Cumberland.	
'35c	Weston, Joseph	Mass. line	Private	74	Cumberland.	
'35c	Weston, Samuel	Mass. line	Private	67	Lincoln	d. in 1829.
'35c	Wetherall, Charles	Mass. line	Private	69	Somerset	d. July 16, 1833.
'40	Wetherel, Obadiah			95	Kennebec	Res. Albion.
'35d	Wetherell, John	Mass. mil	Private & Sergeant	76	Kennebec.	
'35d	Wetherill, Obadiah	Mass. line	Lieutenant	87	Somerset.	
'35d	Weymouth, James	N. H. line	Private Seaman	75	Somerset Kennebec.	
'40	Weymouth, James			80		
'35c	Weymouth, Moses	Mass. line	Sergeant	92	Waldo	Res. Belmont.
'35c	Wheler, John	Cont. navy	Mariner	84	York.	
'35d	Wheelwright Joseph	Mass. mil	Private	83	Kennebec.	
'40				88	York.	
'35c	Wheelwright, Sam	Mass. line	Sergeant		York	Res. Wells.
'40	Wheler, John			90	York	d. Feb. 24, 1831.
'40	Wherren, Peggy			79	Franklin	Res. W lton.
'35c	Whidden, James	Mass. line	Private	62	York	Res. Elliot.
'35c	Whidden, Solomon	Mass. line	Private	80	Somerset	d. Mar. 30, 1828.
'35c	Whitcomb, Thomas or Whiten,	N. H. line	Private	88	Somerset.	
'35c	White, Benjamin	Mass. line	Private	95	Somerset	d. June, 1824.
'40	White, Charles			90	Kennebec	d. Dec. 17, 1833.
'35c	White, Charles	N. H. line	Private	89	Waldo	Res. Belmont.
'35d	White Charles	Mass. state	Private	77	Kennebec.	
35c	White, George	Mass. line	Captain		York.	
'35c	White, John	Mass. line	Private	79	Hancock	d. May 20, 1826.
'35c	White, John	N. H. line	Private	74	Lincoln	d. Nov.14, 1822.
'35d	White, John	Mass. mil	Private	76	Lincoln	d. Sept. 3, 1832.
'35d	White, John	Mass. mil	Private	72	Lincoln.	
'35d	White, Joseph	Mass. line	Private	73	York.	
'35c	White, Joshua	Mass. line	Private	75	Somerset	d. April 21, 1828.
'35d	White, Simpson	Mass. line	Private	80	Somerset.	
'35c	White, William	Mass. line	Private	66	Lincoln	d. March, 1827.
'35c	Whiteham, Jerry	Mass. line	Private	82	Somerset	d. Sept. 4, 1822.
'35c	Whitehouse, Daniel	Mass. line	Private	79	Kennebec.	
'35c	Whitehouse, Eben'r	N. H. line	Private	77	York	d. June 4, 1832.
'35c	Whitehouse, John	N. H. line	Private	65	Kennebec.	
'35c	Whitehouse, Samuel	Mass. line	Private	78	York	d. Jan. 31, 1824.
'35c	Whitehouse, Samuel	Mass. line	Private	74	York	d. Sept. 4, 1837.
'40	Whitehouse, Susannah			84	Somerset	Res. Smithfield.
'40	Whiten, Samuel			83	Franklin	Res. Wilton.
'00c	Whiting, John	Mass. line	Private	76	Somerset.	
'40				82	Somerset	Res. Hartland.
'35d	Whiting, Sampson	Mass. line	Private	77	Oxford.	
'40	Whiting, Sampson			75	Oxford	Res. Denmark.
'35d	Whiting, Samuel	Mass. line	Private	76	Kennebec.	
'35d	Whitman, Jacob	Mass. line	Private	80	Oxford.	
'40				86	Oxford	Res. Buckfield.
'35d	Whitmore, Andrew	Mass. mil	Private	72	Lincoln.	
'35c	Whitmore, Daniel	Mass. line	Private	75	Waldo.	

List.	Name.	Service.	Rank.	Age.	County.	Remarks.
'40				81	Waldo	Res. Unity.
'35c	Whitmore, Joseph..	Mass. line	Private....	79	Hancock.	
'40				84	Hancock....	Res. Deer Isle.
'35c	Whitney, Abraham.	Mass. line	Private....	80	Kennebec.	
'35	Whitney, Daniel....	Mass. line	Private....	71	Cumberland.	
'35d	Whitney, Daniel....	Mass. mil.	Private....	71	Penobscot.	
'40	Whitney, Ebenezer.			79	Kennebec....	Res. Cinton.
'35d	Whitney, Ebenezer.	Mass. state....	Private....	71	Lincoln.	
'40	Whitney, Eleanor...			57	Kennebec....	Res. Dearborn.
'35d	Whitney, Isaac.....	Mass. line	Private....	85	Cumberland.	
'40	Whitney, Isaac.....			83	Lincoln......	Res. Lisbon.
'35d	Whitney, Jacob.....	Mass. mil.	Private....	71	Somerset.	
'40	Whitney, Jacob...			77	Franklin.....	Res. Phillips.
'35c	Whitney, Jesse.....	Mass. line	Private....	77	Cumberland.	d. Jan. 19, 1831.
'35c	Whitney, Jonathan.	Mass. line	Private....	70	Oxford.	
'35c	Whitney, Joshua...	Mass. line	Private....	59	York........	d. Feb. 25, 1832.
'35c	Whitney, Micah....	Mass. line	Private....	79	Somerset....	d. Jan. 19, 1832.
'35c	Whitney, Phineas...	Mass. line	Private....	84	Oxford......	d. May 21, 1830.
'35d	Whitney, Phinehas.	Mass. mil.	Private....	85	Somerset....	d. Nov. 13, 1832.
'35d	Whitney, Samuel...	Mass. line	Private....	75	Kennebec.	
'35c	Whitney, Samuel...	Mass. line	Private....	65	Lincoln.	
'35c	Whitney, Stephen..	R. I. line	Private....	78	Cumberland.	
'35d	Whitney. Uriel.....	Mass. line	Private....	72	Cumberland.	
'35d	Whitney, Zebulon..	Mass. state...	Private....	86	Cumberland.	
'40	Whitten, Jane......			78	Lincoln......	Res. Topsham.
'35c	Whitten, John.....	Mass. line.	Private....	61	Cumberland.	
'40	Whitten, Richard			77	Waldo.......	Res. Troy.
'35c	Whitten, Richard...	Mass. line	Private....	69	York.	
'40	Whitten, Solomon..			86	Somerset....	Res. Skowhegan.
'35c	Whittington, Rob't.	Mass. line	Private....	80	Kennebec....	d. Aug. 19, 1830.
'35d	Wiggen, Nathan....	Mass. mil.	Private....	73	York.	
'35c	Wiggin, Benjamin..	Mass. line	Private....	83	Cumberland.	d. Feb. 16, 1828.
'40	Wiggin, Nathan....			80	York........	Res. Parsonsfield.
'35c	Wiggin, Phineas....	N. H. line	Private....	63	Lincoln.	
'40	Wight, Joseph......			82	Cumberland.	Res. Raymond.
'40	Wilber, Thomas....			74	Somerset....	Res.NewPortland.
'40	Wilbur, Asa........			80	Kennebec....	Res.Augusta.
'35d	Wilbur, Thomas....	Conn. state....	Private & Corporal...	71	Somerset.	
'35d	Wilcox, John......	R. I. mil......	Private & Matross...	76	Kennebec.	
'40				80	Kennebec...	Res. Monmouth.
'35d	Wild, Benjamin....	Mass. mil.	Private....	72	York.	
'40	Wildes, Benjamin...			78	York........	Res. Kennebunkport. Same as preceding
'35c	Wilkins, Edward...	Mass. line	Musician..	77	Penobscot...	d. Mar. 9, 1831.
'35d	Wilkinson, Joseph...	Mass. state....	Private....	79	York.	
'35d	Willard, Ezra......	Mass. mil.	Private....	73	Somerset.	
'40	Willard, Ezra......			72	Somerset....	Res. Mercer.
'35c	Williams, Amos....	N. H. line	Private....	69	York........	d. Jan. 7, 1825.
'40	Williams, Anna....			79	Somerset....	Res. Anson.
'35c	Williams, Benjamin	Mass. line	Private....	65	Kennebec.	
'35c	Williams, John.....	Mass. line	Private....	74	Lincoln.	
'40				79	Lincoln......	Res. Wiscasset.
'35d	Williams, Joseph..	Mass. state....	Private....	83	York.	
'40				90	York........	Res. Wells.
'35c	Williams, Joshua...	Mass. line	Private....	87	Hancock.	
'35c	Williams, Lemuel...	Mass. line	Private....	70	Somerset.	
'35c	Willis, James.......	Mass. line	Private....	69	Kennebec...	d. Jan. 18, 1830.
'40	Willis, Sarah......			79	Cumberland.	Res. Minot.
'35c	Willman, Joseph....	Mass. line	Private...	73	Lincoln.	
'40	Willman, Martha...			77	Waldo......	Res. Searsmont.
'35c	Wills, James.......	Mass. line	Private....	76	Kennebec.	
'35c	Wills, James.......	N. H. line	Private....	58	Kennebec.	
'40	Wilson, Betsey.....			82	York........	Res. Kittery.
'35c	Wilson, Edward....	Mass. line	Private....	72	Cumberland.	
'35d	Wilson, John.......	Mass. mil.	Drummer..	79	Hancock.	
'35d	Wilson, John.......	Mass. mil.	Private....	76	Lincoln.	
'35c	Wilson, John.......	Mass. line	Private....	70	Somerset.	
'35c	Wilson, Joseph.....	N. H. line	Private....	74	York........	d. July 22, 1823.
'40	Winch, Anna......			80	Franklin.....	Res. Freeman.
'35c	Winch, Joseph.....	N. H. line	Private....	86	Somerset.	
'35c	Winchester, Silas...	Mass. line	Private....	78	Penobscot.	
'35c	Wing, Gideon......	Virginia line...	Private....	77	Kennebec....	d. Feb. 24, 1821.

List.	Name.	Service.	Rank.	Age.	County.	Remarks.
'35d	Wing, Moses	Mass. line	Surgeon's Mate	75	Kennebec.	
'35c	Wing, Nathan	Mass. line	Private	72	Somerset.	
'35c	Wingate, John	Mass. line	Surgeon	75	Kennebec	d. July 25, 1819.
'35d	Wingate, Jonathan.	N. H. line	Private	76	York.	
'40				82	York	Res. Parsonsfield.
'35d	Winn, Jonathan	Mass. mil	Private	76	York	d. Jan. 30, 1833.
'35d	Winn, Joseph	Mass. mil	Private	85	York.	
'35d	Winship, John	Mass. mil	Private	72	Cumberland.	
'40	Winship, John			80	Cumberland.	Res. Otisfield.
'35c	Winslow, Benjamin.	Mass. line	Private	75	Lincoln.	
'35c	Winslow, David	N. H. line	Private	68	Lincoln	d. in 1828.
'40	Winslow, Elizabeth.			75	Cumberland.	Res. Freeport.
'35c	Winslow, Ezekiel	Mass. line	Private	76	Lincoln.	
'35d	Winslow, George	R. I. state	Sergeant & Fifer	76	Lincoln.	
'35c	Winslow, John	Mass. line	Private	65	Cumberland.	d.July 14, 1823.
'35c	Winter, Joseph	Mass. line	Musician	67	Oxford	d. June 13, 1832.
'35d	Wise, Daniel	Mass. state	Private & Seaman	73	York.	
'40				78	York	Res. Kennebunk.
'35c	Wiston, William	Mass. line	Private	83	Cumberland.	
'35c	Witch, James	Mass. line	Private	70	Cumberland.	
'35c	Witham, Andrew	Mass. line	Mariner	80	York.	
'35c	Witham, Bartholomew	Mass. line	Private	78	York.	
'35c	Witham, Caleb	Mass. line	Private	70	Lincoln	d. Aug. 5, 1822.
'40	Witham, Elizabeth.			83	York	Res. York.
'35c	Witham, James	Mass. line	Private	77	York	d. Dec. 2, 1833.
'35c	Witham, John Spicer	Mass. line	Private	84	York	d. March ,1824.
'35c	Witham, Joshua	Mass. line	Private	61	Lincoln	d. May 8, 1825.
'35c	Witham, Nathan	Mass. line	Private	81	York.	
'40	Withee, Uzizeel			75	Somerset	Res. Hartland.
'35c	Wither, Uzziel	Mass. line	Private	69	Somerset	Same as preceding.
'35d	Withee, Zoe	Mass. line	Private & Bombard'r.	72	Kennebec.	
'40				78	Franklin	Res. Industry.
'40	Witherell, John			82	Kennebec	Res. Monmouth.
'35c	Wixon, Shubael	Mass. line	Private	68	Kennebec	d. Oct. 4, 1831.
'35d	Wood, Enoch	Mass. line	Private	74	Kennebec.	
'35c	Wood, Isaiah	Mass. line	Private	74	Oxford.	
'35c	Wood, Jesse	Mass. line	Private	69	Kennebec.	
'40	Wood, Josiah			92	Oxford	Res. Porter.
'35c	Wood, Josiah	Mass. line	Private	79	Cumberland.	
'35c	Wood, Nathan	Mass. line	Private	61	Somerset.	
'35d	Wood, Samuel	Mass. mil	Private	75	Kennebec.	
'40				81	Kennebec	Res. Winthrop.
'35c	Wood, Silas	Mass. mil	Private & Corporal	81	Somerset.	
'35c	Wood, Stephen	Mass. line	Private	84	York.	
'40	Wood, Sybil			81	Somerset	Res. Norridgewock.
'35d	Woodard, Samuel	Mass. mil	Private	83	Cumberland.	d. Oct. 21, 1832.
'35c	Woodberry, Benjamin	Mass. line	Sergeant	74	Cumberland.	
'35c	Woodbridge, Christopher	Mass. line	Captain	74	Lincoln	d. March, 1825.
'35d	Woodbury, Benjamin	Mass. state	Private	72	Oxford.	
'40				78	Oxford	Res. Buckfield.
'35c	Woodbury, Ebenezer	Mass. line	Private	74	Cumberland.	
'35d	Woodford, Joseph	Cont. mil	Private	73	Cumberland.	
'40	Woodford, Joseph			78	Kennebec	Res. Readfield.
'35c	Woodman, Be'jamin	R. I. line	Private	79	Kennebec.	
'35c	Woodman, Ephraim	Mass. line	Private	75	York.	
'35d	Woodman, James	Mass. state	Private	81	York.	
'40				87	York	Res. Buxton.
'35c	Woodman, John	Mass. line	Sergeant	69	York.	
'35d	Woodman, Joseph	Mass. state	Private	85	Cumberland.	
'35d	Woodman, Joshua	Mass. state	Private & Seaman	81	Cumberland.	
'40	Woodman, Joshua			83	York	Res. Buxton.
'40	Woods, Jesse			75	Franklin	Res. Wilton.
'35d	Woodson, Samuel	Mass. line	Private	78	York.	

List.	Name.	Service.	Rank.	Age.	County.	Remarks.
'35c	Woodward, Benjamin............	Mass. line.....	Sergeant 5th. Regt......	....	Lincoln.	
'35c	Woodworth, James.	Mass. line.....	Sergeant...	80	Lincoln.	
'35c	Woodworth, Joseph	Mass. line.....	Captain...	74	Kennebec....	d. July 4, 1824.
'35c	Worcester, William.	Mass. line.....	Private....	89	York.	
'35d	Works, James......	Mass. line.....	Corporal & Private....	83	Kennebec.	
'35c	Wormel, Nathaniel.	Cont. navy....	Marine........	....	Penobscot.	
'35c	Wormell, John.....	Mass. line.....	Private....	74	Oxford.	
'35d	Wormwood, James..	Mass. mil......	Private....	81	York.	
'40	———			87	York........	Res. Cornish.
'35c	Worster, Thomas...	Mass. line.....	Private....	80	York.	
'40	Worster, William...	....	....	86	York.........	Res. Sanford.
'35d	Worther, Benjamin.	Mass. line.....	Private....	75	Kennebec.	
'40	Worthing, Isaac...	....	....	78	Waldo......	Res. Palermo.
'35c	Wright, Daniel.....	Mass. line.....	Private....	78	Cumberland.	
'35c	Wright, Joel.......	Mass. line.....	Private....	82	Oxford......	d. Feb. 16, 1824.
'35d	Wright, John......	Mass. mil......	Private....	76	Lincoln.	
'40	———			82	Lincoln......	Res. Woolwich.
'35d	Wright, Joseph.....	Mass. line.....	Private.... Drummer..	72	Lincoln.	
'35d	———			78	Lincoln.......	Res. Woolwich.
'35d	Wright, Joseph.....	Mass. line.....	Private....	70	Cumberland.	
'40	Wutting, Thomas...	....	....	72	Franklin.....	Res. Wilton.
'35d	Wyatt, Benjamin...	Mass. mil......	Private....	72	Penobscot.	
'35c	Wyer, Isaiah.......	Mass. line.....	Private....	71	Oxford.	
'35c	Wyman, Daniel 2d.	Mass. line.....	Private....	79	Somerset.....	d. Jan. 16, 1827.
'35c	Wyman, Daniel 1st.	Mass. line.....	Private....	66	Kennebec.	
'35c	Wyman, Dean.....	Mass. line.....	Private....	67	Somerset.....	d. Aug. 10, 1831.
'35c	Wyman, Henry....	Mass. line.....	Private....	58	Somerset.	
'40	Wyman, John......	....	....	64	Somerset.....	Res. Skowheagn.
'35c	Wyman, Reuben...	Mass. line.....	Private....	71	Somerset...	
'40	———			77	Somerset....	Res. Fairfield.
'35d	Yates, John........	Mass. mil......	Private & Mariner...	80	Cumberland.	
'35d	Yeaton, Jonathan...	Mass. mil......	Private....	76	Kennebec.	
'35c	Yeaton, Paul.......	N. H. line.....	Private....	70	Kennebec.	
'35c	Yenlin, William....	Mass. line.....	Private....	75	Somerset.	
'35d	York, Benjamin....	N. H. line.....	Private....	73	Oxford.	
'40	———			79	Oxford......	Res. Mexico.
'35d	York., Isaac........	Mass. line & mil...........	Private....	71or 76	Cumberland.	
'40	———			81	Cumberland.	Res. Standish.
'35d	York, John........	Mass. line.....	Private....	86	Oxford.	
'35d	York, Solomon.....	Mass. state.....	Drummer..	71	Hancock.	
'35d	York, William R....	Mass. line.....	Private....	77 or 81	Cumberland.	
'40	———			83	Cumberland.	Res. Falmouth.
'35c	Young, Abraham...	Mass. line.....	Private....	74	Cumberland.	d. Feb. 19, 1828.
'35d	Young, Beniah.....	N. H. line.....	Private....	71	Lincoln.	
'35d	Young, Benjamin ..	Mass. mil......	Private & Corporal...	85	Somerset.	
'40	Young, Hannah....	....	....	83	York........	Res. York.
'35d	Young, James.....	Mass. mil......	Private....	74	Kennebec.	
'40	———			80	Kennebec....	Res. Fayette.
'35d	Young, Nathaniel..	Mass. line.....	Private....	73	Oxford.	
'35c	Young, Richard....	R. I. line.....	Private....	87	Lincoln......	d. June 27, 1824.
'35d	Young, William....	Mass. mil......	Private & Corporal...	82	Somerset.	
'40	———			87	Somerset....	Res. Starks.
'35d	Young, Zebulon....	Mass. line.....	Private....	72	Penobscot.	
'40	Zouldthwai', Elizabeth.............	....	....	62	York........	Res. Biddeford.

www.ingramcontent.com/pod-product-compliance
Lightning Source LLC
Chambersburg PA
CBHW070517090426
42735CB00012B/2820